BEER GHOSTS

BEER GHOSTS

IN SEARCH OF LOST HOPS AND THE WOMEN WHO GREW THEM

JENNIFER A. JORDAN

THE UNIVERSITY OF CHICAGO PRESS
Chicago and London

The University of Chicago Press, Chicago 60637
The University of Chicago Press, Ltd., London

Published 2026
Printed in the United States of America

35 34 33 32 31 30 29 28 27 26   1 2 3 4 5

ISBN-13: 978-0-226-85164-8 (cloth)
ISBN-13: 978-0-226-85165-5 (ebook)
DOI: https://doi.org/10.7208/chicago/9780226851655.001.0001

Library of Congress Cataloging-in-Publication Data

Names: Jordan, Jennifer A., 1970– author
Title: Beer ghosts : in search of lost hops and the women who grew them / Jennifer A. Jordan.
Other titles: In search of lost hops and the women who grew them
Description: Chicago ; London : The University of Chicago Press, 2026. | Includes bibliographical references and index.
Identifiers: LCCN 2026008525 | ISBN 9780226851648 cloth | ISBN 9780226851655 ebook
Subjects: LCSH: Women hop pickers—Wisconsin—Social conditions—19th century | Hops—Harvesting—Wisconsin—History—19th century | Hops industry—Wisconsin—History—19th century
Classification: LCC HD6073.H58 J64 2026
LC record available at https://lccn.loc.gov/2026008525

♾ This paper meets the requirements of ANSI/NISO Z39.48-1992 (Permanence of Paper).

Authorized Representative for EU General Product Safety Regulation (GPSR) queries: **Easy Access System Europe**—Mustamäe tee 50, 10621 Tallinn, Estonia, gpsr.requests@easproject.com
Any other queries: https://press.uchicago.edu/press/contact.html

For Dan

CONTENTS

PROLOGUE

THE SPIRIT OF ELLA

Whether it's a boozy barrel-aged stout, a citrusy India pale ale (IPA), or a crisp, light macrobrew, when a person drinks a beer, they are drinking a landscape. All beer is the result of the interactions of sun, soil, plants, and water, as well as the work of chemists, brewers, plant breeders, politicians, and marketing folks. Drinkers of stouts, IPAs, and lagers all, in turn, shape landscapes with their taste for this particular drink because the yeast, water, grains, and hops all come from somewhere, and that somewhere changes over time. Each of these ingredients has a powerful story to tell, but I am especially interested in *hops*, the funky-smelling cone-shaped blossoms of the hop plant that give beer bitterness, flavor, and aroma. Whereas so many of the world's hops today come from the Pacific Northwest, New Zealand, Bavaria, and points in between, for a very brief moment in the nineteenth century, most of the hops grown in the United States came from Wisconsin.[1] Until the early twentieth century, people picked hops in much the same way they had for the previous millennium—by hand, one cone at a time. Most of the hands picking hops in nineteenth-century Wisconsin belonged to young white women who flocked to the hopyards in the tens of thousands at the height of the 1860s hop boom (figure P.1).[2]

The landscape of my adopted home state reveals little of this history on the surface. In fact, I might never have noticed the ghosts of

FIGURE P.1. Hop pickers posing in the Laffan Hop Yard. Photo by H. H. Bennett, Wisconsin Dells, Columbia County, Wisconsin, ca. 1880. Wisconsin Historical Society, W012OCJ.

the women of the hop fields if I had not come across a chance paragraph in Richard Unger's book *Beer in the Middle Ages and the Renaissance* (2004). While discussing something else entirely, Unger briefly mentioned farmers growing hops centuries ago in northern Germany, not far from the Baltic Sea.[3] I had only ever thought of German hops growing in the southern part of the country, where the hop industry thrives to this day—sunnier places like the Hallertau and the Bavarian town of Spalt, with its distinctive houses built with peaked multilevel attics for hop drying. Yet here was robust evidence of hops once growing elsewhere, then vanishing without a trace—or so I thought. Given my long-standing interest in cultural memory and forgetting, and a growing interest in beer history, my research antennae perked up and I began to wonder where else hops might once have thrived. When I set out on this path, I had no idea that I was living just one hundred miles or so east of a place that was briefly one of the most important hop-growing regions in the world: southwestern and central Wisconsin.[4] The hop industry of Wisconsin receives passing mention in the many histories of beer and hops in the United States, but most of them focus on the alpha and omega of US hop growing—New York state in the nineteenth century and the Pacific Northwest region in the twentieth and twenty-first centuries.[5] I also had no idea that women would be the backbone of Wisconsin's hop trade. But this story has much to teach us about the history of beer, the power of consumer tastes to affect landscapes and laborscapes, the often-hidden work of women in broader agricultural systems, and the hubris of thriving agricultural industries in the face of obvious warnings of coming cataclysms.

I began to search for information about hop growing in Wisconsin, and one source that appeared in my results was the Seymour family papers. When I put in my request for the cardboard box of ledgers and other documents at the Wisconsin Historical Society, I did not know whether it would be of use. Archival research can involve many haystacks and few needles. The guide to the file's contents contained the word *hops*, but that single word in an index could mean anything from a brief mention to a treasure trove. When the archivist brought the box to my table, I slowly unpacked its contents. Sitting in the quiet reading room, I opened an envelope and slipped out a small ledger, which turned out to be the diary of a young hop picker named Ella Seymour. After reading through this bittersweet document, I continued to leaf through the soft manila folders full of fragile pages and brittle ledgers, and to my surprise, a photograph (figure P.2) fluttered out of the pages and onto the table where I sat, Ella gazing out at me from more than a century and a half in the past.

In the second half of the nineteenth century, a rising tide of beer swept across the United States. The breweries of Milwaukee, St. Louis, Chicago, and so many other US cities churned out ever more beer with each passing decade. In Milwaukee, the smokestacks and chimneys of Pabst, Schlitz, Blatz, Miller, and the other breweries of this rapidly growing city sent smoke and steam into the air, while draft horses hauled mountains of kegs to taverns and beer gardens around town,

FIGURE P.2. Ella Seymour, date unknown, photographer unknown. Probably the late 1860s in Sauk County, Wisconsin. Wisconsin Historical Society, box 1, Seymour Family of Dellona, Sauk County, Wisconsin, Papers, 1842–1986, Call Number M93-113; W01CDME.

and to the train depot and harbor to be shipped to far-off places. The more research I did, the more I realized that Ella and young women like her made this beer possible.

(Hard) cider and whiskey had long filled the mugs and tumblers of US drinkers. Cider was comparatively easy to make with even mealy or overtart apples, and whiskey was relatively easy to store and transport.[6] But the second half of the nineteenth century gave rise to a beer boom on a national and global scale, in particular the crisp and drinkable lager that had originated in central Europe.[7] Brewers mashed unprecedented quantities of barley and tossed millions of pounds of hops into their kettles as they sought to meet the ever-growing demand for their product. To keep the beer flowing, the brewers relied on a steady supply of grain and hops grown by farmers both in and out of state. Although the state of New York had long been the leading hop producer in the United States, Wisconsin gave it a run for its money in the 1860s. As we shall see, from the late 1830s until the end of the nineteenth century, Wisconsin farmers grew hops for brewers near and far, coming to a dramatic crescendo shortly after the American Civil War. Brewers across Wisconsin, around the Midwest, and as far away as New York, London, and Liverpool bought up bale after bale of Wisconsin hops.[8]

On July 19, 1873, two months after Frederick Pabst, of Pabst Blue Ribbon fame, took over as president of his father-in-law's Phillip Best Brewing Company, and as the future Pabst Brewery was beginning its meteoric rise to become one of the biggest breweries in the country (and in the world), Ella Seymour turned twenty-one and began to keep a diary.[9] About 130 miles west-northwest of Milwaukee's rowdy taverns, the polkas and chatter of its beer gardens, and the beery, smoky fumes of the great breweries on the Lake Michigan shore, in Dellona Township, Sauk County, Wisconsin, seated somewhere in a house that has long since been torn down, Ella began to fill the margins of a small ledger with details of her days.[10]

Living just a few miles from today's Wisconsin Dells, she kept a careful record of how frequently she and her sister Ida (figure P.3) picked raspberries and currants, the timing of her father Silas's harvests, the illnesses of her youngest brother, Arthur, and when relatives and neighbors came calling. A month or so after the diary began, Ella wrote, "Aug 22nd, Ida and I took up the carpet, ma mopped the floor, & we cleaned the windows. Aug 23rd, Arthur don't seem to be much better. He is a very sick boy. We have been cleaning today

FIGURE P.3. Sisters Ella (seated) and Ida Seymour, date unknown, photographer unknown. Probably the late 1860s in Sauk County, Wisconsin. The only known copy is in a self-published book held at the Wisconsin Historical Society library: Ruth Seymour Burmester, *A Barn on the Place* (1996), 1-19.

as much as possible. Have the bed steads all up for hop picking." For me—a historical sociologist on the hunt for historical hops—this last sentence shone like a beacon the first time I read it. Without Ella and her ilk, in Wisconsin and around the world, those churning breweries would have ground to a halt. Brewers needed hops, and hops were only possible because of the laborious work of picking the hop cones one at a time. As I read through Ella's diary, often stopping to puzzle over the nineteenth-century handwriting, I began to see the cycle of the seasons of hop growing, as she repeated descriptions of harvest preparation and completion each August and September. The litany of chores I had seen in the 1873 entries repeated itself a year later: "Aug 28 [1874]. I washed 10 windows & a door. Ma, with Ida's & Walter's help cleaned the kitchen chamber, ready for hop picking. Aug. 31 Pa went after hop pickers. We washed, ironed & churned. Sept 1. Ironed, baked & c, & e. Hop pickers came just dusk."

What could building bedsteads, churning butter, and baking bread have to do with hop picking, and why is Ella—a mostly forgotten young woman who died not all that long after this diary entry—a protagonist in the history of beer? A person who likely never left her home county, didn't live to see her thirtieth birthday, and quite possibly never had a sip of beer (at one point in her diary, she announced that she had taken a temperance pledge) occupied an essential role in the flourishing beer trade of her time. The history of beer is incomplete without the history of Ella and the others who labored in the hop fields and in the quarters of the hop pickers, because women mattered throughout the hop industry of the day: as pickers, as hostesses engaging in an immense amount of domestic labor to keep this seasonal labor force happy and healthy, and as the bearers of the hop farmers' children, who would become the farmers' in-house pickers as soon as they were grown enough. The great sweep of industrialization happening in nineteenth-century brewing rested on a solid bedrock of women's work and the intimacy of sharing homes with dozens of strangers every harvest season. Women have long played key roles in brewing, not only as pickers of hops and hosts of pickers, but also as *brewsters* (women brewers, a term dating from circa 1300), on bottling lines, in taverns, and beyond, through the present day.[11] The private labors of Ella and her metaphorical sisters fueled the agricultural and industrial enterprises of nineteenth-century beer, as they did to varying degrees in other arenas as well.[12]

Even the most fecund farming couples would have had trouble creating enough of their own farmhands to pick a large commercial hop crop. Many hop farmers had to rely on hiring outsiders to work alongside their own families in the busy weeks of the harvest. In nineteenth-century Wisconsin and in New York state—the most significant hop-growing region in the nation for most of that century—many farmers relied on young white women to do this work and hosted them in their own homes.[13] New York used several other widespread models of hop-picking labor, including hiring more itinerant laborers who self-provisioned, and, as became very common on the West Coast, Indigenous families who would self-provision as well, discussed in more detail later in this prologue.[14] In Wisconsin, hosting young women became a predominant labor practice for most farms with a hop crop too large to be picked by family alone, and the farmer's wife had the primary responsibility for hosting these hop pickers. As one former picker later recalled:

> When I was about sixteen or seventeen years old, it was time for me to go out and earn a little money. . . . I worked picking hops for the Allens in Allenville. . . . This hop-picking was lots of fun. It lasted two weeks, and we got room and good board and working with a group of young people all day, kidding and laughing. . . . When the hops were ready to pick, there were young men who would pull up both poles and vines and bring them to where we were picking. These were called "box tenders." We girls picked the hops off the vines and put them into boxes, being paid by the box. We had a place to eat and sleep in a building attached to the house.[15]

They needed three meals a day, clean water and outhouses, and a safe and comfortable place to sleep—sometimes in a newly built building, other times in the attic or bedrooms of the farming family. Those bedsteads mentioned in Ella's diary were for the girls and women who would fill the Seymour house at the hop harvest—as many as thirty-five pickers for the harvest of 1867.[16] Some farms, including the Seymours,' hosted so many pickers and cooked such large quantities of food that they built whole new "summer kitchens" to accommodate the work, and dishes and cutlery had to be borrowed from neighboring farms.[17]

The annual harvest in August and September brought upheaval to the rhythms of farm life, and a unique and lucrative opportunity for women from far and wide. The picking itself was very similar to the way that hops had been picked for centuries. The pickers would pull each cone off the bine (not technically a vine) by hand in the hot summer sun or the earliest days of fall. One picker recalled it being hard work but noted that they sang in the fields and had plenty of fun alongside the work.[18] At the peak of Wisconsin hop production, the demand for this work in the brief weeks of the harvest gave tens of thousands of women well-paid work and an often pleasant diversion, as hop pickers could expect good food and entertaining dances after a long day of picking. Wisconsin's hop-growing farmers depended so much on this temporary work force that they competed with one another to draw these much-needed workers to their farms—better food, better beds, better bachelors at the barn dances.

This moment of opportunity for the pickers fundamentally increased the workload for the women of the house, as farmers hosted thousands of young women from nearby towns or more distant cities such as Milwaukee, making room for them inside their own homes. Hops poured into the voracious breweries of Milwaukee and beyond because farmers' wives and eldest daughters set up bedsteads and plump *ticks* (homemade mattresses or pallets consisting of a fabric case and straw or other filling), baked untold numbers of loaves of bread, cleared the barn for nighttime dances, protected sleeping young women from adventure and misadventure, administered to illness, and washed endless piles of bedding by hand.

At the Seymour farm in Sauk County, Wisconsin, by the last week of August 1873, the hops were coming on strong. The pending arrival of the hop pickers sent Ella, Ida, and their mother, Mary Ann, into a frenzy of chores: "Pa and Lon started for hop pickers this morning. We arranged beds, cleaned windows, and Ida mopped some. . . . Mertie [Merton, a younger brother] churned, Ma baked some yesterday and baked more today. I ironed nearly all the white clothes. The pickers got here about eleven o'clock P.M. Most of them were old pickers of ours." Ella and Ida, guided by their mother, hosted the hop pickers whose labors made the mugs full of lager and ale possible on down the line, and the two sisters and their mother all picked hops themselves once the harvest started. In 1873, the Seymour family's pickers stayed until September 5, at which point the hopyard had been picked clean and

Ella and her mother and sister were exhausted: "The pickers started for home early, and so all the hurry & bustle is ended for this season. P.M. The beds are down the floors are mopped, & we can breathe more freely. Windows cleaned also." Ella's experience echoed that of countless farm families across Wisconsin and, to varying degrees, around the hop-growing regions of the world.[19] This book is not simply the tale of a solitary hop farmer's daughter. It is the story of a thousand Ellas, the swamps and valleys they inhabited and altered, and the women's work that drove so much of the nineteenth-century beer trade.

SETTING UP HOPS

The unique properties of the plant that sent Ella's household into such a flurry of chores and visitors each August offer some clues about this annual work. Hops have played a role in the brewing of much of the world's beer for roughly a thousand years.[20] There are very important exceptions. Gruit, chicha, millet beer, and sake, among others, all qualify as beer, all are beverages with long-standing traditions, and none use hops.[21] But for much of the past millennium, a significant amount of the world's beer has been almost unthinkable without a single, unusual plant: *Humulus lupulus*, the hop. The mothers and fathers of today's hops once inhabited wild thickets in China, meadows in ancient Rome, and river bottoms in Europe, and they later grew in cultivated hop gardens in dooryards and European monasteries. As far as archaeologists and historians can determine, beer existed for thousands of years before anyone ever added hops to a brew kettle. Even after hops had become more common in brewing, the unhopped ale called *gruit* still experienced widespread popularity, often brewed with bog myrtle and other herbs that lent bitterness to balance out the sweetness of the malt.[22] But hops conquered much of the beer world by the eighteenth century, especially in Europe and North America.

Hop cones are, to say the least, aromatic. They give off a range of scents depending on the variety, but grassy, citrusy, funky odors all come into play. Some people adore this sensory experience, others not so much. I share handfuls of commercial hop pellets and my home-grown hop cones with the students in my beer seminar each fall, and there is always a very strong difference of opinion as to whether or not that's a pleasant experience. Hops bring alpha acids and essential oils to beer. The alpha acids generate bitterness, effective in balancing out the sweetness of the sugary malt in beer. This bitterness is released in the boil, with more or less bitterness depending on the kind of hops.[23] Many traditional central European varieties, often known as noble hops, give off notably less of this bitterness than the wildly popular Pacific Northwest varieties that grace so many of today's beers. The flavors and aromas that come from the hop cone's essential oils, and comprise a vital part of the sensory experience of an IPA, for example, would be harmed by boiling, so for this element of a beer, brewers often add these hops after the boil.[24]

The papery green cones grow on long bines that clamber clockwise up any support they can find. These cones hold the true treasure from a brewer's and beer drinker's perspective—a waxy yellow substance called *lupulin* that nestles at the base of each petal or bract. Lupulin is the primary source of the bitterness, aroma, and—in the days before pasteurization—preservative qualities that hops bring to beer. Across the Northern Hemisphere, the hop harvest has long taken place in August and September, varying slightly depending on the weather that year, the location, and the hop variety. Today that harvest is far more mechanized—still hard work for those involved, but requiring far fewer hands than the Wisconsin growers at the heart of this book needed back in the day.[25] Once the hops began to ripen, the pickers had to get to work soon enough to avoid rot, pests, and bad weather. Once picked, the hops had to be brought immediately to the nearest hop kiln for drying before being pressed into sacks and shipped onward to breweries in adjacent towns and far-flung cities. Many farmers across the United States in this era added hops to their existing crops in the hopes of increasing revenue, or managing falling prices or yields for their existing crops, with varying degrees of success and failure.

White settler farmers rapidly filled the Ho-Chunk cornfields, ancient prairie, and fertile river bottoms of the southwestern quadrant of Wisconsin with their own field crops including corn, wheat, and oats, and eventually hops and other cash crops. The land on which Wisconsin hops bloomed was and is home to Ho-Chunk, Potawatomi, Menominee, and other Indigenous nations.[26] In 1839, Wisconsin farmers grew more than 200,000 bushels of wheat on just over 15,000 acres of this land. In 1849, they harvested 4.2 million bushels on more than 300,000 acres—a staggering increase in a relatively short period, involving a huge change in land use, population, and ecosystems, particularly "south of Green Bay and east of the Wisconsin River."[27] Wisconsin had just over 1 million acres of "improved" land in 1849 as well ("cleared land used for grazing, grass, or tillage, or lying fallow").[28] By 1869, that figure was 5.9 million acres, and by 1880, there were 9.2 million acres of "improved" land.[29] Even in the 1850s, wheat was both widely planted and not always a successful crop in terms of yield or price. Many farmers had quickly exhausted much of the rich soil they had initially encountered, and they could not always rely on their wheat harvests, so to pay their bills and attempt to turn a profit, they sought other agricultural endeavors including flax, wool, ginseng, tobacco, sugar beets, and hops.[30] Many farmers turned to milk, cheese, and butter alongside wheat and other field crops, but despite Wisconsin's modern-day reputation for cheese, the dairy industry did not fully take hold until the 1880s, with 90 percent of farms having dairy cattle by 1899.[31] We can see similar cycles of boom, bust, and diversification in Kansas, for example, with the failure of corn followed by an overreliance on soft winter wheat.[32]

The hop boom of the 1860s bore similarities to other agricultural and botanical booms, such as tulips, coffee, rubber, and cinchona bark.[33] Individual farmers, speculators, and whole companies set their sights on a given crop as a solution to profitability, sometimes with marked success but often followed by a precipitous drop in price. Historians James Webb's and Stuart McCook's accounts of the volatile history of coffee production bear a particular resemblance to hops, as European growers planted crops in colonized settings in the hope not of subsistence, but of cash, and wealth. Coffee failed in Ceylon (now

Sri Lanka) and India because of rust, not unlike the blight that eventually laid waste to acre upon acre of hop fields in the United States. But even when coffee cultivation began to find a successful foothold in the Americas, other problems arose. While blights posed an obvious danger to profits, widespread bountiful harvests leading to overproduction also threatened to cause a free fall in prices. These boom-and-bust industries may fade from memory in a given place, when the crop has moved on to more successful settings, but they can leave their mark on individual lives and local landscapes, as well as larger industries. In nineteenth-century Wisconsin, hops fit into a broader strategy of settlers trying to make money off the prairies, oak savannas, swamps, and woods the US government had taken from Indigenous nations and made available to mostly white settlers, many either Yankee or European, although there were a handful of Indigenous and Black men who filed claims as well. One of the earliest Black settlers was Charles Shepherd, who moved to Wisconsin in 1848 after being freed from slavery and bought 200 acres of land in Pleasant Ridge.[34]

While many hop fields fit into land that settlers had already plowed up for other commodity crops, there was at least one relatively unique ecological effect of hop cultivation. Because the plants grow best when twining up toward the sun on some kind of support, sometimes growing a foot a day, these farmers and the people they hired chopped down millions of tamarack (or larch), birch, and other saplings to make hop poles, leaving an indelible mark on the hop fields and on surrounding woods and wetlands. Settlers sought out all kinds of timber. The demand for fencing, construction, and firewood, as well as the building of barrels, looms, and wagons all put pressure on the local supply of trees, but hops were unique in the need for such a large number of very young slim trees in such a concentrated time frame and the very sudden rise in demand in the 1860s as the industry boomed.[35] Within a couple of years, hop growing must have denuded the surrounding swamps and forests in the pursuit of millions of hop poles. By the peak of the boom, people had to search farther and farther afield for the necessary poles.

Beer brewers near and far needed hops to make their customers happy. But they needed specific varieties of hops. While there were hops that grew in the river bottoms and woods of North America long before European colonization, such as *Humulus lupulus* var. *lupuloides*, most brewers rejected them as too pungent, preferring to rely on the more conventional brewing hop, *Humulus lupulus* var. *lupulus*, and in particular on a variety long popular in the hopyards of New York. All the evidence I have found suggests that the hop variety "Cluster" and its relatives were the dominant hops grown in this period in Wisconsin. However Cluster itself is, in the words of hop geneticist Josh Havill, "shrouded in mystery": "'Cluster' as we know them in North America are not always the same Cluster that have been grown elsewhere. Cluster itself just represents what was likely a 'found' hop that was more productive than the potential counterpart that was growing in their field originally. Recently, genetic evidence firmly demonstrates that this variety is of hybrid origin, between European and North American populations, consistent with the idea that this was likely a 'found' hop with proximity to commercial production. This process, however, was likely reiterated multiple times across space and time."[36] For a brief time in Wisconsin, hops, primarily Cluster and its kind, solved the problem of profitability for many farmers in the state. And while some of these farmers lived in quite isolated settings for varying stretches of time, many quickly plugged into global circuits of trade, consumption, and information via the post office, trails, roads, shipping lanes, and eventually the railroad.[37] Likewise, as provincial as Ella may have been, she occupied a key position in the global networks of industrializing beer production and the growing thirst for lager. Because brewers of the day bought hops from a range of places, in local and international marketplaces, the hops picked by Ella and her compatriots found their way to towns and cities at home and abroad.

Ella's story exposes patterns that aren't always visible in the landscape. But by linking the archive with the landscape, I began to see the faint outlines of these beery ghosts. Across Wisconsin, individual brewers, historical societies, artists, and landowners have continued to tell parts of this story.[38] I joined in their efforts to recall the history of this plant in Wisconsin by turning to local, state, and national archives, some physical and some digital. I used letters, diaries, ledgers, photographs, and maps carefully indexed and archived by generations of professionals. Books both old and new, scholarly articles, and nineteenth-century newspapers all inform this work. These sources surprised me with their richness, but—like so many archival records—they are also full of silences, the result of both intentional and unintentional omissions.[39]

Perhaps most significantly, Lee Grady at the Wisconsin Historical Society changed the entire course of this book when he said one day, "Well, have you looked at the Agricultural Census?" Reader, I had not, and I didn't even know what it was. Yet today I stand before you as a person who used the immense bound volumes of the Census of Agriculture—the US Census Bureau's agricultural census taken every ten years in conjunction with its main population census—held at that archive to create my own database of more than four thousand nineteenth-century hop farmers.[40] To date, the 1850, 1860, and 1870 volumes of the Wisconsin Census of Agriculture on which I relied—a handwritten record that includes the farmer's name, their township, and the quantities of various crops they harvested since the previous June—have not been digitized. Many states do have digitized individual-level agricultural census data, much of it available on Ancestry.com, but not Wisconsin. And although the overall aggregated statistics are available for counties and states through the United States Department of Agriculture (USDA), to find the identities of individual farmers I had to leaf through thousands of pages of handwritten census forms to find anyone who reported a hop harvest in the previous year. As one guide to the genealogical use of the census declared, "agriculture [census] schedules are little known and rarely used."[41] Yet page by page, sitting at a table at the Wisconsin Historical Society Archives in Madison, Wisconsin, I did indeed make use of them, reading through the records of every county that had reported a hop harvest in 1850, 1860, or 1870. The preprinted census pages in these enormous books are filled with the inky scrawl of clerks and enumerators, some with better handwriting than others. I sought out tiny, handwritten numbers in the "Hops" column, entering the quantity into my database along with the farmer's name, county, and township. These sparse records of farmers and their harvests told me exactly who was growing hops and where, unlike the aggregated harvest data available through the USDA website, and cited throughout this book whenever I am discussing larger-scale analyses. But the database I created is unique in at least two ways. First, it contains each individual farmer and the amount they harvested, information only available in these handwritten volumes or on a very low-quality microfilm. Second, my database also goes one step further. While the agricultural census largely omitted women, I entered every single farmer's name into the digitized and searchable population census records available on Ancestry.com to track down the farmers' wives and households, as well as their birthplaces. Combining these two sources provides a far more complete picture of the people doing the work of raising hops, revealing the larger household often so fundamental to the success of this crop. Ella's diary and other histories of hop picking had quickly made clear to me that the farmer's wife mattered as much to the production of hops as the farmer, and so I sought to discover the full households of hop growers, rather than the sole male name listed in the Census of Agriculture. Although Ella's individual story is unique and illustrative, the census places her in context, surrounded by thousands of other hop-farming families. In most cases, I only know these households as handwritten entries in the census rolls. There are only a handful of diaries, letters, and memoirs detailing the life of the hop picker in nineteenth-century Wisconsin.[42]

When I wasn't knee-deep in archival documents, digitized newspapers, and aging library books, I set out into the landscape itself, scouring the countryside of the hop-growing counties for remnants of the past industry. The graveyards were an obvious place to start, and I walked among the headstones, where I saw the same names I had seen in census records and property maps, engraved in mossy stone. Nearby, however, I also found living remnants of this past. Hops are rhizomatic, so some of the tangle of roots underground grew, expanded, adapted, and survived the transition from hops to today's fields of corn and soybeans, creeping out of the earth on the edges of fields and roads. I used tax records, Google Earth, and old plat maps to find old hops growing up alongside the fields of former hop farmers.[43] From time to time, local newspapers have used these hops as an inspiration to inform their readers about the local hop history, and craft breweries have tracked down these old bines, using them as a source for a historical beer.[44]

When I sit in the archive reading the ledgers of historical breweries, I can almost see, hear, and smell the bales of hops trundling down the newly laid railroad tracks, into the jostling, bustling city, full of mustachioed men in wool suits and warehouses packed to the rafters. I can hear ships' riggings creaking in the harbor and see steamships trailing columns of smoke behind them as they set off across the blue expanse of Lake Michigan laden with bales of hops and other crops. The stark numbers in my spreadsheets, government census reports, and the ledgers of farmers and brewers are abstractions of ecosystems. These seemingly dry statistics teem with life at the ground level. The slim lines of reports charting the rise and fall of harvests and prices represent acre upon acre of living, growing plants, and agronomic gambles on their futures. Hop bines unfurled in the solstice sun, and a few months later legions of calico-clad women entered the fields of August to pluck the fragrant cones. Oblong bales of gunnysacked hops piled up in the train station to be sent off in a cloud of soot and steam by locomotive to Milwaukee, St. Louis, Chicago, and New York, and even sometimes onward by ship to Liverpool. The fields hummed with life in the hot summer. Insects, fungi, unseen mites, and bacteria led full lives in the roots and leaves of the plants. Birds and skunks and badgers picked through the plant matter and insects at the base of the plants.[45]

The landscapes of Milwaukee and Wisconsin yield only the smallest clues about what once happened here. Today everyone in this story is a ghost. The up-and-coming brewers of Milwaukee and beyond, folks like Valentin Blatz, Frederick Pabst, and Joseph Schlitz, relied on Ella and young women like her. We only have a few pages of Ella's life, but it is enough to turn our attention to a story that tends to be hidden in the vivid accounts of the rise of the beer barons and the flood of beer rising across the planet in the late nineteenth century. Ella calls upon us to consider the bigger webs of agricultural and ecological change that we inhabit and the ways that the things we eat, drink, wear, or drive all have corresponding landscapes and laborscapes.[46] Much as Anna Tsing finds the imprint of late capitalism in the pursuit of mushrooms in damaged forests, Wisconsin's hop boom and bust reveals the workings of late nineteenth-century systems of agriculture and the movement of goods and people across territories to generate profit and meet consumer demand—and the centrality of women to these endeavors.[47]

Ella teaches us that what happens inside houses matters for what happens outside them. The work of women in the fields and the home helped fuel the ascent of the nineteenth-century beer industry. The macro only happens through the micro. The hops that found their way into nineteenth-century brew kettles came from very real places and were made possible by the work of very real people. Along the way, these very real people encountered pirates, wolves, and hopyard romances. It all came to an end in verdant cemeteries and abandoned hop plants curling up the trees along today's fields of corn and soybeans, and in stories that families and communities may still tell each other today, here and there.

The story of Ella and her hops originates not in Wisconsin but in New York. Both of her parents were born there, and the ancestors of the hops they grew came from there as well. The Seymours acquired their first hop rhizomes in the early 1860s from a nearby farmer, Jesse Cottington, with direct connections to New York's prime hop fields. It was decades earlier, however, that the first brewing hops arrived in Wisconsin, in the form of roots grubbed up in New York not far from where Cottington later acquired his own rhizomes. These first commercial hops to be grown with brewing in mind in Wisconsin came ashore on June 9, 1837, sixteen years before Ella's birth, in the luggage of James and Elizabeth Weaver as they disembarked the schoo-

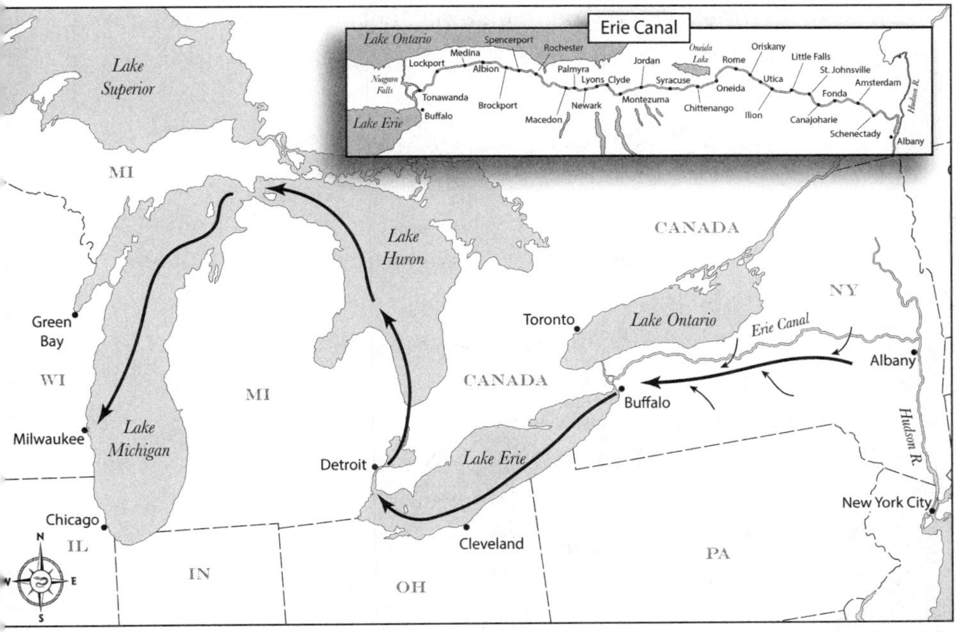

FIGURE P.4. Map of the Erie Canal and Great Lakes route from Albany, New York, to Milwaukee, Wisconsin. Map created by John Wyatt Greenlee, Surprised Eel Mapping, 2025.

ner *Julia Palmer*, a journey that had begun in Oneida County, New York, followed the Erie Canal to Buffalo, and then sailed first across Lake Erie, then up Lake Huron, and down and across Lake Michigan (figure P.4). As central as Ella and the rest of the Seymour family are to understanding the origins of Wisconsin hops, they were by no means the first hop farmers in the state. That title (for now) goes to James and Elizabeth Weaver, who, along with their extended family, played a starring role in the rise of Wisconsin's hop industry. James and Elizabeth arrived in what would later become Waukesha County eleven years before Wisconsin became a state, two years after the state's first documented brewery opened in Mineral Point, and two or three years before the first brewery opened in Milwaukee.[48] The Weavers matter both because they brought the first brewing hops to Wisconsin that we know of, and because they became a dynasty of growers and dealers, shaping the industry in the state and supplying the growing beer trade.

Both the farmers and the plant material that anchored the Wisconsin industry had roots in New York.[49]

SIDEBAR: HOP BOTANY, VARIETIES, AND HUSBANDRY

The plant carried in the Weavers' luggage, and causing so much extra work for Ella each August, is in the Cannabaceae family, although without the psychoactive properties of its better-known cousin, cannabis. The hop species is divided into five subspecies. Most of the hops used in brewing today trace their lineage to wild European hops that were slowly domesticated and then fanned out across the world. The first hops to grow in the territory that we now call Wisconsin were wild, indigenous North American hops, *Humulus lupulus* var. *pubescens*, but they have been of little use to brewers. Elsewhere in North America, other varieties of native hops grow, including *Humulus lupulus* var. *lupuloides* on the East Coast and *Humulus lupulus* var. *neomexicanus* in parts of the Southwest, and are similarly largely (although not entirely) uninteresting to most brewers.[50] The globally preferred brewing hop is *Humulus lupulus* var. *lupulus*, brought to North America by European colonists. Cluster—the star of the show in so many nineteenth-century US hop fields—appears to be a cross between a *lupulus* and a *lupuloides*.[51] This was most likely the hop that Ella Seymour and her family and most of the farmers in this book grew and picked, and it was perhaps the most important North American hop in the nineteenth century.

Hops prefer deep, alluvial soil for their long thirsty roots. They need something to climb, and there should be good air circulation between the plants. And they require the daylight that falls between the 30th or 35th and 55th parallels in each hemisphere, and in places with the right combination of weather patterns. In the wild, new growth twines up the previous year's growth, while cultivated hops are generally cut all the way to the ground at the end of the growing season and regrow from the ground up in the coming spring and summer, as much as a foot in a day at their peak.[52] The female plants are the plants of interest to brewers, as they produce the lupulin-rich cones. Each day as the summer draws to a close, the yellow lupulin in the heart of the cone grows yellower, less grassy, ever closer to the ideal balance of acids and oils preferred by brewers and beer drinkers. Harvest too soon and the lupulin will be underdeveloped and not up to the task of delivering its bittering and aromatic properties to the beer. Harvest too late and the grower may lose the entire crop to aphids, hail, mildew, or rot. Hops are *dioecious*—that is, unlike most plants, there are separate male and female plants, and they cannot self-pollinate. But they can reproduce asexually through their rhizomes, with or without human help. To get what humans want from hops, growers often plant them in a botanical nunnery, reproducing them either with the asexual act of grubbing up the rhizomatic roots and chopping them up to make new plants or by taking slips of plant and rooting them in a sterile hothouse.

Early European settler depictions of the landscape of North America repeatedly remarked on the presence of hops, perhaps as shorthand for fertile land and growing conditions that might favor other plants brought from Europe. Hops grew in the French settlement at Vincennes, in what would become Indiana, in the eighteenth century.[53] In the vicinity of St. Louis, French military officer and explorer Georges-Henri-Victor Collot described the vegetation he saw on his 1796 journey through the area, including hops and dozens of other named plants.[54] President Thomas Jefferson mentioned wild hops as he reported the findings of the Lewis and Clark and other expeditions in 1806: "wild mint of three kinds, coloquintida (bitter apple) growing along the river side, clover, sheeps clover, life everlasting, wild liquorice, mary gold, missletoe, thistle, wild hemp, bulrush, dittany, white and red poppy, yellow jessamine, poke, fern, capillaire, honeysuckle, mosses, petu to make ropes with, wormwood, hops, ipecacuanha, persicaria, Indian turnip, wild carrot, wild onion, ginger, wild cabbage and bastard indigo."[55] In his diaries written between 1809 and 1811, Scottish naturalist John Bradbury wrote of his travels along the Missouri River, "I had an opportunity of going ashore, and found the soil to have the appearance of greatest fertility. On the sides of the hills I noticed an abundance of the hop plant, (humulus lupulus)."[56] Such early hop sightings also included the river and creek banks of Wisconsin.[57] A book of advice for Europeans seeking to settle in the Midwest reported, in the 1850s, that "there are currants of all varieties but only in the gardens. At least I have not yet encountered any in the woods although I have been assured that there are some growing wild. Raspberries in some neighborhoods, particularly northern ones, grow wild. Wild hops are also found, especially along the streams."[58] Whereas these wild hops might have found their way into a hearthside brew kettle or two, the increasing numbers of brewers and beer drinkers in the region in the mid-1800s preferred the hops being grown in New York state, which were taking root in Wisconsin during that period.

The nineteenth-century approach to hop cultivation was widely circulated in newspapers and pamphlets. Farmers would plant rhizomes "several feet apart in hills to allow for proper drainage, light, and cultivation. Then the farmer had to wait, for hops yielded in the second year, and only after three years would there be a full crop.... From first planting, hops [*sic*] yards had to be plowed, grubbed, and fertilized in the spring to ensure proper growth."[59] Farmers needed to combat weeds, and keep the soil rich and the hop roots happy, in part by digging them up in the spring to prune them back, in turn yielding more rhizomes to sell on to neighbors or to use in additional hop acreage. Poles needed to be set in the hills, as the hops grow best when supported by something they can climb, spiraling clockwise toward the sun. The young shoots would need to be tied to the poles—often the work of the women and children of a household, although sometimes outsourced to hired hands. While picking required the largest labor force, smaller quantities of (often female) workers were required at other parts of the season. According to Belle Cushman Bohn, the daughter of hop farmers, who herself tended hops, "When the vines were long enough to twine around the poles, a girl or woman cut off the top of an old yarn sock, drew it over her left arm, and raveled it as needed to tie the vines to the poles. The workers were busy nearly every day twining and tying the new growth, and many of them, I remember, complained of sore fingers as the vines were rough and scratchy."[60] One recollection outlined three increasingly risky stages of tying hops to the poles: "first, from the ground; next, from a step ladder, and last from a horse's back. The food for the help was much the same at all meals, such as you would expect at any picnic dinner of the present day. We paid $1 a day to young ladies for tying them [the hops] to the pole."[61] Ella, her sister, and their mother tied hops in her father Silas's hopyard as well. Silas or hired hands or elder sons would grub up older fields to create hop root cuttings for sale or for expanding the farmer's own hop acreage and to refresh the plants. A local newspaper article advised, "Grubbing should be done by the 10th of May, the roots cut and assorted, and the good ones placed in a pit in the ground or in a coal cellar, to preserve them from growing as much as possible."[62]

When the farmer decided it was time to harvest, and the picking crew had arrived and settled in, a man in the role of pole puller would cut the hop bine at the root and lift the hop-covered pole, setting it across a four-sectioned wooden box for picking. As one former hop picker recalled (albeit in a novel she later wrote), "The brawny, young giants tugged and dragged [the hop poles out of the ground] all the while pouring out a steady stream of profanity."[63] Four women would stand at the box, picking each hop cone by hand and dropping it into their section of the box. A box tender—sometimes (but not always) the same person as the pole puller—would bag up the picked hops, transport them to the kiln, and in some cases fetch water for the pickers. When all the cones had been removed, the pole would be stripped of the remaining bines, and, as long as it was still in reasonably good shape, stacked to be used again the following year. Such stacks are visible in several of the photographs in this book.

Then as now, hops need to be dried very soon after picking, as their moisture content makes them prone to rotting. As I discuss in more detail in chapter 7, Wisconsin farmers built hop houses or hop kilns of stone, brick, or wood, where "hops were laid out on canvas cloth that was placed across slats above stoves in hop kilns, dried slowly using sulfur to cure them, then pressed into large bales. Each step required specialized knowledge, and badly prepared hops had little value."[64] Bales varied in weight, between 180 and 200 pounds or so. European bales were often much heavier, the hops packed into much larger sacks, so the bale is not a useful measure across national borders.

Not only were many beloved varieties a century or more away from being bred, variety—as we understand it today—was simply not as meaningful a category to the industry. Quality and region provided much of the categorization of hops of the day, and sometimes a farmer's name. In newspaper and government reporting on the hop market in the 1850s–1870s period, the main focus of this book, there was comparatively little mention of variety. That started to change later in the nineteenth century, and indeed, many of the big developments in brewing (such as refrigeration and more systematic hop breeding) started to take off in the 1880s, just over the horizon from the period of this book. In the time just before and after the American Civil War, journalists, dealers, and government analysts tended to focus on location, age, and quality more than variety, although sometimes location was something of a proxy for variety. As Emmet Wells, a widely published hop dealer, explained in 1868:

> The comparative value of hops is determined by their color, strength, and aroma. The grades indicating the different qualities, usually adopted in the markets, are the fancy, prime, common and mouldy goods and though no commodity is so difficult to grade from sample as hops, yet the distinguishing characteristics of the different grades may be set as follows: Prime hops must be reasonably unbroken, clean and of a uniformly lively light yellow color, though it is regarded as no disparagement to show brown tints at the tips of the leaves, such being held an evidence that the hop was mature and that it has been bleached with brimstone [sulfur].[65]

Much of this assessment of quality relates to the picking itself, as well as the speed and skill of drying. That same year, a reporter from Waupaca County described the various qualities of hops, emphasizing clean picking and skillful drying:

> They must be of medium size and well charged with lufulia [lupulin], the yellow dust that envelops the seeds and lower half of the leaf. They . . . must possess largely the peculiar aroma of the hop. The fancy grades possess all these qualities . . . and must especially excel in fragrance and further must possess an assurance of superior excellence from the previous reputation of certain districts or individual growers. Common hops are those deficient in any of the requirements of prime hops and most frequently are not lacking in strength but are deteriorated by slovenly picking and unskillful curing. . . . Fancy hops are mainly consumed by eastern brewers for fine liquors to whom hops of undoubted excellence are not only desirable but necessary, as their reputation and success in business depends upon the quality of their hops.[66]

Today's beer brewer may be puzzled by these categories that were the common parlance of the nineteenth-century hop trade, but these judgments of quality show a direct connection between the work of the pickers and the experience of the beer drinker. Here, however, we can also discern a phenomenon familiar to today's brewers as well: Some hops are best suited as *bittering* hops, the first to enter the brew kettle—with high alpha acids whose bitterness remains in the beer, even if the aromas are boiled away. These hops contrast with the *aroma* hops, added at later stages of brewing to keep the aroma created by the hops' essential oils. As we will see, based both on brewery ledgers and on import and export figures, brewers of the 1860s and 1870s bought all kinds of hops from all kinds of places, depending on price, availability, consumer demand, suitedness to a particular brew, and other factors.

Many US hops in the time frame of this book would have been

Cluster or its kin with some important exceptions (in particular, the range of varieties began to expand as the nineteenth century came to a close, and as hop production increased on the West Coast).[67] According to a later *Yearbook of Agriculture*, "In the important years of production in New York several varieties grown included English Cluster, Grape, Canada Red, Palmer Seedling, and Humphrey Seedling."[68] Another source indicated that "two varieties of the hop are principally grown in New York, being known as the large and small cluster," helpfully adding that there is little difference between the two "excepting the one is larger than the other."[69] To date, I have not found a single mention of German hops being grown in this era in Wisconsin, and few examples of anything but New York hops being grown. That doesn't mean there were no German hops, but in many years of research I have not seen a convincing reference to people planting German varieties of hops, or any of the hops traditionally associated with German, Czech, or Austrian lager. At least one group of Flemish immigrants did bring their own hops and grew them somewhat commercially: "The Vander Kelens brought seeds of the rich hops of Flanders. For many years, the good home-brew quaffed in the community was made from these hops. . . . [The family] grew hopvines around the back porch and on a string framework 9-feet high in the fields. The rows were always planted in a North-South direction to get the most sun. The harvested hops were piled in a shed on slats with a drying-fire underneath. Then they were bleached with sulfur; Sulphur-saturated rags were burned on wires around the stove for one day."[70] Were I an enthusiast of nineteenth-century Belgian hops, I would scour the margins of the Vander Kelens' former farms in Brown County, Wisconsin. I might look in Sections 7 and 8 of Humboldt Township.

PART 1

GROUNDWORK

1

SCOW AND SCHOONER

From New York to Wisconsin

Returning to the year 1837, the Weavers who were introduced at the end of the prologue merit our attention for three reasons. First, they are the earliest known growers of the hop plant *Humulus lupulus* var. *lupulus* in Wisconsin. Second, their journey illustrates the journeys taken by Ella Seymour's parents and thousands of other subsequent hop farmers. Third, and above all, James Weaver (figure 1.1) did not arrive alone. Even if it is only his name and the names of his brothers and sons that appear in the original handwritten volumes of the Census of Agriculture and in the brewery ledgers, James traveled in the company of his wife, Elizabeth, and a slew of daughters whose work made his relative fame and fortune possible. One source suggests that the Weavers brought hop roots for their own home brewing of ale.[1] Yet James Weaver—an experienced hop grower with a well-established network of hop dealers and growers back in New York—may have had bigger plans, envisioning a future where there would be demand for his hops on a commercial scale. He was not wrong, and eventually hops made many members of the Weaver family quite wealthy. They became growers and dealers for breweries across Wisconsin, their surname peppered across the surviving ledgers of the Pabst and Blatz breweries.[2] Despite the later dominance of Sauk County in terms of hop production, Wisconsin's hop industry originated near the small

FIGURE 1.1. James Weaver. Western Historical Company, *The History of Waukesha County*, 130a.

town of Sussex, in Waukesha County, around nineteen miles northwest of the port of Milwaukee.

The sort of hops found in the Weavers' luggage had been popularized in the previous decades of the nineteenth century by the hop growers of New York state, and especially the region the Weavers had just departed. Their family's well-documented journey to Wisconsin resembles the journeys of thousands of eventual hop farmers who traveled from New York to Wisconsin. They, and later New York immigrants to Wisconsin, brought with them both the literal roots of the hop industry and a deep familiarity with the needs of this plant—from properly training them up poles to constructing kilns to dry them for baling and transport, working with the hop dealers who delivered much of the harvest to breweries, and hiring and hosting young women from neighboring farms and towns to harvest their hops.[3]

Like many of the early hop growers, the Weavers were both born in England— in their case, Sussex, James in 1800 and Elizabeth in 1802—and they spent considerable time in the hop-growing regions of New York before coming to Wisconsin. The Census of Agriculture listed farmers born in New York and England as the main growers of Wisconsin's hops in 1850 (the first year data were collected on hops in Wisconsin).[4] James Weaver married Elizabeth Fielder in 1822. Before they ever thought of heading to Wisconsin, the extended Weaver family sailed from the United Kingdom to New York, departing from Rye Harbor on March 10, 1830, on the brig *Emma*, and arriving in New York City on April 19, 1830.[5] They made their way to Oneida County, not far from Utica, New York, where James became a hop farmer, as his father had bought a farm for him that had already been planted in hops.[6]

Oneida County supplied more than 38,000 pounds of hops to the US brewing industry in 1840, and New York was the single most important hop-growing state until the early twentieth century.[7] Places like Oneida County were not simply supplying local breweries—they grew such large quantities of hops that even in the first half of the nineteenth century they were exporting well beyond their borders, in the United States and abroad. With "the relaxation of the British Corn Laws in the late 1840s [that] created a ready market for American hops," and with the growth in demand for beer at home and abroad, raising hops could be very profitable, as in a good year an acre of hops brought in far more cash than an acre of wheat.[8] But the industry was (and still is) a fickle one, with stark fluctuations in prices shaped by everything from changing consumer tastes to wars near and far, mildew, aphids, hailstorms, temperance movements, and even ill-timed bumper crops that led to a crash in prices as high-quality hops flooded the market. The hop-growing counties of New York had cracked the code, for a while, and New York reigned supreme in hop production from the early nineteenth century into the early twentieth.[9] The first documented hopyard in New York dates to 1808, when James D. Coolidge planted hops in Madison County, which later became a center of the industry alongside Oneida County.[10] At the time, many brewers were still importing English hops. By the time the Weavers arrived in New

York, a successful—and cutthroat—industry reigned, relying primarily on hops like Cluster and employing thousands of young women among the hop-picking labor force.[11]

After a few years of tending hops in New York, the Weavers began to consider a move to land ceded to the United States in Treaty 187, signed by representatives of the Chippewa (Ojibwe), Ottawa, and Potawatomi Nations.[12] This 1833 treaty included 5 million acres in southeastern Wisconsin and northern Illinois, some of which later became the home of the hop industry, as well as the wheat, corn, and other field crops that often predated hop cultivation on a given farm. The Weaver family could plan a Wisconsin future only because of these US efforts to envision and render land empty that was not empty at all but instead full of homes, cornfields, gardens, well-built trails, graves, and memories. James's brother John and sister-in-law Melinda preceded James and Elizabeth in journeying to the lands of Treaty 187, following a brother-in-law who had already headed west.[13] When they reported back that it looked to be a promising place to settle, James and his wife Elizabeth and their many children soon followed.

In 1875–76, Melinda Weaver wrote a small book, *Memories of Early Days*, recounting her first years in Wisconsin, including the journey west, which illuminates the path followed by her own family and by so many of the people who later came to grow hops in Wisconsin and who occupy the pages of this book. Melinda's own description of her journey helps us better understand how people like Ella's parents, Silas and Mary Ann Seymour, and the hops that moved from New York to Wisconsin and supplied the early breweries made their way across the Great Lakes. Melinda's experience may have been unique, but many of the wives and daughters at the heart of this story followed a similar path, as did the hops themselves.

On a September day in 1836, Melinda Weaver stood on deck aboard the becalmed schooner *Alleghan* on a glassy Lake Michigan, eight months pregnant and in the company of two toddlers. She found herself in the middle of an unexpectedly lengthy journey from her former home in New York to Wisconsin. Melinda's route was unique in some ways (more pirates, less wind), but otherwise many of the Yankee and

European immigrant settlers traveling into newly ceded territory in Wisconsin experienced a similar journey. Melinda and women like her teach us that the men whose names fill the handwritten pages of the Census of Agriculture that I read at the Wisconsin Historical Society Archives were rarely traveling alone, and often had wives and children in tow. Then as now, the census boxed people into its categories, in the form of preprinted census sheets that constrained how the census taker could list people, products, and property. The population census smoothed, and continues to smooth, out the edges of the complexity of marriage, gender, sexuality, and family, as well as race and ethnicity. The stark columns can obscure a range of ways of loving and being, and the census is full of secrets, many of which may never be revealed.[14] The Census of Agriculture schedules leave just enough space to enter the name of a solitary person in the farmer column (occasionally squeezing in the surnames of two business partners), who, in Wisconsin in 1850, 1860, and 1870, was almost always a white man. Women have played central roles in agriculture both around the world and throughout history, yet the people who appear in most of the nineteenth-century US agricultural records in Wisconsin were by and large male and white. But many of their lives were intimately intertwined with the lives of women and children. English lacks a word for *farmer* that is not implicitly male. (Think of "farmer" versus "farmer's wife"—how often have you heard "farmer's husband"?) But these farming endeavors were often conducted with the money and intention of a married couple, where the wife may have had a strong role in decision-making and even an important role in the physical labor of farming. Many such couples journeyed together on scows and schooners, westward to Wisconsin.

In the many years before Wisconsin could grow enough hops to meet the demand of Wisconsin brewers, hops themselves traveled very similar routes, arriving by steamer or schooner in the ports of Milwaukee, Southport (today's Kenosha), and Racine along the western shore of Lake Michigan. Ads for "eastern" hops, shipped from New York, checkered the local papers.[15] Milwaukee brewers, and anyone else coming into town for other supplies, could buy hops by the bale (usually 180–200 pounds) or smaller quantities at a range of drugstores, general stores, and breweries. At varying points in the 1840s and 1850s, Cunningham's, Daggett & Richardson's Variety Store, A. F. Clarke's, E. Hathaway (who also sold yeast), and the Eagle Brewery all sold hops. By September 1848, William Cunningham had ten bales of hops on hand for sale at his store at 151 E. Water Street.[16] In April 1850, L. J. Higby of Milwaukee had a whopping twenty-eight bales of hops on hand, all shipped into town from Oneida County, New York—that is something like 5,600 pounds of hops, enough for three thousand to five thousand barrels of beer.[17] Wells & Hill had seventy bales of hops "1st Sort New York" on hand in December 1851, and Dousman & Co. was selling "a choice lot of hops" in January 1853.[18] The brewers and hop farmers of Wisconsin, as isolated as they may have been geographically, avidly read newspapers that obliged them not only with ads for imported hops and other goods but also with reports of the hop markets in New York, England, and Germany.

Melinda and John Weaver did not plant hops themselves, but they forged the path for John's brother James to become the first hop grower in Wisconsin, and one of the most influential, prolific, and successful ones at that. James Weaver sent his brother and sister-in-law on ahead of him in part because their family was smaller—just two very young children and one on the way. Melinda and John departed from their home in Augusta (in Oneida County), New York, on September 1, 1836. They traveled fourteen miles in two wagons laden with their worldly possessions to Lenox Basin, where they boarded a canal boat bound for Buffalo. Construction of the Erie Canal had concluded in 1825, and shortly thereafter steamships had begun to navigate the Great Lakes, providing ever-swifter connections between New York and points west. In the 1830s, trade picked up, with ships sailing from Buffalo, Cleveland, and Detroit.[19] By 1835, about 150 brigs, steamboats, and schooners worked the ports of Lake Michigan.[20] Most of the hops that ended up in Milwaukee beer at the time would have traveled a route similar to that of the Weavers themselves, via the Erie Canal and the Great Lakes (as illustrated by figure P.4 in the prologue). Cargo tended to travel under sail, and passengers tended to travel under steam, as apparently the steamships provided a slightly smoother and more comfortable ride than sail-powered vessels.[21] In the 1830s, the quantity of shipping escalated along with the increase in settlers. Between 1835 and 1836, shipping went from arrivals of 80 schooners and 2 steamboats at the port of Milwaukee to arrivals of 19 steamboats and more than twice as many sailing vessels; by 1839, there were 182 steamboat arrivals and 118 sail arrivals.[22] In 1837, the steamer *James Madison* brought a thousand passengers and four thousand barrels of freight into the port. That is a massive change in just a few years, one that made the coming boom of breweries and hop fields possible.[23]

Long before travelers or cargo reached the port of Milwaukee, the ride along the Erie Canal may have been the pleasantest part of the journey, at a gentle clip of 4 miles per hour thanks to the horses or mules pulling the vessel. Canal or packet boats typically had one large interior space that would be divided with blankets into sleeping quarters. Passengers spent much of the journey sitting on the roof of the boat if the weather allowed, except when approaching low bridges, when everyone had to scramble out of the way.[24] The packet boat dropped off John and Melinda Weaver and their two small children in Buffalo, where they boarded the steamer *Monroe* to travel the length of Lake Erie, from Buffalo to Detroit, a journey that lasted from 8 a.m. Tuesday to 2 p.m. Thursday.[25] The *Monroe* had a fairly substantial seventy-one berths.[26] By the time the Weavers arrived in Detroit, they had missed the boat they wanted to catch to Milwaukee. As luck would have it, a storm blew another ship, the schooner *Alleghan*, into the Detroit harbor in the middle of the night, so they boarded that ship even though its destination was Chicago rather than Milwaukee. The *Alleghan* struggled mightily to get to Chicago, although it met a far better fate (at least on this journey) than the hundreds of vessels that lie at the bottom of the Great Lakes.[27] Early in the journey, the ship hit a sandbar. An hour after the crew had laboriously dug the *Alleghan* free of the sandbar, the wind died. Melinda recalled, "We had to lay there still until the next day at three o'clock when a steamboat came puffing along and took our schooner on one side and the brig *Illinois* on the other, and towed both vessels about six miles." A few hours later, the wind died again. Later in the season the wind picks up but can quickly become the "Witch of November," a howling gale that has sent many a vessel to the deep cold bottom of the lakes, perhaps most famously the wreck of the *Edmund Fitzgerald*. On this particular journey, aboard the *Alleghan* early enough in the fall to avoid the gales, the wind continued to disappoint, Melinda recounted, including "three days in one place by the side of the Manitou Islands and within a mile of the shore."[28]

Then came the pirates. As Melinda remembered, "When we first started from Detroit the captain told us that if we had good weather and favorable wind, and didn't get taken by pirates, he hoped to get us to Chicago in a week. We all thought he was joking about the pirates, but he said that it was no joke at all, for there had been a pirate vessel on the lakes that summer." The pirates had been arrested but then freed for lack of evidence. Sure enough, a few days into Melinda's journey across Lake Michigan, the captain of the *Alleghan* saw a vessel that was not included on his exhaustive list of "every vessel that had gone before him for the last month." The unknown vessel pursued theirs at varying speeds, and at one point "the captain ordered his men to clew [adjust the sail] and load all the guns belonging to the vessel . . . and likewise requested the passengers who had guns with them to do the same."[29] The captain was concerned enough to keep the night watch himself, not his usual habit. But, for whatever reason—perhaps the bristling armaments on this ship's gunwales—that was the last they saw of the mystery vessel.

Immigrants to Wisconsin from New York, Vermont, and other points east reported similar journeys, albeit rarely with pirates astern: dirty taverns, kidney-jostling stagecoach rides, the bustle of the Buffalo port as steamer agents competed for passengers, and sailing across some of the largest lakes in the world, subject to alternating bouts of terrifying storms and windless days.[30] One traveler described sending his belongings on the brig *Neptune* to Milwaukee, while he took a steamer to Detroit. At one point pretty much everyone on board was seasick. They all slept belowdecks, in various states of undress that ran counter to the conventions of Victorian modesty. By the 1850s, the railroad was in place, and many travelers opted for the train rather than the Erie Canal and the Great Lakes—the train was more expensive but faster and more comfortable.[31] Even after the railroad reached all the way to Milwaukee, Great Lakes shipping continued to be important for both passengers and cargo, and goods and people would have encountered these conditions whether heading east or west. Agoston Haraszthy (whom we will meet again later, as some sources list him as the first hop farmer of Sauk County) wrote a vivid recollection of the journey traveling from the East Coast to Sauk County, including a woodsy route, some of which the Weavers may have followed, between downtown Milwaukee and the village of Waukesha.[32] Haraszthy's journey across Lake Huron included his steamer colliding with a heavily laden salt ship that promptly sank with its $11,000 cargo, although the crew made it safely to Haraszthy's steamer.[33] Soon enough, his captain had come to the aid of the steamer *Cleveland* (which had itself carried hops across the Great Lakes), which had run aground. Crossing the Great Lakes was no pleasure cruise in the nineteenth century.[34]

By this point, more than three weeks had passed since Melinda's family had left their New York home. While the pirates had disappeared over the horizon, the lack of wind on the lake continued to pose a problem. The breeze picked up again, then died down again, this time leaving them in a fogbank. Even though the *Alleghan* captain's compass had inconveniently ceased to function, he managed to guide his ship through the gloom and into the port of Milwaukee. Given how many of his passengers had Milwaukee as their final destination, the captain had decided to make an unscheduled stop there rather than head straight to Chicago. His Milwaukee passengers disembarked into a rowboat that shuttled them back to the Milwaukee shore as a storm gathered. Like many of the Lake Michigan ports, Milwaukee posed challenges to the captains and crews of approaching vessels, including a sandbar blocking the entrance to the confluence of the

Milwaukee, Menomonee, and Kinnickinnic Rivers.[35] But it was the best option for miles around, according to one scholar who studied the port's history: "Ships passing from Lake Huron through the Straits of Mackinac found Milwaukee the only haven between the Manitou Islands and Chicago and it was customary for them to run for Milwaukee in inclement weather."[36] The broad bay provided more protection than the rest of the western shore of Lake Michigan, but it was still completely exposed to easterly storms.

On any given day today, landing in a rowboat on the often choppy Milwaukee shore would be a challenge—much less nearly two hundred years ago for Melinda: at night, in an oncoming storm, while more than eight months pregnant and wearing a floor-length skirt, with two toddlers in tow. Once the Weaver family and their possessions were on reasonably dry land, they left their belongings on the darkened shore and took shelter in a stranger's nearby cabin. Melinda had insisted on bringing furniture with them on this entire journey, so there must have been a stack of their furniture at the base of the bluffs as well. The roar of the waves driven into shore by the howling storm was so loud that it kept her awake all night, even from the relatively safe confines of the cabin.

Heading west to his intended homestead, John left Melinda and their two small children in Milwaukee, where she soon gave birth to their third child, on October 13, 1836.[37] (I have no idea how many midwives were in Milwaukee at the time, but later city directories listed more than a dozen in town in the late 1850s.[38]) A slightly later description portrayed Milwaukee in the following way, which must have resembled what John and Melinda experienced: "The magnificent city was then a hamlet, no pier had been constructed, and the passengers were therefore taken ashore, at the mouth of the Milwaukee River, on an old flat-bottomed scow. As there was no bridge across the Milwaukee River, they were taken over by means of a crude ferry-boat drawn by hand, along a rope stretched from shore to shore. . . . What is now the most valuable portion of the city was then a tamarack swamp, made joyous at evening by the croaking of hundreds of frogs. Where the great railroad depots, the principal factories and Pabst's brewery now stand."[39] Likewise, rich expanses of *Manoomin* (also spelled *Manomin* or *Mnoomin*, and commonly if incorrectly called wild rice) lined the rivers and wetlands, harvested by canoe by Potawatomi and other Indigenous residents of this area at the convergence of three rivers that later became the "Machine Shop of the World."[40]

John returned to collect his growing family at the end of February 1837. They spent three days traveling from Milwaukee to Lisbon (see figure 1.2), presumably in bitter cold but with comparatively easy travels by sleigh across snowy prairie and frozen rivers.[41] Sleighs and sleds brought welcome speed in the depths of winter, but sleighing became dangerous in March as the ice would start to break up on the many rivers that needed to be crossed. One of Melinda's neighbors set out with a team of oxen to buy grain in Milwaukee, but on the return trip the ice had started to break up: "Then he took the ox whip himself and hurried the team along as fast as possible, for he had seen cracks in the ice, when he crossed the river, and water above the ice, half way to his boot tops, and when they got back there, the water was deeper and the cracks in the ice wider."[42]

The Weavers moved to a cabin they shared with two other families, and with various claim-seeking men. These dwellings were made of the forest timber and with the labor of bodies, built without a sawmill nearby—each board sawed by hand. Wolves were frequent visitors, including one night when Melinda "heard the wolves howl nearly all night."[43] From day one, the Weavers had neighbors. According to one history of Waukesha County, "When the first white settlers came to Waukesha County, in 1835 and 1836, there were many small camps and a few large Potawatomi villages on the banks of its streams and lakes. The principal villages were at Waukesha and Pewaukee, near the center of the county; at Mukwonago, at its southern boundary line, and at Muskego Lake, in its southeastern corner."[44] The Weavers lived near a major Ho-Chunk village and traded flour for venison with their Indigenous neighbors.[45] They planted familiar crops on unfamiliar land—potatoes, turnips, corn, beans, and later buckwheat and oats. By 1860, various members of the Weaver family were growing wheat, corn, oats, potatoes, barley, fruit trees, and hops; shearing sheep for

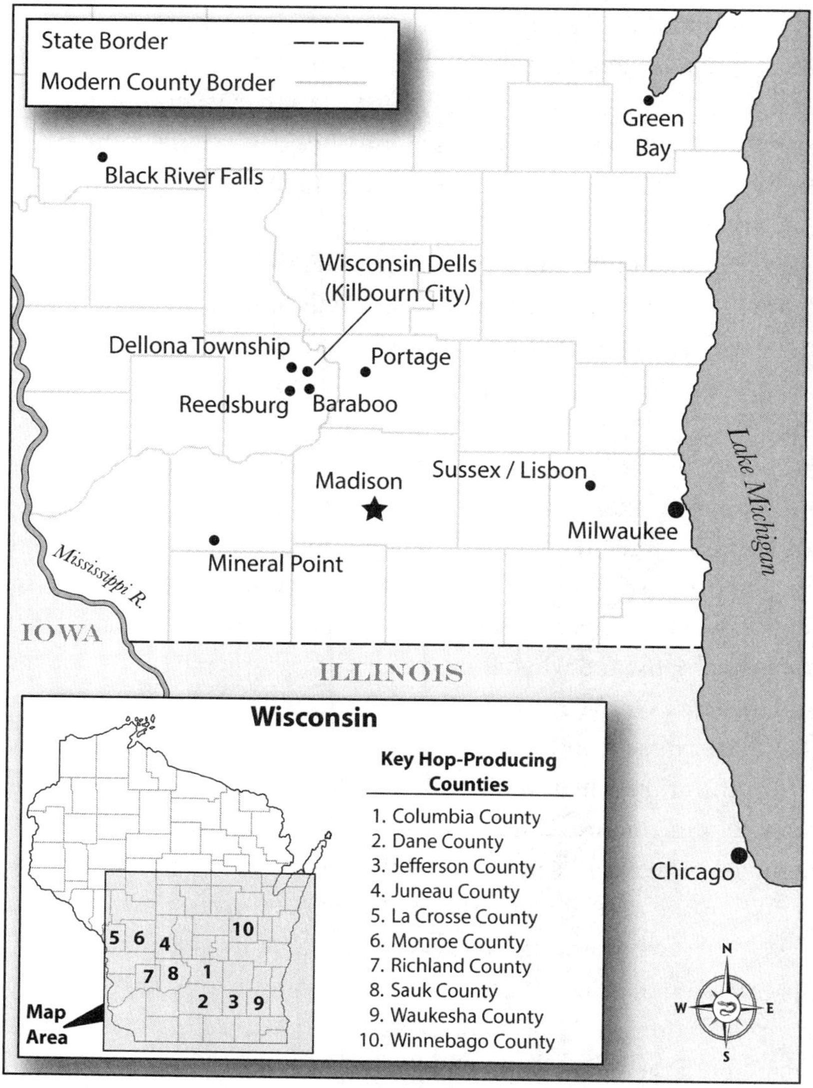

FIGURE 1.2. Map of key locations in Wisconsin. Map created by John Wyatt Greenlee, Surprised Eel Mapping, 2025.

hundreds of pounds of wool; and producing hundreds of pounds of butter and cheese.[46] Women were actively involved in gardening and in fieldwork. Melinda recounted, "In harvest time we could and did carry sheaves [presumably of wheat] together and shock them, and sometimes help load and stack, and pick up potatoes, husk corn, feed swine."[47] The Weavers kept sheep at one point but lost many of them to wolves. When Melinda arrived, the land felt like wilderness to her because she couldn't (or chose not to) recognize the trails, the blazes, the edible or otherwise useful plants, and the filigree of use and memory that lay across the land. She and most of the other white settlers put themselves at odds with the people whose land they occupied. She had no knowledge of the nearby sacred fishing sites, the caches of corn and dried roots and fish. She entered a land rich in Indigenous cornfields, gardens, sites of worship, villages and sugaring camps, and even racetracks.[48] It was only a wilderness in her mind and in the words of US lawmakers and boosters.

By and large, Wisconsin's cultivated hops fit into land that settlers had already cleared for wheat and other field crops in the wake of treaties signed by Ho-Chunk, Potawatomi, and other Wisconsin nations in the 1830s across southern Wisconsin—treaties often broken in later decades by the US government and the mostly white settlers it aided. The Ho-Chunk Nation was not a signatory to Treaty 187 of 1833, not because Ho-Chunk people did not inhabit this land but because of the arbitrary boundaries that had been created by the 1825 Treaty of Prairie du Chien.[49] And the treaties to which the Ho-Chunk Nation was a party, including the land that would become Sauk County, Ella's home and the later heart of the hop boom, were all signed under varying degrees of duress. Regarding the treaty of 1837, twenty-first-century historian Amy Lonetree wrote, "Ho-Chunk leader Dandy described what compelled the men to relinquish control of our homelands after long, painful negotiations: '[T]heir [Indian] agent told them . . . if they did not sign the treaty, he would . . . kill them.'" She added, "Close to one thousand people died as the result of the horrific journey and poor living conditions on the Iowa reservation in the summer and fall of 1840. I cannot even imagine the pain my ancestors felt as they faced leaving their beloved homelands."[50]

As journalist and professor Patty Loew observed, "According to the origin stories of most Indian nations in Wisconsin, the tribes have been here 'from the beginning of time.'"[51] The official Ho-Chunk Nation website asks its readers to "please understand that our oral tradition states 'we have always been here' and more than likely, will always be here. Our history is not told in history books, but spans back beyond possibly three ice ages. The Ho-Chungra have traditional lands that go from Wisconsin, Minnesota, Iowa, Missouri and Illinois."[52] As Lonetree wrote of her ancestors, "Ho-Chunk claims to this land are deep and long-standing; we originated near present-day Green Bay, Wisconsin, known as Mogašuuc in our language, or the Red Banks. For countless generations, we occupied more than ten million acres of land in what is now Wisconsin and northern Illinois." Starting in the 1830s, she continued, "invasion, diseases, warfare, forced assimilation, loss of land, and repeated forced removals from our beloved homelands left the Ho-Chunk people in a fight for their culture and their lives. . . . Yet, in the wake of these devastating events, the Ho-Chunk people survived and managed to remain in Wisconsin" even in the face of "deliberate acts of ethnic cleansing and genocide . . . committed against Indigenous people throughout the United States. . . . We are not sure how many of our people died during these removals or where they are buried. . . . These massive losses have never been fully acknowledged."[53]

JAMES AND ELIZABETH WEAVER AND THEIR HOPS ARRIVE IN WISCONSIN

John Weaver's brother and sister-in-law James and Elizabeth Weaver decided to follow John and Melinda out to this land a few months later. Like John and Melinda and their children, James and his family traveled the Erie Canal and the Great Lakes from Oneida County, New York. They arrived in the port of Milwaukee on June 9, 1837, aboard the *Julia Palmer*. The *Julia Palmer* was a rare vessel on the Great Lakes—a full-rigged ship, one of only three sailing the lakes in the 1830s.[54] Launched in 1836, it was nearly brand new when the Weavers stepped aboard. Nine years after the Weavers' journey, a Michigan newspaper described the ship thus: "The Julia Palmer is well found in every particular, and is as fine a heavy weather vessel as any ship that floats upon any sea—has good upper cabin state rooms and family saloons, as well as single berths, ladies' cabin and steerage cabin, all well ventilated, and will accommodate one hundred cabin passengers. Freight in large quantities can be stored under decks."[55] In part because the full-rigged ship required an extensive and expensive crew to run, it was soon converted to a sidewheel steamer, and at one point it was carried overland into Lake Superior. The *Julia Palmer* ran into many problems over the years, including a close call in a November gale, when an eyewitness described being "driven in a northeasterly course, every other minute apparently buried in the sea, with the water sweeping our deck . . . [and with] snow, rain, sleet, and hail, and the most dismal fowling wind, that ever moaned the requiem of shipwreck. . . . And thus, for seventeen hours . . . did she wrestle with her fate."[56] Although the ship survived that incident, it eventually met its match and now rests on the bottom of Lake Superior, just off Michigan's Upper Peninsula.[57]

Soon after James and Elizabeth Weaver entered the port of Milwaukee and traveled on to the future Waukesha County, they planted the hops that they had brought from New York, and Elizabeth gave birth to baby Ruth, their tenth child.[58] They reportedly sold early harvests for a dollar per pound, a fantastic return on their efforts—nearly double the price paid at the high point of the hop industry in the 1860s. The history of the Weavers is well documented thanks to the survival (and subsequent digitizing and transcribing) of many letters and the extensive work of the Sussex-Lisbon Area Historical Society.[59] Since the early years of growing hops in New York, Weaver paid attention to the international hop market, peppering relatives back home with requests for information about the English hop harvest.[60] His letters convey the constant gamble in hop growing, the endless series of decisions about when to sell, when to harvest, when to hold out for more money, and when to get while the getting is good. The letters reflect the pulses of the seasons, the swing of the earth around the sun, the cycles of the solar system, bodies, and lives, and the ways the harvests thousands of miles away could impact a remote farm in Wisconsin.

Of the 119 hop growers in Wisconsin in 1849, a dozen were apparently unmarried, and the rest had at least one adult woman in the household.[61] The patriarch James Weaver relied on the labor (reproductive and otherwise) of Elizabeth, who bore sixteen surviving children from 1821 to 1845—at the very least more than two decades of gestation and lactation. The women are less obvious in the historical record, but their work anchored the rise of settler agriculture and the subsequent hop industry. These relationships were varyingly economic and emotional connections, and the risk of losing an emotional and economic partner lay close at hand. James Weaver wrote to his beloved English cousin Richard Hardeman in December 1839: "My wife [Elizabeth] was confined last July of another son and was sick [a term for labor at the time] for 12 hours and I [had] 16 miles to send for a doctor but we got through before eny doctor got there and she got a long pretty well the first week and then was taken vey dangerus ill and I got the doctor out as soon as I could and I did the best I could for her my self which I [knew] was my duty to do and I be happy to say the Almighty [h]as restore her to her health [again] in which I feel very thankfull for. [Had] I but lost my wife I should have been undon[e]. I know I should of known the lost of a good one."[62] To understand much of nineteenth-century agriculture in the upper Midwest, and the hop boom in particular, we have to take into account these domestic arrangements, this overlay of love and work and money. Indeed, one of James's sisters-in-law perished three weeks after delivering a baby—James's fears of loss were very real (as, of course, were any fears Elizabeth may have had).

Elizabeth's youngest child was born when she was forty-four. The longest she went between births was twenty-four months, which happened twice. The shortest she went was with her final three children, with just fourteen months elapsing between each of these births (all of which took place in her forties).[63] The bodily work of making new people overlapped with the physical labor of running the household. In correspondence with his relatives, Weaver detailed his pigs, chickens (his wife skillfully turning two chickens into thirty-three chickens!), as well as his wheat, oats, barley, peas, buckwheat, potatoes, turnips, and wild hay. The loss of his wife would have been ruinous. Her labors were vital to the family's economic survival, even as he loved her deeply. He closed his detailed letter to his cousin Richard, "I be sorry to send you such a small sheat of paper but I have now long sheat by me so please to exquse bad spaling."[64] The census records of hop farmers reveal some small families and childless households, but there are many expansive families where every child seems to have survived (with each child's birthdate one or two years after the previous child's), and cases where the wife died and the farmer remarried, creating an even larger family.

The Weavers' large nuclear family and nearby extended family played to their advantage. While they grew many other crops, the Weavers formed a hop-growing and hop-dealing dynasty in Waukesha County, as many sons became hop farmers or dealers (or both), and daughters married other hop farmers and dealers.[65] By the time the *Atlas of Waukesha County* was published in 1873, the Weaver surname marked many properties in and around Lisbon and Sussex, and even more of those names have Weaver connections in the form of Weaver daughters married to local farmers.[66] Documents like that atlas and other aging records stored in the analog embrace of well-tended archives or the hum of unnamed server farms were once powerful mechanisms of expropriation and ecological change—and foundational for the beer industry in the US at the time.

In 1836, shortly before the Weavers journeyed across the Great Lakes, surveyors including Garrett Vliet and John Brink surveyed Waukesha County and produced the maps that made the Weavers' land claims and farms possible.[67] Thomas Jefferson initiated US surveying with the Land Ordinance Act of 1785 and the Northwest Ordinance Act of 1787. The surveying that shapes the state to this day began in Wisconsin in 1833 and lasted until 1866.[68] The surveyors had notebooks printed up in Milwaukee with which to document the locations they traversed. Those notebooks are now one of the best remaining sources of information about this moment in Wisconsin's natural and social history, as the surveyors recorded the trees and other ecosystems they encountered, as well as Indigenous villages, sugar works (maple sugaring camps), and effigy mounds, among other sites.[69] Yet as meticulous as these lists of trees may have been, they barely scratched the surface, simply noting the trees standing nearest the section corners, as well as streams, and occasional mentions of other trees and landscape features.[70] The surveyors developed an intimate, physical knowledge of the terrain to create the grid that Wisconsinites still inhabit today—the warp and weft of townships, sections, and plat lines making it possible to turn tamarack swamps, oak savannas, and Ho-Chunk homes and fields into white settlers' real estate and commodity crops.

Hops primarily grew in the land of black, white, and bur oak, as well as maple, elm, and American basswood. Much of the understanding of nineteenth-century Wisconsin ecosystems comes from this "witness tree data" from the General Land Office's public land survey. "In forested regions, they used trees as witness markers for corners," twentieth-century botanist John T. Curtis reported. "On the other hand, in treeless areas such as prairies, meadows, or barrens, they built a mound of earth at the corner point and simply stated that the corner was in an open area."[71] Much of what became hop country was in the area of Western Coulees and Ridges, with oak savannas, including one of my very favorite trees, the bur oak. One of the surveyors' notebook pages created in March or April 1832 lists bur oak as the dominant tree and includes "Indian sugar works," which implies both Indigenous presence and maple trees. The land was full of trees, and full of people who lived with those trees—tending them, using them in a variety of ways, dwelling among them.[72] These surveyors' notebooks, left by the white men who set out to survey the terrain step by step, allow us a glimpse into what has changed. After the arrival of white settlers, "besides elimination of most prairie, savanna and pine ecosystems, fossil pollen studies show us that relative abundances of species changed about five times as much since the 1800s as changed in the preceding 3000 years."[73] These quadrants scratched out by a handful of men on foot and on horseback created a physical and bureaucratic framework for subsequent agriculture, including hops.[74]

The surveyors' grid accomplished two distinct and contradictory things: It irrevocably altered the existing ecosystems and communities while simultaneously creating one of the most complete records of the vegetation at the time.[75] This type of mapping reimagined the land as a set of squares and enabled a radical shift in property relations and property values, as well as a stark change in the arrangement of human, nonhuman animal, and plant life in this space—indeed, all types of life, microbes and fungi as well, just less visible to the naked eye. Increase Lapham was one of the central surveyors. Known for his interest in botany and geology, he also actively undid the landscape as he found it. Soon after he arrived in Milwaukee in 1836, staying at a house where he "could look south down the river and see smoke curling up from wigwams and a canoe here and there gliding among the wild rice marshes," he "got right to work laying out and leveling streets . . . so that the high places could be graded off and the swampy places filled in. . . . He worked westward on the hard ridge between swamps and into the timber, laying out on the complex topography the simplicity of level streets and town squares" atop land that had long been home to Indigenous communities.[76]

The Weavers and the settlers who became their neighbors set out to remake the terrain of their new home in the forms of houses, fields, and woodlots more like New York's rural and agricultural topography than the oak savanna and prairies they had entered. Their work of breaking prairie and clearing forest, planting wheat and hops, and grazing livestock led to the loss of oak savanna and wolves, as well as many of the cornfields, fishing and hunting grounds, berry patches, and other places tended by Ho-Chunk, Potawatomi, and other Indigenous communities of the area.[77] Knowing what the maps look like, moving through the landscape along freeways or along bike paths built on old rail lines, it is possible to feel the precise quadrants laid out across the terrain, contested from time to time by the meandering diagonal flow of a river. Some of the smaller quadrants have been hollowed out with quarrying. Expanses of the former Weaver properties are now a stone company. Curving suburban subdivisions now fill most of the quadrants once farmed by the Weavers, a landscape of large, well-constructed new houses, multifamily buildings from multiple decades, and more modest single-story ranch developments.

Before European colonization of North America, there were some fifty million acres of oak savanna in the United States.[78] Today in Wisconsin there are just remnants, a few stands of gnarled, spreading trees above low-growing grasses. Nineteenth-century records repeatedly recount oak savannas looking like orchards or like carefully cultivated landscapes—which they often were. One set of descriptions comes from the person many people claim was the first to grow hops in Sauk County, Agoston Haraszthy. In 1844, Haraszthy depicted a stand of oaks not all that far from where the Weavers lived: "Having traveled twenty miles [from Milwaukee to a point somewhere around today's Waukesha] we crossed a brook which separated a dense forest from a sparse one where the oak trees exist in small numbers on the so-called 'oak openings.' . . . Let us imagine an English park on which thinly-scattered ancient oaks tower over a beautiful green meadow. Such are the oak openings; here and there spreading white oak trees four or five feet in diameter stand 200 to 400 feet from each other, surrounded by grass six feet tall. We stopped and for some time feasted our eyes on this marvelous work of Nature."[79] Others described the "homestead-like expression they give to the landscape" and "the park-like openings of spreading oak trees scattered in a sea of prairie grasses and wildflowers."[80] Traveling between Madison and Lake Winnebago, the surveyor Franklin Hatheway saw a landscape of "open prairie, which was dotted here and there with groves of burr oak, in the distance resembling cultivated orchards."[81] Part of the reason for this landscape was fire, both human-set and lightning-set. The thick bark of these old oaks could withstand the low flames of a prairie fire, while sugar maple and basswood forests rise up where they are better protected from frequent fire, either by fire suppression or natural firebreaks such as rivers and lakes.[82]

As a Californian from a land of salty Monterey pines, gnarled cypress, and coastal live oaks, I marvel at this 1880 list of trees in Waukesha County's (now almost completely destroyed) oak prairies: "burr-oak, white-oak, pin-oak, poplar, aspen, shell-bark hickory, pig-nut or bitter-nut hickory, crab-apple, chokecherry, black cherry, wild plum, sumac, hazlenut [*sic*], sugar-maple, red maple, elms, basswood or linden, ironwood, black ash, butternut," as well as willow, cedar, and larch or tamarack.[83] This diverse tree ecosystem contained a phenomenally sustaining larder and supply of raw materials: calories from nuts and fruit, habitat for other calories, materials for shelter, containers, weapons, and tools. Beneath or between the trees in the foregoing list, six hundred kinds of plants grew in Waukesha County, including many that can be used medicinally or for food: cowslip, gold thread, golden seal, bloodroot, prickly ash, snakeroot, tea, grape, wild pea, wild bean, groundnut, strawberry, red and black raspberry, prickly gooseberry, wild red and black currant spikenard, sarsaparilla, wild coffee, high-bush cranberry, puke weed, ginseng, wild hop, Jack-in-the-pulpit, wild asparagus, sweet flag, wild rice, and "fifty species of wild grasses. Many of these are gone, but they, with the carices, which were used for hay, formed a most valuable wild product in early times, as farmers could cut fodder enough without waiting to make 'tame' meadows."[84] This was, and is, a landscape in flux. Time is deep in Waukesha County, as it is everywhere else. These lists of nearly vanished plants and trees speak of an era long ago, but even more perspective appears in the paving stones and bedrock of Waukesha County, full of cuttlefish fossils from an ancient sea, and coral fossils scattered from Menomonee Falls to Pewaukee.[85]

Hops were just one of a multitude of plants brought from elsewhere and inserted into the biome of Wisconsin, and the United States.[86] Flax, weeds, wheat, apple trees, and other plants moved into new ecosystems, sometimes of their own accord, through spreading seeds or rhizomes, or with the help of birds and mammals who ate them and then via their droppings planted them somewhere else, or through the actions of humans moving across the terrain, sometimes with a single plant, sometimes with a grand scheme of botanical (and often commercial) transformation.[87] All those hops in all that beer come from somewhere. Acre by acre, field by field, with hardly a machine in sight, these settler farmers flung their bodies and the bodies of their wives and older children into the work of clearing and cultivating by plow, axe, oxen, horses, and the sheer power of a pair of biceps and a youthful body.

At the time the Weavers and their hops landed in Milwaukee in 1837, soon traveling on to what would become Waukesha County, commercial brewing in the place now known as Wisconsin had begun just three years earlier and on a relatively small scale. But soon after the Weavers' arrival, with the wave of Yankee and European settlement flowing along the Erie Canal and across the Great Lakes, masons, carpenters, and smiths began to construct breweries across the state. Steamships and schooners brought farmers and brewers as well as hops, grain, and even yeast.[88] The hop industry in Wisconsin was in its infancy, but the beer trade grew swiftly. The first brewery in Milwaukee is a slightly controversial topic, but it seems to have been either the brewery founded in 1840 by Richard Owens, William Pawlett, and John Davis or, according to Leonard Jurgensen via beer historian Doug Hoverson, the one established by the German brewer "Simon (or Herman) Reutelshofer (sometimes called Reuthlisberger)."[89] Owens brought 130 bushels of barley via ship from Indiana for his first brew. I have found no specifics on where his hops came from, but my money is on hops also arriving by ship, from New York state.[90] The 1840s saw the arrival of more German brewers, and by 1848, the year Wisconsin became a state, there were forty breweries across Wisconsin. In the late 1840s, Best & Co., the earlier incarnation of Pabst, advertised "Superior Ale, Porter, Beer, Rye and Corn Whiskey! . . . under the management of an experienced Brewer and Distiller from Germany." That same year, Eagle Brewery on Chestnut Street promised to keep "constantly on hand Milwaukee, Eagle and Scotch ale."[91]

The Weavers were atypical, but their story captures much of the physicality and place shaping of the hundreds of other experienced or would-be farmers who set off down the Erie Canal and across the Great Lakes to turn oak savannas and maple forests into wheat and hops. At the time the Weavers arrived in Wisconsin, the demand for hops across the United States had not yet begun to skyrocket, and New York was meeting much of the domestic demand. Several changes occurred in the 1840s that increased demand for hops in the US, including the repeal of the Corn Laws, allowing English brewers to import US hops, German immigration contributing to a rise in beer consumption, and the rising popularity of lager.[92] These hops then journeyed into breweries and beer mugs near and far. Today the lands that Weaver and his large family occupied are subdivisions dotted with housing from various decades of the twentieth century, as well as a park, a quarry, a bike path, and a Piggly Wiggly grocery store. Richard Weaver's plot, for example, became the Hamilton Heights subdivision.[93] Across the planet, many people inhabit these kinds of agricultural palimpsests. We live our lives atop uneven layers of past ways of living. Sometimes the past is nearly invisible; other times it peeks through into the present. Remnants and relatives of the hop plants still grow at the edges of suburban backyards in Sussex. The Weavers left their still visible mark on the landscape—in surviving houses, property lines, hop plants curling up along the edges of subdivisions, and the cemetery.

2

AXE AND CRADLE

Breaking the Land and Making Ella

Whereas the Weavers were both old hands and early adopters of hops, Ella's father Silas J. Seymour spent many years of farming in Wisconsin before jumping on the hop bandwagon. His path more closely resembles that of thousands of hop farmers I found in the handwritten records of the US Census Bureau's decennial Census of Agriculture held at the Wisconsin Historical Society Archives, who added hops to an existing lineup of crops as they faced falling wheat prices, chinch bug infestations, and other challenges. Understanding how Silas (eventually) came to be a hop farmer illuminates the origin stories of thousands of other farmers, and the way their earlier actions contributed to the rise and fall of Wisconsin's hop industry. That is, in order to explain the appearance of tens of thousands of young women in the Wisconsin hopyards in the boom years of the 1860s, and how Wisconsin came to be such a central if short-lived node in the global hop supply, it is instructive to turn to the younger years of Silas. I can take advantage of his unusually rich archival remains to chart the changes he made to the land that later enabled the rise and fall of this particular agricultural venture. The story of Silas captures the existing ecosystems and agricultural practices as hops began their ascent, and it shows the dramatic effect of a wife on his comfort and productivity, a pattern echoed out across other settler households.

Silas arrived in the new state of Wisconsin in 1849 at the age of twenty-five. Ella was just a gleam in his eye, and hops were not yet on his agenda. At that time, the Weavers and Waukesha County eclipsed all other Wisconsin families and counties with regard to hop production. But change was afoot. Silas was one of thousands of agents of that change. To the best of my knowledge, Silas did not plant hops until 1861, twelve years after arriving in Sauk County. Everything he did in the interim laid the groundwork of the hop farm at the heart of this story, and that same work happened on farms across the state. Staking a homestead claim on Indigenous land, chopping down trees, planting crops from back home, marrying, having babies—this acre-by-acre transformation of the land as well as the creation of large families of hop pickers built the industry on which nineteenth-century breweries and beer drinkers came to rely. This chapter also reveals how marriage matters, as both a social and an economic arrangement, and how both farming and marrying laid the foundation for the emergence of widespread hop cultivation in much of the state. The hop boom did not come out of nowhere. It entered an already existing set of landscapes and social relations—farms, families, transportation networks, breweries, beer drinkers, banks, prairies, and trees.

Born in 1824, in Pompey (in Onondaga County), New York, not all that far from Syracuse, Silas left home at fourteen to find work on the Maumee River and the Erie Canal but returned after a few years, working jobs closer to home, including a stint as a schoolteacher. For reasons not entirely discernible from the written record (perhaps a mix of restlessness and a desire for a farm of his own), on May 1, 1849, Silas and his sister Elizabeth departed New York for Wisconsin. Several relatives of his parents' generation were already in Wisconsin, and he followed their lead. Silas and Elizabeth rode a stagecoach to Buffalo (perhaps from Covington, as that is where their parents lived) and then traveled to Wisconsin via the Great Lakes, arriving in Milwaukee a mere eight days later, on May 9—a much faster journey than Melinda Weaver had experienced back in 1836. Silas was rightly optimistic that the Ho-Chunk lands he had his eye on would be available to him to farm. While in Milwaukee, Silas bought Increase Lapham's 208-page tome on Wisconsin as his guide to this territory.[1] This book shaped countless settlers' plans as they moved from New York and other places into the stretch of land we now know as Wisconsin.[2] Silas left Elizabeth with relatives in Aztalan, fifty-four miles west of Milwaukee, and then walked nearly sixty miles to Fort Winnebago (today's Portage, Wisconsin), presumably along existing Indigenous routes. Once Silas had identified the land he wanted in Dellona, adjacent to Reedsburg, he then walked sixty miles south to the Mineral Point land office to register for his land patent.[3] Here, men (almost exclusively), most (but not all) of them white, crossed the threshold of this small log building to make fateful claims to tracts of land that surveyors had marked subtly in the landscape, with an occasional blaze on a tree, a boundary stone, or a pole stuck in the earth. Silas's marker stone has gone missing in the meantime.[4]

Silas's early letters to his family from Dellona record the way that a solitary body could wreak such change on a tract of newly surveyed land. He busied himself with near-constant physical labor. Depending on the season, he spent his days chopping down trees or plowing fields, a relentless project of turning the existing fields and forests into sources of familiar food, livestock feed, and cash. On February 3, 1850, Silas wrote to his sister Elizabeth (or Lib), "I have cut and drawn timber enough for 1800 or 2000 [fencing] rails—and want to get enough for about 2000 more but the sleighing is about gone. . . . I expect to finish my house in the spring."[5] The rails—long, narrow pieces of split timber often used for fencing—were winter work, when the trees were bare and the snow cover meant he could use a sled to move the rails out of the forest and into the places he needed them. Although the following description is of a settler's work near Buffalo, it captures much of Silas's work as well: "One of the most important things which the emigrant looked out for in selecting a farm was an ample supply of oak, elm, ash, or walnut, for rail-making purposes. Then, when winter had put an end to other work, laden with axe, and beetle, and iron wedge, and wooden wedge, he tramped through the snow to the big trees, and perhaps for months did little else than convert them into great, three-cornered rails, twelve feet long, and facing six or eight inches on each side. In the spring these were laid in fence."[6] Silas's arrival in this assemblage of forest and prairie was a fateful moment in the history of this place. Silas "breaking" acres of prairie for wheat and other field crops, felling trees, and building his own home made possible the later hop boom that enabled the flourishing of beer in the nineteenth-century United States, repeated across farm after farm. On the individual level, the work and the changes it enacted on the land may have only been a matter of acres, but in the aggregate—whole counties and states full of people engaged in similar work—the changes were monumental: "The population of Wisconsin increased from 3,245 in 1830, to 305,391 in 1850, and to 1,315,497 by 1880. In the same intervals, the acreage devoted to crop production increased from about 400,000 to 2,900,000 to 15,300,000."[7]

Yankee and European settlers like Silas and the Weaver families immediately changed the landscape with their axes, their plows, and their bodies.[8] These settlers dismantled existing forests and cut through the ancient tangle undergirding the prairies, long shaped by Ho-Chunk residents and other Indigenous communities. Silas and his compatriots brought new plants and trees and repurposed existing ones. The trees found a range of uses in a variety of industries: "butts for woolen mill looms from hickory . . . barrel hoops from bitternut hickory, barrel stave bolts from basswood, beer keg stave bolts from white oak, and poles for hop vines from poplar, oak, and especially tamarack."[9] Many of those products of the forest went straight to the beer industry, one way or another. The ledgers of Blatz and Best in the 1860s and 1870s bristle with purchases of barrel staves, wooden bungs (the cork-like stoppers that seal the barrels), and cordwood. The Weavers of Waukesha County and many other hop farmers had a fondness for tamarack hop poles, and the felling of thousands of saplings for hop cultivation each year had a secondary impact on local forests and wetlands, beyond the hop fields themselves.[10] (But more about the tamaracks later on . . .) Hops were not a part of Silas Seymour's original plan, as he and his fellow settlers planted a few subsistence crops and a succession of cash crops, constantly calculating how best to make money off of this land. As the prices for Wisconsin wheat dropped, they sought new and, they hoped, lucrative crops to add to their fields, including sugar beets, tobacco, ginseng, and hops.[11] All this work made hops possible, even if hops weren't initially part of most farmers' plans.

At first Silas lacked a primary component in this endeavor. As a solitary man, he found himself sorely missing not only companionship but also someone to do the work of sewing, laundry, cooking, and other material and economic support that, at that time and in that place, most settler men expected of their wives. In the fall of 1849, Silas Seymour built a shanty in the woods close to where he was cutting wooden fence rails, a mere 10 feet by 12 feet.[12] He was not especially happy or comfortable in the shanty, writing to his sister, "Well, now Lib, to tell you the truth, this batching is hard business and I am heartily sick of it. I have kept 'batch' [done his own housekeeping] some 4 or 5 weeks and don't like it at all. . . . I see some *lonesome times*. I find it very difficult to get candles and what little I read evenings is by firelight."[13] He complained about his lack of earthenware and other comforts, and in these early bachelor days, Silas relied on his sisters for some of his creature comforts. Elizabeth made him a "quilt, bedtick, etc.," just one of many examples of how the work of settler farming was difficult or impossible without women's labor.[14] Silas had marriage in mind as he soon set to work building himself a roomier log cabin to replace the shanty.

By the autumn of 1849, a post office had been built in nearby Reedsburg, making correspondence easier, although it was still a trek to the small town and "there was not a house between my place and Reedsburg." The few settler neighbors he had were "[New] York State folks" like himself, and a few Irish immigrants.[15] Silas wrote to his family back east about his hopes for a road that would further ease transport, communication, and trade: "I expect (if they laid the road where I wanted it) to build in a little grove of oaks and poplars on the prairie."[16] This road later became a county highway, which, according to Silas's granddaughter Ruth Burmester, "followed the old stage route of the 1850s and 60s . . . up the valley through our meadow and just below the house and row of Norway Spruces that made the windbreak on the west of the homestead, and on over the hill northeast. The same trail over which Papa [Silas's son Merton] as a boy had seen loads of hops go to market."[17] I have scouted out the Norway spruce and bur oaks of the former Seymour property on Google Earth and on the land itself, and many still stand. The spruce once sheltered the now-vanished farmhouse and outbuildings from the prevailing westerly winds. The oaks that flank each side of the road predate the Seymours, resistant to the fires that once moved through this landscape. They outlived Silas and his family by decades, heading toward centuries, and I hope they will outlive me as well, if all goes well for the trees.

Silas provisioned himself with a mix of supplies he had brought along with him, foods foraged from the surrounding woods, and his early crops. In his letters he described raising a successful potato crop and gathering hazelnuts and wild onions. For decades this family shared a taste for the foods they could forage in the surrounding landscape. They sought out what must have been the same raspberry, cranberry, hazelnut, and onion plots tended by Ho-Chunk neighbors and their ancestors.[18] As much as he appreciated the plants that grew in the nearby woods and fields, he quickly set about the business of importing new flora and, eventually, fauna. Silas asked his sisters in New York to send currant seeds, and they obliged in September 1849: "We send some currant seeds. If they do not satisfy you, we will send some more in the next letter."[19] That letter took its sweet time getting to Silas, and the folks back home wondered in a subsequent letter in November 1849 whether the weight of the currant seeds had caused the delay.[20] Decades later, Silas's daughter Ella mentioned picking and preserving currants—could they have been from the same seeds?

These siblings carried on a cheerful, affectionate exchange. In December 1849, sister Elizabeth wrote from Koshkonong, Wisconsin, "I think you must either have had the *blues* or else had a great quantity of *housework* on hand when you wrote that letter to me for there was not a dozen lines in it. Now Sile, if you ever write me such a short letter as that again I will write an answer so long that you will not dare do it again."[21] Many of the family's letters were full of jokes and gossip, including frequent mention of Silas's marriage prospects. One sister back home wrote, "Mary Ann [Conine] had made [Silas's parents] a visit. She sent her love to western folks—I suppose YOU come in for a share of course."[22] Mary Ann's stepmother Betsey had recently "[run] away from her husband and stayed two months" with another man, quite a scandal in that time and place, and indicative of a less than happy situation at the Conines' place, as Mary Ann and her sister moved out when Betsey returned.[23] At one point sister Clarissa offered to choose a wife for Silas, "and somebody besides M.A.C. [Mary Ann Conine] . . . tho' she is good enough for anybody."[24] Silas did include a brief mention of his future wife in a letter to his sisters, though he seemed to be hedging his matrimonial bets: "If you see Caroline Tyrrell give her my respects and Miss Hollister and Miss Conine too. Love to all from Silas J. Seymour."[25] Silas's pursuit of a wife came from a longing for companionship, and for help with the chores, as his letters reveal his frustration with chores like cooking for himself ("baching"), his reliance on his sisters for many of his textile needs, the lack of homemade candles, and all the other household tasks that tended to be split between settler spouses of this era. Marriage was conducive to the predominant system of farming in Wisconsin, and to the later work of hop growing.

Alongside such mild secondhand flirtations, these letters included details of daily life ("Pa is peddling and Ma weaving"[26]) and litanies of illness and death in close succession. Silas's brother reported on the death of a relative's wife, noting without embellishment that their baby "is now about 7 weeks old. It was the cause of her death." A pair of twin boys died of cholera (likely cholera infantum, or "summer complaint").[27] A stagecoach rolled over on an uncle and killed him. Writing from New York, Clarissa reported her own challenges, particularly with regard to dental health (and drug use!): "I have had the toothache for 2 months about ¼ of the time and have had 2 extracted and another lifted. The last mentioned has ached full gallop for three days. . . . I am taking Opium for it and that seems to relieve me. I am also taking Dr. Watter's medicine and I think it helps me. I have the shakes now occasionally but not so hard as I had it in the spring."[28]

In 1851, Silas paid his neighbor Mrs. Deborah Pelton $2.87 to make him a new coat, trousers, and vest of her homespun fabric.[29] He entrusted her husband Hiram with the care of his crops, donned his new suit, and returned to New York to marry, finally acting on what must have been a long-standing affection: "In May, 1851, Silas J. Seymour wrote from Wisconsin to his sister Clarissa that he was planning a short visit to Wyoming County [in New York state]. 'I am questioned almost every day about what I am going east for . . . & I have now a *Stereotyped answer*. That is: that I am going to bring up a CARGO of *Old Maids*. Now I want you to *drum up* all you can, who wish to get *good husbands* and have them ready to embark . . .' . . . He then departed for New York, where one 'old maid,' the twenty-four year old Mary Ann Conine, was 'ready to embark.'"[30] Mary Ann's sister wrote in August 1851, when Mary Ann was obviously planning a wedding and a one-way journey to Wisconsin, "I supposed Mary is thinking of something more important than writing is it so Mary? You are very busy without doubt."[31]

Silas and Mary Ann married in a small ceremony at Silas's parents' home on September 23, 1851, went on a brief honeymoon, and had a party in Wyoming County, New York, when they returned from their short trip. By October 20, they had returned to Wisconsin—their journey, and their wedding, likely timed to beat the arrival of the oncoming November gales. According to Burmester's writings, "They had come by lake boat to Milwaukee, and on up into the Baraboo country by wagon, ox-drawn." Silas brought his new bride "over the Lakes to Milwaukee, over corduroy roads, through [oak] openings, across the prairies and bluffs, down Indian trails and paths, to the grove of burr oaks where his cabin stood and here they made their home."[32] As Mary Ann herself described it, in contrast to Melinda Weaver's crossing of the lakes:

> We had a very pleasant trip, by water, from Buffalo to Milwaukee. Here we found a neighbor of my husband, waiting to take us & our goods to that place. I never felt like going into ecstacies over that part of our journey. It was made in a lumber wagon, with a high spring seat, on which I sat with the driver, while my husband sat wherever he could find a place. The owner of this conveyance, made several purchases in Milwaukee, among them a barrel of salt, which he placed under the seat.

FIGURE 2.1. Mrs. S. J. (Mary Ann) Seymour. Reedsburg Old Settlers Portraits, OS-416. Photo by E. R. Curtiss, Madison, Wisconsin, date unknown (possibly the 1870s). "Reedsburg Old Settlers," Reedsburg Public Library, accessed August 16, 2025, https://content.mpl.org/digital/collection/RPL/id/7557/rec/3.

On the way we were obliged to pass over several Corduroy bridges. These were made of logs . . . over which no earth had been placed, & every time we passed over one of these logs our seat came down solid on this barrel of salt. I really envied my husband the comfort he took on these occasions, for he walked. We were five days coming from Milwaukee. How well I remember the first view I had of my new home which was from the top of the hill east of here. It was a small log house about 16 feet square, consisting of two rooms one above the other. But it was *home*, & with it I tried to be content.[33]

FIGURE 2.2. Silas Seymour. Reedsburg Old Settlers Portraits, OS-415. Photo by E. R. Curtiss, Madison, Wisconsin. "Reedsburg Old Settlers," Reedsburg Public Library, accessed August 16, 2025, https://content.mpl.org/digital/collection/RPL/id/7544/rec/2.

Mary Ann brought a collection of textiles, food, seeds, and tools to make her new home more familiar, and productive, including "her sea-shell quilt, her blue-and-white wove coverlet, seeds and 'piney' [peony] roots, dried apples, calico, candle molds, spinning wheel, the flax wheel, Abigail Bates's [her mother's] cradle" as well as plum and cherry pits.[34] Note two separate spinning wheels, one for the fibers of flax and the other for the fibers of wool. She brought her mother's cradle in anticipation of bringing babies into the world, and bedclothes to keep them warm.[35] As the newlyweds Mary Ann and Silas (figures 2.1 and 2.2) made their way to the Dellona cabin, "the heavy things they left at Aztalan with Uncle Eben against the time when Silas could come down with his ox-team and fetch them to Dellona. They rode on with Hiram Pelton, Silas's neighbor."[36]

Mary Ann's presence changed Silas's workday and comfort level right away. The day after they arrived back at the cabin was a Monday, wash day, so Mary Ann did the washing in an iron kettle. They had no chairs, instead sitting on two benches that Silas built, and a "lounge" upholstered with a straw tick. Ruth Seymour Burmester, Silas's granddaughter, remembered "the long wooden bench made by Grandfather Seymour in his first years in the wilderness here: a length of oak log, the top half hewed and hacked off to make it level, with four legs (bark still clinging tightly) of ash sapling . . . used now by Mama [Blanche, Silas's daughter-in-law] as a wash bench."[37] When Mary Ann took up the laundry—as well as the cooking, spinning, weaving, butter making, and so on—Silas had more time for chopping wood, making fences, plowing, and the other labors taken on by settler men of his day in Wisconsin.

In her fortieth wedding anniversary speech, Mary Ann declared, "I think I never enjoyed any summer of life better than the first one I spent here."[38] This recollection might contradict other information contained in family letters about how Mary Ann was so homesick that she would take herself into the woods—out of earshot of Silas—and sob.[39] Yet both accounts could easily be true. Many people telling the story of their lives forty years after a given event might emphasize the enjoyment over the sobbing, and joy and sorrow can dwell in close proximity in our days and in our hearts. "There had been raised on the place that summer some very fine Pumpkins. These I cooked very nice & dry & we used them on our bread for butter. Our neighbors did the same, so we were in style. . . . We brought from Milwaukee as we came ten lbs sugar and one of tea. This lasted us till spring. *Then* things began to improve," and they made enough butter to have it with every meal.[40] Once settled in Dellona, Mary Ann "made her own soap, her candles and her yeast. She dyed and spun and wove, made cloth, made bread of coarse-ground flour, dried apples, corn, and berries for winter. Carried water from a spring until menfolks made a dug-well beside the log house."[41] Mary Ann's presence left Silas more time in which he mowed "his grass with a scythe and raked the hay with a hand rake; cut his grain with a cradle and bound it by hand; threshed with a flail."[42]

Silas faced delays in retrieving Mary Ann's heavier belongings: "Winter set in before he could make the trip, and the spring was very wet, and cold and he did not go until June. Twas high time, indeed, for the first week of July baby Ella was born and they needed Abigail Bates's cradle to put her grandchild in. . . . Baby Ida came three years later."[43] After the birth of Ida on March 2, 1855, Mary Ann suffered from an infection. Her sister Emily wrote, "I think it strange that you have such feavers after your confinemet it must be owing to bad management from hired girls or unskilled physicians we have many more doctors than good ones."[44] Both girls must have been born in the log cabin, but by the time baby brother Merton was born, "he came to life in a fine new frame house that Silas had built."[45] Merton remembered his mother spinning yarn and then using it to make her own stockings: "Spun the yarn, after she'd washed and carded the fleece of their own sheep."[46] She had her hands full with textiles and babies, although there was a decade gap in infants—the youngest two children, Walter and Arthur, were born ten years apart, when Mary Ann was thirty-five and forty-five, respectively. There may have been a decade of abstinence or a series of miscarriages; there is no way to know.

This is the story of a single marriage, but it resembles the thousands of marriages that operated at the core of the later hop boom. As for thousands of other Wisconsin farmers, hop cultivation made its way into existing farms and households, integrating into already present arrangements of land, labor, and families. Given the quantity of women's labor necessary for the hop harvest—in picking and in hosting pickers, as well as raising future hop pickers—it should come as no surprise that only 19 of 369 people listed as harvesting hops in Wisconsin in 1860 lived without an adult woman in the house.[47]

The arrival of settlers like Silas left its mark in history books and archives, but also in soil cores where the sudden profusion of ragweed pollen indicates the presence of Yankee and European agriculture.[48] These settlers brought in a variety of weeds along with crops, including "Kentucky bluegrass, redtop, timothy, and other grasses, and white sweet clover, white clover, and other legumes . . . asparagus, the common apple, marihuana [*sic*], horseradish, buckwhite, parsnip, and carrot."[49] I have never seen mari*h*uana in the wild here, but I have definitely seen rogue apple, parsnip, and carrot. By naturalist Kenneth Lange's calculation, the area that later became the heart of Wisconsin's hop industry was 67 percent oak savanna and oak forest, and 22 percent swamps and marshes, with the rest covered in other types of forest and prairie.[50] The surveyor W. H. Canfield (son of a hop farmer, creator of the 1859 map that has guided much of my research, and a frequent overnight guest at Silas Seymour's place[51]) portrayed the nearby prairies as full of "myriads of flowers of every shape, shade and color, and the luxuriant grasses. . . . a handsome picture set in a beautiful frame."[52] Above all, wheat was on the vanguard, accompanied by oats, barley, and corn. Hops were not on the front line of colonizing plants in mid-nineteenth-century Wisconsin, but they benefited from these earlier endeavors as fields were already cleared of tree stumps and the deep roots of perennial prairie plants.

Silas's son Merton, who outlived his sister Ella by many decades, took it upon himself to preserve the memory of his father and held onto all that he could, and he took over from Silas as the farmer on this land. Merton's daughter Ruth Burmester recounted a moment when her maternal grandmother tidied up a shelf full of Merton's many papers while he was away from the house, including tossing papers into the cast-iron stove. When Merton returned, he feared that they had destroyed his treasured papers and that his mother-in-law had thrown these remnants of his father's life into the flames, but then his wife found a bundle of papers in the pockets of a horsehair coat of his. I am inclined to believe that we have Merton to thank for so much of this information, with the sheaf of rolled-up papers in his coat pocket, his presentations to the Old Pioneers society, and his eagerness to hold onto the objects and documents of his father Silas's life.

Settlers like Silas translated the whole terrain into cashbooks, daybooks, and ledgers, as well as letters and diaries. These account books contain stories of relationships with people caught up in webs of debt and credit that connect them to each other across time and space. They created sets of documents that allowed them to chart their monetization of the land and its fruits. Some of this tallying happened in families, but these private records echo the scrupulous recordkeeping pursued by the US Census Bureau as it sought to capture every bushel of peas and pound of hops grown in the expanding farmlands of the nineteenth century. In Wisconsin, a tiny fraction of these private family documents remains, and so some families and some tracts of land speak much more loudly today than others. Many such documents instead ended up being used to start fires in kitchen stoves or got stuffed into the rafters or behind wall panels to add a bit of insulation.[53] The archiving of the Seymour family files allows for a deeper understanding of the day-by-day rise of the hop industry in Wisconsin. A series of actions and decisions made by one household combined with the actions and decisions of thousands of other households to lead to a rising wave of hop cultivation.

The year of Silas's arrival, the state's entire hop harvest amounted to nearly 16,000 pounds, gathered in August and September, and most of it grown by the Weavers and their kin and neighbors in Waukesha County. New York state harvested more than 15 times as much hops, 2.5 million pounds, that same year.[54] The comparatively meager Wisconsin harvest was not nearly enough to supply the state's booming brewing industry. As immigration to Wisconsin increased along with the demand for beer's raw ingredients, more and more farmers began introducing hops into their fields. The Seymours spent the 1850s clearing land, growing a range of crops, adding more livestock, and birthing babies. By 1859, Silas reported the following harvest to the census taker: 80 acres of "improved" and 85 acres of unimproved land. He owned three horses and five "milch cows" (the term used in the census for dairy cattle), as well as two oxen and six other cattle. He had nine swine and a modest collection of just seven sheep (that same year one of the Weavers had seventy), but those sheep produced twenty-five pounds of wool. His field crops included 585 bushels of wheat and 300 bushels of what the census listed as "Indian corn"—maize, as well as 410 bushels of oats and 80 bushels of potatoes. He reported just two gallons of wine, but an impressive four hundred pounds of butter and twenty pounds of honey.[55]

Like so many Wisconsin farmers, Silas faced growing pressure to make money from his land, as the success of and demand for Wisconsin wheat declined in competition with more productive states. One of his strategies to make up for unpredictable wheat profits was to plant hops. As far as I can tell, the Seymour family first grew hops in 1861 and continued to grow them until the mid-1870s. The source of Silas Seymour's original acres of hops? His neighbor, hop grower and hop dealer Jesse Cottington, who sold a pile of gnarled hop rhizomes to Silas Seymour on May 16, 1861, just a few weeks after the opening shots of the Civil War were fired.[56]

PART 2

LOST HOPS AND LAGER BEER

3

HOPS ON THE RISE IN THE 1850S

> To Jesse Coddington [*sic*] belongs the honor of introducing the culture of hops in Sauk County. Although others may have commenced about the same time, good authority seems to have placed his name first on the list.[1]

One summer day, thanks to helpful archivists and librarians, as well as a Library of Congress map and the online property tax records of Wisconsin counties, I was able to pinpoint the location of Jesse and Rebecca Cottington's farm. While the Weavers may have originated the Wisconsin hop industry, it was Jesse and Rebecca Cottington (figure 3.1) who brought the industry to bloom in Sauk County and who played an outsize role in the 1860s boom. I set out westward from Milwaukee and eventually pulled my car onto a very narrow shoulder on a country road in Sauk County, across the street from the address my research had pointed me to, and began scouring the exposed rock for any sign of hops. Roadside verges aren't a central data source for most sociologists, but to be fair, my entire research career—since at the very least 1995—has included not only archives, libraries, and interviews but also moving my body into the literal field, to see what's up. Working on my long-ago dissertation and my first book, my faux combat boots traced overlapping paths in the jumbled concrete of 1990s Berlin, notebook and camera in hand, abandoning my dad's Canon AE-1 for a compact SureShot that I could slip into the pocket

FIGURE 3.1. Rebecca and Jesse Cottington. Reedsburg Old Settlers Portraits, OS-520. Photo by Kellogg, Reedsburg, Wisconsin, 1893. "Reedsburg Old Settlers," Reedsburg Public Library, accessed August 16, 2025, https://content.mpl.org/digital/collection/RPL/id/7789/rec/23.

of my leather jacket to photograph the swiftly changing city. For the next book I donned hiking boots and a sun hat to haunt the orchards and berry patches of farms and gardens growing heirloom fruits and vegetables, braving sunburns, rainstorms, and mosquitoes. Now I seek hops in parks, verges, and ditches. I enter the thicket, the woods, the swamp, the valley, the fields. On this particular day I waded into the brambles and nettles and followed vines up the rock face, continually disappointed to find the wrong arrangements of leaves. Wild grape and cucumber vine can be deceptively hop-like to the eager hop hunter. I wasn't quite dressed for this work, a mistake I somehow made repeatedly, with bare ankles and arms, and (correctly, it turns out) nervous about wild parsnip and ticks. The mark the wild parsnip left on my pale skin on an earlier hop hunt took a couple of years to fade. The nettles and blackberries I didn't as much mind. Their sting and scratch are more temporary than other dangers of a Wisconsin ditch. As I continued my search, I finally saw a set of hop leaves emerge out of the tangle of plant life, possibly a remnant or relative of what may have been Jesse and Rebecca Cottington's hops.[2] A month later I returned to the same spot and was rewarded with the sight of cluster upon cluster of rich green hop cones hanging from the bines that clambered up the rock. The Cottingtons' hops, perhaps, the rhizomes reproducing themselves below the earth over decades and heading toward centuries.

Once I saw the cones, I traced the spiraling bine to its roots. I had bought an old trowel at a thrift store in a nearby town, but I quickly realized it was easier to just reach my hand into the earth and yank out a chunk of rhizome. I brought it home in a bucket, planted it in my garden, and waited. And waited. The first spring, I started to give up hope, but finally I saw the telltale shoots emerging from the thick East-side clay that counts for soil on that corner of our lot. That first summer, the bine grew six feet tall or so but never flowered. The following summer, the bine grew much taller, but still no cones appeared. The third summer, the plant grew back even taller but failed to blossom for months after the other hop plant in our yard, a Saaz—one of the traditional European varieties—grown from a cutting given to us by another brewer's household, had already set burr and even started to form cones.[3] I began to wonder if somehow I had grabbed the rhizome of a male plant rather than a female plant, despite the unpopularity of male hop plants in nineteenth-century US hop culture, as they were useless for brewing and caused the female hop plants to produce unwanted seeds. But finally, impossibly late in the season, burrs suddenly emerged on the Cottington(-adjacent) hop, which soon became slim fragrant cones. We harvested an ounce or so, which we brought to a neighborhood brewery along with our two pounds of Saaz, on the day of its annual "backyard brew" where anyone with hops growing in their yard could donate their harvest to the brew kettle and go home with a free six-pack a few weeks later. The Cottingtons' bodies lie in nearby Reedsburg's Greenwood Cemetery, which bristles with the names of hop farmers and their kin. But it is possible that relatives of their hops may live on—on the side of a Sauk County road, in my Milwaukee garden, and in a fresh-hopped Milwaukee beer. This is a tenuous connection, but it is one way that plants push themselves into the future, these rhizomes thriving across time, reaching out to me through the archive and from beneath the surface of the earth.

Hops came on slowly in nineteenth-century Sauk County, but the industry took off there with the Cottingtons. Despite the county's eventual utter dominance of the industry, it lagged well behind other counties until the 1860s.[4] Agoston Haraszthy, the exiled Hungarian aristocrat we first met in chapter 1, may have brought the first eastern or European hops to Wisconsin, as well as planting grapes at what is now Wollersheim Winery. He also reportedly brought Zinfandel to California after leaving Wisconsin in 1848, and he definitely founded the Buena Vista Winery in Sonoma, California. Born in 1812, Haraszthy died in Nicaragua in 1869.[5] According to one account, his "restless spirit [was] quenched in the waters of Central America, where he was swallowed by alligators."[6] Haraszthy supposedly planted hops in Sauk County in 1842, yet the census takers of 1850 recorded no hop harvests in Sauk County, so his attempts to initiate a hop industry in that county did not take hold, and Jesse and Rebecca Cottington more clearly deserve the title of founder of the Sauk County hop industry.

Ten years later, in 1860, the census takers found twelve hop farmers in Sauk County, who harvested a total of almost 20,000 pounds of hops in 1859. Another ten years later, in 1870, there were more than twelve *hundred* hop farmers in Sauk County, who harvested more than 1.2 *million* pounds of hops—a stunning transformation of an agricultural sector, with a massive impact on the social and physical landscapes of this place. One source of this avalanche of hops was the Cottingtons' hopyard, in walking distance of Silas Seymour's farm.[7]

The Cottingtons arrived in Sauk County in 1851, not long after their neighbor Silas Seymour. Publicly available records on the Cottingtons are fairly scant compared with the Seymour family, and despite the Cottingtons' obvious importance to the industry. In fact, the Wisconsin Historical Society holds the official biographical sketch of Jesse Cottington in a file titled "Dictionary of Wisconsin Biography Rejected Entries."[8] Despite the sparse archival record, I do know that Jesse and Rebecca brought both skill and hop rhizomes to Wisconsin and set about importing the trade Jesse knew well in New York to his corner of Sauk County. The ghost of Jesse himself would remind me that it wasn't only him doing this work. His wife Rebecca played, in his view, an equal role in the work of his life. No one even bothered to draft a biographical entry (rejected or not) for Rebecca, despite her role in the rise of Wisconsin hops. I know about her work thanks to a grainy microfilm of state probate records. Jesse bequeathed one dollar to each of his children and grandchildren, and the rest of his wealth to his wife—because, in a statement as rare as it was accurate, "she has contributed to its accumulation as much as I have myself."[9]

The Cottingtons' path to Wisconsin resembled the Weavers', including the transatlantic and Great Lakes journeys and the profiting from Ho-Chunk land made available through wars, forced exile, and treaties. Jesse was born in Sussex, England, in 1816, and died in Reedsburg, Sauk County, Wisconsin in 1893. Jesse and Rebecca married either in May 1834 or May 1838.[10] Upon arriving in the United States, they settled in a hop-growing region of New York in 1841, with three little ones in tow, and four more children were born while the family lived in New York.[11] Jesse became manager "of the widely-known Palmer hop yards at Waterville, Oneida County, N.Y., a position he held for seven years," and a yard that later supplied hop rhizomes to Wisconsin's growing industry.[12] This was the same county where the Weavers had lived—about ten miles from the Weavers' origin point of Marshall, as the crow flies, although most of the Weavers were in Wisconsin by the time the Cottingtons got to Oneida County.

The 1850 census taker captured a momentous New York harvest at the hands of Jesse: 20,000 pounds of hops. Jesse and his family gathered extensive knowledge about caring for this somewhat finicky plant, producing hops that were of great interest to brewers and forging networks they would continue to use once in Wisconsin. This man—or, more accurately put, this household—knew how to raise a profitable hop crop and brought this knowledge to Wisconsin. Both the Weavers and the Cottingtons had acquired hop-growing skills as well as connections with other hop farmers and dealers that carried on after they left for Wisconsin.

Soon after the census taker came through in the summer of 1850, Jesse and Rebecca must have begun planning their move to Wisconsin. The Cottington family arrived in Sauk County in 1851, just two years after Silas Seymour. After a brief stay in the township of Westfield, south of Reedsburg, the Cottingtons bought a farm in Section 26 of Winfield Township, Sauk County, in February 1852.[13] Much of the area was a swamp of black alder at the time.[14] Like Silas, Jesse set about chopping down trees, plowing up prairie, and building log structures on Ho-Chunk land, albeit (unlike Silas) with a wife and children already on hand, many of whom were old enough to assist in the work. A Works Progress Administration profile on leading figures in the county recounted how, soon

> after his arrival in Winfield Cottington procured from the Palmer yards in New York enough hop roots to plant a half-acre. It was from this yard, rather than the earlier but experimental plantings of Auguston [*sic*] Haraszthy on Sauk Prairie that the hop-growing industry which flourished during the 1850's and 1860's developed. . . . From his original stock were propogated [*sic*] many of the hop yards which eventually made Sauk County the principal hop-producing region of the nation. For many years, as agent for the Palmer yards, he supplied planting roots for a wide area embracing Sauk, Dane, and Columbia Counties, becoming equally known as a grower, root-salesman, and dealer in hops. He also unsuccessfully tried to adapt native wild hops to commercial culture.[15]

This is pretty convincing evidence that much of Wisconsin's hop crop was the variety Cluster and its relatives, the rhizomes imported from major New York hopyards. According to a nineteenth-century local history, "The variety of hop grown around Reedsburg is the English Cluster, the same as is grown in Waterville, Oneida County, N.Y., because . . . cuttings were brought from that locality."[16] The Cottingtons became a central conduit for New York hop rhizomes to spill across the Great Lakes and into the Wisconsin hinterland.

But the Cottingtons started small, when Jesse wrote to Palmer's hopyard in Oneida County, New York, ordering up enough hop roots to plant a half acre in 1852, with the first harvest in 1853.[17] The hops were dried in a hop kiln made of logs.[18] The first shipment of hop rhizomes for the Cottington farm was sent from New York to the port of Milwaukee, and either Jesse or his eldest son, Amos, drove 120 miles to Milwaukee to pick up the roots.[19] The following version of the events is so specific (the wheels!) that I am inclined to believe it was Amos:

> The roots were shipped to Milwaukee by boat, and brought from Milwaukee by wagon to Reedsburg. Mr. Amos Cottington brought them to his father's in Winfield, Section 26, in a home-made wagon, composed of a dry-goods box, supported on running gear, the wheels of which were formed of sections sawed from the end of a log. Mr. C. planted about an acre of hops from these roots, but from being so long on the way, many of them had become damaged, and failed to grow. He built a hop-kiln of logs, size 12x24 feet, without windows or stove. By burning a pit of charcoal, he procured fuel with which he could dry his hops. The charcoal was burned on the ground floor, in such a manner as to produce the desired effect. As he had no press, the hops of the first picking were stamped by foot into a sack, the first crop yielding only 150 pounds.[20]

It is unclear who did the stamping—Jesse himself? His many children? This would have involved someone with sufficient body weight climbing into the hop sack and stamping the dried cones as someone else slowly poured hops into the sack around them. With larger harvests, such work would be done with mechanical hop presses. Jesse had been around some of the best hop kilns and hop presses in the world, in the heart of the US (and global) hop industry in Waterville, so even if things started out rather do-it-yourself for the Cottingtons in Sauk County, they had the knowledge and experience to eventually get the right gear in place. But Jesse's start in Wisconsin hops was comparatively modest.

That first sack of handstamped, log cabin kiln-dried hops had a long journey to market in Columbus, Wisconsin, in the autumn of 1853. According to my sources, this sixty-mile journey "is worthy of mention. A friend, Mrs. Van Camp, was going to Columbus on a visit"[21] (she "had to go thither on business and was glad to have them as company"[22]). "Her conveyance, one horse and wagon. Mr. and Mrs. Cottington, with the sack of hops, accompanied her. After various mishaps, capsizes and breakdowns, the party reached Columbus, where the hops were sold for 30 cents per pound [a good price!]."[23] They returned home with forty-five dollars' worth of gold.[24] I have not seen a mention of which brewery Jesse was selling to on that trip. Following the sale of that first sack, "Mr. Cottington found a market for his hops only by giving a guarantee to a brewer in Madison, and one at Portage [both much closer than Columbus], that his hops were all right—equal in quality in all respects, to a New York hop, and that he would pay any damage arising from using them. For the first *fifteen years* of growing, he made contracts at a fixed price at 20 cents a pound."[25] I don't think he intended to seed a boom. He had a steady business of his own, with few competitors in the vicinity. In terms of his customers, I can only speculate. It is possible that the Portage brewery was "a small wood-frame building on Jefferson Street," the Epstein Brothers Brewery, Fort Winnebago Brewery, or "The Old Red Brewery."[26] The Madison brewer he was selling to may have been Frederic Sprecher, or a brewery built alongside a mill in 1849, owned at least briefly by two fellows named Tibbits and Gordon, and then John Keyes.[27]

One late summer day I visited the (un-air-conditioned) warehouse which the Reedsburg Area Historical Society uses to house an extensive collection of objects and exhibits. One tiny corner of the building held hop- and beer-related objects. For an industry that once shaped the region, there are few surviving material objects, something Wisconsin hop grower James Altwies had warned me about in the earliest stages of my research, as he showed me around his hop cultivation greenhouse on an icy winter afternoon. Despite its modest size, the Reedsburg Area Historical Society held the largest collection of Wisconsin hop paraphernalia I had ever seen. There was a framed tribute to Jesse Cottington, donated by his descendants. It had pictures of Jesse and others, dried hop blossoms, newspaper clippings, and a photo of a hop house. The exhibit includes a cast-iron stove for drying hops, which would have been set up on the ground floor of a hop house. And I saw three things I've never seen before in this state, although I have seen them elsewhere—a hop pole, a hop pole hole digger, and a hop pole lifter. While the state's antiques fairs and swap meets are full of old farm equipment, most of it is from grain growing and dairying. The unique tools required by the cultivation of hops have long since vanished, or molder in barns and attics. And those that remain, such as a hop hook or grubber, might be unrecognizable to most of us as connected to the long-ago hop industry.

The Cottingtons continued to make money off of hops in subsequent years. Their neighbors took notice and started converting portions of their farms to hops as well. Some even "gave up the traditional crops and planted their fields with the brewer's root."[28] The New York town where Cottington learned the hop trade, Waterville, is about thirty miles east of Pompey, where Silas Seymour was born, but that was a significant distance in that day and age, and there is no reason to assume that Cottington and Seymour had known each other in New York. However, in Wisconsin, Silas certainly knew Jesse and Rebecca, as well as their son Amos, whose name graced the pages of Ella Seymour's diary in the 1870s. She mentions A. Cottington coming to appraise the hops, as well as visiting A. Cottington in September, and a Mr. and Mrs. Cottington coming by to visit in a very cold January. While their crop started small, by the 1860 census, the Cottington household produced 2,800 pounds of hops. Still, because six of their seven children were still living at home, many old enough to assist with picking, and their grown children would be starting their own families nearby, it is unlikely they would have had to hire pickers. Like the Weavers, the Cottingtons had produced their own hop-picking crew through the act of reproduction, but both families would have been very familiar with the practice of hiring young women to pick hops, based on their experiences in the hopyards of New York.

HOPS BEYOND THE COTTINGTONS

The largest concentrations of hops in Wisconsin occurred on the southwestern side of the S-shaped *tension zone* that runs diagonally across the state, with distinctly different plants and animals above and below. The tension zone is the place where northern and southern flora and fauna mingle, the overlapping of the northern mixed forest and the southern broadleaf forest:

> Southwest of the tension zone, indigenous vegetation consists of prairie species, mostly grasses and tall herbs, and oak savannas. This vegetation distribution is a response to prevailing air masses. During the winter and spring, arctic air is more frequent to the north of the tension zone, whereas Pacific air is more common to the south of the tension zone. . . . In 1850 an estimated 2 million acres of native treeless prairie covered the southern third of the state and from the Mississippi River into west-central Wisconsin . . . today only a scattered few thousand acres of indigenous prairie remain, and most of the original oak savanna has become dense stands of white and black oak.[29]

The Weavers were the first, and in the early days the most prolific, hop farmers in Wisconsin. The only other clearly commercial hop growers in the state by 1849—the year of the first Census of Agriculture to collect details on hop production—were two farmers in nearby Jefferson County.[30] (The decennial census was always reporting the previous year's harvest, so the 1850 census numbers covered the hops harvested in the autumn of 1849.) My best guess as to the Weavers' customers is that in the earliest years they were selling to breweries in Milwaukee, as the first brewery in Waukesha County didn't open until 1848. Initially transportation challenges would have limited their markets, but the Weavers actively advocated for a plank road—a technique that involved laying shorter horizontal planks atop longer planks running in the direction of the road—and for a true harbor to be built at Milwaukee, in part to ease the sale and export of their crops.[31] More than a decade after James Weaver and his hop roots arrived, "between 1848 and 1853 the plank road fever swept Wisconsin."[32] This surge of building included nineteen miles of plank road to Waukesha. Plank road fever was of limited duration, however, as a rail line was built from Milwaukee to Waukesha by 1851. The track inched across central Wisconsin for the next six years, finally arriving in Prairie du Chien, on the banks of the Mississippi, in 1857. The railroad came to Spring Green in 1855, and to Kilbourn City (the later center of the hop boom, today known as the Wisconsin Dells) two years later.[33] The train linked to stagecoach lines, all of which brought a stream of "lawyers, doctors, preachers, newspapermen, lumbermen, and settlers seeking places of abode in the new country. There came, too, the homeseeker from across the sea in singular garb, clinging tenaciously to his queer looking hand-baggage. In the '50's and '60's many raftsmen floated down the Wisconsin River to some snubbing-post along the stream and then sought the highway conveyance on the return. During the Civil War soldiers were frequently passengers from the railway station to their homes in the interior, bringing back . . . not infrequently an empty sleeve or pantaloon."[34] Wheat was the main driver of this trade route, but hop harvests followed along the plank roads, railways, and docks created for the transportation of wheat and other large-volume crops.

By 1849, James Weaver and his family were raising large quantities of a range of agricultural goods, including 500 bushels of wheat, 500 bushels of oats, 100 pounds of wool, 50 pounds of "Irish potatoes" (this is the official term used in the Census of Agriculture, presumably referring to white or golden potatoes as opposed to sweet potatoes, which are the next column in the census), 75 bushels of barley, 250 pounds of butter, and 20 tons of hay.[35] Weaver even won a state fair prize for his hops in 1852.[36] One mystery of the Weavers' hop harvests in the 1840s and 1850s is who picked their hops. If one picker could pick around 400 pounds of hops during a three-week harvest, then in 1859, James would have needed 16 pickers. Two grown sons had planted hops on their nearby farms as well. James's eldest son, Thomas Weaver—thirty-seven at the time, and with a household of his own—would have needed 4.5 pickers, and younger son William Weaver would have needed 3.5 pickers. Given the number of young adults and teenagers, as well as two hired hands, in these households, and the presence of many other close relatives who were not growing hops but might have been available to pick at harvest time, it is plausible that in the earlier years they could rely on household members and nearby relatives to pick the harvest. In 1849, Waukesha County's hop production far exceeded the hop production of any other county, producing more than 80 percent of Wisconsin's hop harvest for that census year, thanks in large part to James and Elizabeth Weaver and their relatives.[37] The Weavers grew a full 60 percent of the state's hops that year—9,700 pounds (6,500 of that by James and Elizabeth alone).[38] That amount will seem trivial by the time we get to 1870, but it was enough to brew approximately ten thousand barrels of beer, thus the importance of roads, railroads, and harbors, because sleepy little Lisbon, Wisconsin, had no use for that quantity of hops.[39]

Even as the Weavers, Cottingtons, and others were settling into a successful hop business, only eleven other Sauk County farmers were growing hops by the time of the 1860 census. The records from this time include a mix of those growing just a few pounds for their own use and people growing a commercial crop. I turned to hop expert Stan Hieronymus to help me think about who was a home brewer and who was a professional. Based on the fact that brewers in that general period were using 1–2 pounds of hops per barrel, depending on whether they were brewing lager or not, he pointed out that even a relatively modest harvest of, say, 28 pounds could have yielded 434–868 gallons of beer—likely more than even a very thirsty household could consume. As Hieronymus suggested, perhaps some were growing for local use, or were "semi-pro," or were simply bad hop farmers.[40] As the Weavers and other farmers began to plant hops alongside their other crops, a few people grew commercial crops, but many also grew for their own consumption both early on and much later. The smallest harvest I came across in the census was half a pound—I still can't believe the census taker bothered to write that down! The largest harvest was an astonishing 50,000 pounds at a single farm in 1870.[41] Depending on the time and place, people grew for local breweries a wagon ride away, and then for Milwaukee breweries. As the state's hop industry peaked, they also grew hops for the world market. Contrary to the locavore approach sometimes used today, much of brewing history has involved a fair amount of mobility of raw materials.[42]

Several sources reveal the use of hops (and other plants) in Wisconsin home brewing in the nineteenth century, sometimes using ingredients gathered from nearby forests and prairies. Thurine Oleson remembered her mother brewing beer with "hops, malt, syrup or molasses, and water," including doing their own malting. The brew didn't last very long and wasn't highly alcoholic.[43] The Ragatz family near Sauk City made home-brewed beer with homegrown hops: "Mother made butter and father cheese. He had to learn this from a book but soon mastered the art, and for years 'Ragatz cheese' was in great demand in Sauk City. We grew hops and brewed our own beer. We likewise made wild grape and elderberry wine."[44] Some home brewers simply used hops they gathered from the nearby countryside. In 1857, in Richland County, west of Madison, twenty-five-year-old Hannah Aldrich wrote to her parents back in New Hampshire: "I make beer out of the roots that grow in the woods, of sarsaparilla, spignot, golden seal, hops, anise, and other things. This is recommended to be very healthy to drink along in the spring and summer."[45] Even while these small batches of beer were brewed on hearths and on woodstoves, a handful of farmers was setting the stage for a breathtaking change.

My analysis of the Census of Agriculture revealed four main categories of hop growers in this era (my categories, not theirs): (1) home brewers growing just a few pounds, (2) those whose hops could be picked by existing family and farmhands, (3) those who had to hire pickers they would host in their homes, and (4) those whose hopyards were so extensive that they hired dozens or even hundreds of hop pickers. The first two categories dominated the early years of Wisconsin hop production, and the second two grew in importance as hop cultivation expanded rapidly. The influx of hired pickers in the third and fourth scenarios created an enormous amount of work for the wives and elder daughters of the hop farmers as they often housed and fed all of these pickers in need of a lot of food, beds, and entertainment.

I can't assume a linear increase in either harvests or numbers of farmers, but the end result was a dramatic leap from 1850 to 1860, and an even more dramatic leap from 1860 to 1870. The 1850 harvests ranged from a half pound grown by Moses Pool, a twenty-five-year-old settler from Massachusetts, in Fond du Lac County, presumably for home brewing, to James Weaver's 6,500 pounds in Waukesha County. By 1860, 369 farmers reported an 1859 hop crop to the census enumerator, and fewer than a third of those were growing commercial quantities.[46] Still, in 1859 the state produced ten times as much hops as it had in 1849, 135,587 pounds on 369 farms, including farms growing just a pound or two to the 7,000 pounds grown by Isaac Frank in Jefferson County, on his farm nestled between Goose Lake and Mud Lake in Concord Township.[47] By the time of the 1860 census, once-dominant Waukesha County was growing just over 18,000 pounds of hops, eclipsed by Jefferson County's nearly 50,000 pounds. Even Sauk County had gotten into the game by this point, in part thanks to Jesse and Rebecca Cottington, edging out Waukesha County at 19,000 pounds. Still, as large as these quantities may sound, ten years later they looked paltry by comparison. By the 1869 harvest, Sauk County brought in almost 1.3 million pounds of hops, and Jefferson County reported almost 300,000 pounds.[48]

While it is impossible to know the precise changes in hop cultivation and farmers from one year to the next, there are glimpses of change in newspapers and biographies. For example, in March 1854—the time of year people started thinking about the ground eventually thawing enough to get their hop poles in—A. P. Lyman, who ran a big Sauk County store, was advertising a supply of *ten thousand* cedar hop poles, a quantity so large it surely left its mark on the surrounding countryside for decades to come, given the abrupt loss of thousands of young trees.[49] In Jefferson County, a regional periodical reported, "the tamarack swamps are turning out immense quantities of hop poles, which find a ready sale in the towns of Kushkonong and Oakland, where considerable capital is already invested in hop growing, and where preparations are making for more extensive operations next season. In Milford and Lake Mills large yards have been established, and as the business promises a good profit on the capital and labor invested, from the excellent quality and quick sale of what has been marketed, there is a prospect of our county's becoming somewhat noted for its Hop growing."[50] Even in this time of expansion, the 1850s brought unique meteorological challenges, as "the winters of 1855/1856 and 1856/1857 were among the severest on record in Wisconsin."[51] There was snow in the ravines until mid-May in 1857, and a killing frost on August 29, which surely would have affected the early September harvest. While the cold could be a risk to agricultural endeavors, it brought an ease of distribution in the ice-cold wintertime: Sleigh season was so important that it would get mentioned in the *Milwaukee Daily Sentinel*'s "Commercial" column, reporting on the markets: "A warm and southerly breeze has pretty much used up the sleighing. The roads however are in prime order."[52] Snowy conditions eased the felling and transporting of hop poles alongside other timber harvests.

Each county had its early adopters and most prolific growers, and each entry in the census potentially takes us down a separate archival journey, intersecting with broader sweeps of history. Charles Avery worked in hops in New York state for thirty years before coming to Concord, Wisconsin. As with the Weavers and Cottingtons, he was well acquainted with the New York hop industry, and he imported many of its practices. After three years of farming in Wisconsin, he wrote up a summary of his work in 1853.[53] He described planting six-inch pieces of hop rhizomes eight feet apart and applying lots of manure; he stressed the importance of planting in bottomland. In 1853, he planted eleven acres, including six acres of bottomlands—land that would have benefited from the rich alluvial soils deposited by the changing paths of rivers and creeks. Avery averaged one ton of hops per acre in 1852, relying on the labor of young women: "I commence picking the first of September. Last year I employed on the five acres, sixteen girls for two weeks and three days. Their wages were from two to four shillings per day with board. I dry and press my hops in bales containing about 200 pounds each."[54] This is one of the earlier mentions I have found in Wisconsin of a large crew of nonfamily being hired to pick hops. That brief "with board" contains within it so much labor for the women of the household. Someone (presumably Avery's wife, Louisa—their children were too young to be much help at that point) was cooking and cleaning for these sixteen girls, created safe and comfortable places for them to sleep, washed a tremendous number of dishes, and so on. Charles Avery likely already had seen the widespread employment of young women as hop pickers in New York, and he imported that labor system to his farm in Wisconsin, as did Silas Allen, possibly the first hop grower in Winnebago County.[55]

Hop growers have employed a range of approaches to the problem of who will pick their hops. In other parts of the United States, the hop-picking labor force has at times been far more diverse, and far less dependent on the farmers' wives for their provisioning. The housing and nourishing of hop pickers in such places as California, Oregon, and Washington were much less the responsibility of a farmer's wife, where camping and self-provisioning were more the norm and where the labor force was often far more diverse in terms of age, ethnicity, national origin, gender, etc.[56] In California, in the later nineteenth century and into the twentieth century, pickers included brigades of Chinese, Filipino, and Japanese men as well as Indigenous and white families, almost all of whom self-provisioned. Historian William Bauer's work on Pomo hop pickers is especially relevant as an in-depth contrast to the hostessing happening in Wisconsin.[57]

One of the major sites of seasonal migrant hop picking in beer history has been the English county of Kent, where generations of working-class Londoners journeyed for a few weeks of fresh air and agricultural labor, into the 1950s, often picking alongside locals as well as Romany and Traveller families.[58] At the high point of the industry, eighty thousand pickers traveled primarily from London to Kent, both individuals and whole families.[59] Even George Orwell got in on the action and went hop picking himself, as a self-described "tramp," in 1931.[60] In nineteenth- and earlier twentieth-century England, "for the work of picking women and children were mostly employed, but with a proportion of men, most of whom came from London and other towns. At one period, a strong contingent of Irish made their way annually to the hop-fields and a large number of people came from Wales. Two women or a woman and two or three children would generally pick into a bin, and to every four or five bins there would be a pole puller who would act as measurer and exercise an oversight of the pickers."[61] Some of the practices in England resembled those in New York and Wisconsin, with respect to both the reliance on women and the placement of men in the positions of pole puller and box tender. One difference with the English workforce is that they rarely slept under the same roof as the farmer but either camped or stayed in buildings built specifically to house this seasonal labor force. Germany also saw the arrival of hop pickers, often coming from poorer regions, to work the larger farms, while smaller farms could make do with friends and relatives.[62]

There was an incredible liberty available to so many of the hop-picking young women of Wisconsin—to travel in relative safety, to be welcomed into homes, to freely come and go, to earn money independently.[63] This liberty stands in powerful contrast with so many other ways of being a woman or a worker (or both) in this era, particularly with chattel slavery just a few hundred miles away, and continued dangers and exploitation after 1865.[64] Even hop picking itself varied widely from the relative comfort and autonomy of so much of the Wisconsin workforce, to more exploitative, dangerous and violent settings, whether the deaths of dozens of hop pickers from cholera in 1835 and 1849 in Kent, the Wheatland Hop Riot in California in 1913 (and the terrible living conditions that preceded it), or attacks by white hop pickers against Chinese hop pickers in 1870s California.[65]

One Wisconsin picker recollected later in her life:

> Unlike the pickers in the West, who are described as roaming transients obliged to provide their own shelter and food, the Sauk County pickers were given the best the farm afforded. Men and boys slept wrapped in

> blankets on the hay in the barn. . . . Women and girls were given all the beds in the house, and big, plump ticks [fabric-covered mattresses] filled with straw that made nice, soft beds when spread on the floor of the sleeping quarters. Great preparations had to be made to house and feed from twenty to forty or more people, the number depending on the size of the [hop] yard. Bedding and dishes were loaned by the neighbors to the housewife needing them at the time, then passed on as the crews moved from place to place. For many days before the arrival of the pickers, the women folk were busy preparing edibles of all kinds, for the best was none too good for hop pickers; for if meals were poor, there might be a shortage of help on that particular farm the next year.[66]

Wisconsin hop farmers benefited from the experience of New York hop farmers, and, as we have seen, plant material, people, and information flowed between the two states.[67] In the early days of hops in New York:

> Farmers first tried to maintain the traditions of using only family or neighbors at harvest. Because of this, they generally restricted acreage to a maximum of five acres. But in the middle of the harvest season, labor was difficult to procure; hence, hops growers employed women and children to pick hops. . . . The scale of operations strained household resources. Growers bedded pickers in the farmhouse, barn, or outbuildings, and the farm wife had to work throughout the year to lay in enough foodstuff to feed the pickers, baking bread and pies before the harvest, and then had to cook hot meals for the workers. She also continued her traditional chores in the house, garden, and dairy, a staggering load.[68]

The freedom and comfort were made possible by the hosts seeing young white women pickers as people to bring into their homes, and almost every other category of hop picker as someone to keep at arm's length.

Some of this work reinforced existing connections and provided welcome entertainment, even as it altered existing social structures in this region of New York.

> In other ways, hops fractured traditional relations, having a profound influence on young men and women and generating a new and at times exhilarating peer culture. Young women formed the bulk of the harvesting corps and entered the fields each year to strip the vines. The labor was divided so that a young man acted as box tender for four pickers, usually young women aged thirteen to twenty-five. . . . Not surprisingly, perhaps, spinning girls from local mills formed the first groups of pickers. . . . Young women welcomed hops-picking season because it offered relief from daily household routines.[69]

Thus the textile industry had already created a labor market for young women well before hops took off in New York state, and the phenomenon of many young women setting off to earn their own money away from their families already existed.[70] But many of those workers resided in boardinghouses, and for longer periods. I am unaware of an agricultural setting that involved this scale of women's involvement compared with men's, in this time and place, and that also involved this large labor force living under the same roof as the farming family. Women have long been engaged in agricultural, industrial, and domestic labor—in some cases in the context of chattel slavery, in other cases small-scale family labor, as parts of families in larger picking brigades, and in Wisconsin's hopyards.[71] But to the best of my knowledge, it was relatively rare to welcome a substantial seasonal labor force into the home in this era. Even in New York, farmers distinguished between young white women from the vicinity, who crossed their thresholds and shared the intimacy of their homes, and the generally white pickers from cities, who did not—indeed, whom many farming families regarded as strangers, ill-behaved and at times dangerous.

New York hop harvesting strategies in turn emulated those that had been established at the time in Kent, England, although with some important distinctions: "Hops harvesting in central New York was organized in much the same way as in Kent in England, with women and children pickers predominating and considerable fears of pickers from outside being employed."[72] In New York, "prior to the Civil War, neighbors and young people drawn from nearby towns had picked hops in a festive neighborhood activity that reinforced ties of mutuality. . . . The first 'foreign' pickers were urban working families, and many returned to the same farms each year. Local families felt comfortable with such laborers, and some struck up lasting friendships."[73]

BACK TO WISCONSIN

The growing, harvesting, and crews of pickers were still comparatively small-scale in 1850s Wisconsin, as in the hopyard of Harvey Canfield. Canfield was one of a small group of early commercial growers of hops, acquiring his first hop rhizomes through Jesse Cottington, sent out from the Palmer farm in New York. Canfield was born in Connecticut in 1794 and moved to Onondaga County, New York, during his childhood. He arrived in Wisconsin in 1844. He had all kinds of careers before he found himself raising hops and other crops in Sauk County, including construction on two canals, and being a "gold digger in the Carolinas."[74] His son W. H. Canfield was a surveyor who created the map I relied on most heavily for this book, tacked to the wall of my office and covered in pink Post-it notes. Harvey Canfield's place is marked on the map and has a Hop Yard, just north of the part of Baraboo named Lyons.[75] His hexagonal hop house survived into the twentieth century (figure 3.2). If his household was anything like Jesse Cottington's, his wife Sarah, born in 1798 in New York state, would have contributed a significant amount of labor to the endeavor. While he was one of the earliest and most prolific hop farmers in Sauk County, he died in 1861, well before the boom. One indicator of the rising importance of hop cultivation was the use of prizes for best hops in county fairs, and Harvey Canfield won the prize for best sack of hops in 1859 at the Sauk County Fair in Baraboo (he also won a prize for his beans).[76] The *Baraboo News Republic* from September 1, 1859, listed a premium of one dollar for the prize-winning sack of hops at the Sauk

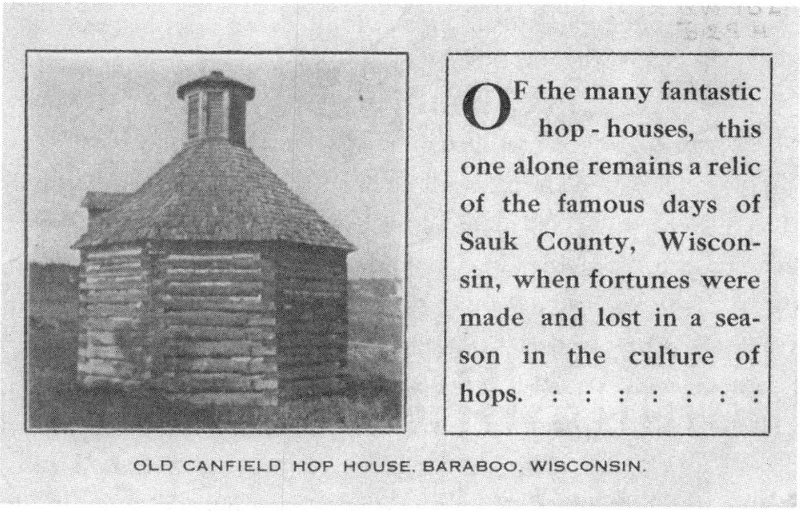

FIGURE 3.2. Canfield Hop House. Photographer unknown, Baraboo, Wisconsin, ca. 1900. Wisconsin Historical Society, W013QKG.

County Fair. This list of county fair prizes reflects local efforts to encourage particular kinds of household production. A few weeks later, on September 29, the newspaper reported the winners of the county fair prizes including awards for flannel skirts, for the best three-year-old Devon bull, and for a bushel of flax.[77] Charles Avery of Concord won a Wisconsin State Fair prize for one bale of hops in 1853.[78]

Much of the story of 1850s hops in Wisconsin took place in Jefferson County. Thirty hop farmers lived in Jefferson County by 1860—paltry compared to a decade later, but every single one of them was growing at a commercial scale. Yale Henry, for example, built a hopyard in Jefferson County in 1852.[79] He was born in Madison County, New York, one of the hop-growing counties, and made the journey to Wisconsin in 1844 when his family left New York. Thirteen of these thirty farmers resided in a single township, Concord. Similar scenes played out across Wisconsin in this time period, as individual farmers, often from New York, integrated hop cultivation into their other farming. Across the state, many farmers and families tracked down hop rhizomes and planted them in the tilled earth. Some invested massively in the prospect, staking their futures on turning a gigantic, if elusive, profit, while others integrated hop cultivation into their cultivation of other crops.

Whereas the 1850 census listed no women as hop farmers, by 1860 I found at least four in my analysis of the handwritten, individual-level census records held at the Wisconsin Historical Society Archives. These four farmers lived in two counties—Mary Tobin (b. Ireland, 1805, 10 lbs. hops), Lydia Parsons (b. 1817, Vermont, 180 lbs. hops) both in Dodge County, and Mary Appleyard (b. 1800, England, 3 lb. hops) and Rebecca Mosaman (b. 1814 Pennsylvania, 1 lb. hops) both farming in Racine County. The census taker actually listed Tobin and Parsons with the occupation of farmer, a relatively rare occurrence in the records I consulted, which much more frequently listed women in the population census as "keeping house," even if they appeared as the farmer in the Census of Agriculture. Each of these pairs was in separate townships, and there is no reason to assume they knew each other. All four of them had multiple children in their households, and I would assume all were widowed, although I can't confirm that definitively with the available records—I would say it is the most socially likely status for them, given the conventions of the day. Unlike the women hop farmers of 1870, discussed in greater detail in chapter 7, these four were growing comparatively small quantities of hops.

Despite the importance of German immigrants in Wisconsin history, in the brewing industry, and as consumers of beer in general and lager in particular, German farmers played no significant role in the initial rise of hop cultivation in Wisconsin. There were over 38,000 Germans in the state in the 1850 census, but only two of them (plus their household members) grew hops. But New Yorkers and people who had passed through New York on their immigration journey played a much bigger role: "There is hardly a doubt . . . that the introduction of this crop is to be credited to the people who were familiar with its culture in the state of New York. At all events, the names of the men who first are mentioned in this connection are without exception the names common in New York settlements."[80] My census analysis bears out this claim. There were more Norwegians (9!) growing hops in

Wisconsin in 1850 than there were Germans, and 34 hop farmers from New York.[81] By 1860, 74 Germans grew some quantity of hops, out of a total of 370 hop-growing households and German farmers became more important in the boom time of the 1860s into 1870.[82] In addition, as noted in the prologue, I have found no archival evidence of German hops growing in this era in Wisconsin. That doesn't mean there weren't any there, but they did not leave the bureaucratic or journalistic impressions left by New York-bred Cluster and similar hops.

In Winnebago County, Silas M. Allen was an early importer and grower of hops. Like Jesse Cottington and James Weaver, Silas Allen had grown hops in New York, and when he set off for Wisconsin, "according to family lore," he filled a barrel with hop rhizomes as he set out on his journey to Winnebago County; he harvested his first crop in 1853, and by 1854, he harvested 6,000 pounds, an impressive quantity for this time and place.[83]

Hop farming was always (and continues to be) a volatile industry, even in the comparatively quiet 1850s. As one Dane County farmer wrote to the local newspaper in 1866, "In 1847 we had a large crop, for which we were offered four cents; in 1857, with a light crop, we sold at thirty-six cents. . . . We made a nice little fortune speculating on the hop one year. We lost it the next."[84] New York was still the leading supplier of US hops.[85] Wisconsin production expanded, but so did overall US production, from 3.5 million pounds in 1850 to 11 million pounds in 1860. In 1850, New York produced more than 2.5 million pounds, and in 1860, it produced more than 9.5 million pounds, primarily in Otsego, Madison, Schoharie, Oneida, Herkimer, and Montgomery Counties.[86] In 1860, Wisconsin was not yet ascendant, and it was tiny Vermont that produced the second most hops—638,677 pounds that year. These ever-increasing harvests were responding to the ever-increasing demand for beer.

The 1850s saw rapid growth in Wisconsin's brewing industry. Although much of my focus is on Best/Pabst and Blatz because of their size as well as the availability of their historical records, many other breweries were integral to this process, including Obermann, Falk, Krug, and Melms. While he credits Len Jurgensen with being even more of an expert on Milwaukee breweries than he is, Doug Hoverson offers a detailed play-by-play of the origins and growth of Milwaukee brewing in his wonderfully encyclopedic book, *The Drink That Made Wisconsin Famous* (2019).[87] Milwaukee's brewers advertised a range of beer styles, including lager but also ales, porters, and even Scotch ales.[88] In the 1850s, Miller was selling Bock and a "Munich Dopple beer."[89] In 1860, Schlitz brewed 4,000 barrels of lager and 2,500 barrels of "young beer," likely ale.[90] Likewise, in 1860, Sands' Spring Brewery advertised "Stock Ale, Burton Ale, Pale Cream Ale, Porter."[91] In 1867, M. W. Powell & Co. had "XX Cream" and "Stock Ale" on hand.[92] From 1840 to 1860, Milwaukee went from zero breweries to thirty.[93] Milwaukee produced 48,900 barrels of beer in 1858, and in 1860, Milwaukee breweries alone used 100,000 pounds of hops. However, the entire state produced only around 135,000 pounds of hops, with nearly two hundred breweries all across the state needing hops.[94] If we compare the rise of the hop industry with the rise of the brewing industry, it is clear that there was no way to meet the brewing needs of Milwaukee with the hops grown in Wisconsin. The breweries of Milwaukee were ascendant *before* commercial hops were widely grown in Wisconsin, and therefore the breweries were getting their hops from New York and elsewhere.[95] As we saw in chapter 1, the newspapers were full of ads for imported hops, such as a German newspaper in Milwaukee that advertised thousands of pounds of hops from the "western parts of the state of New York" in 1852.[96] If you read someone saying the breweries started here because of easy access to local hops, they are wrong—or at least their story is incomplete.

Most of Wisconsin's hops moved along the path followed by the Weavers (described in chapter 1 and illustrated by the map in figure P.1 of the prologue). The demands of Milwaukee's early brewers in the 1840s and 1850s far outstripped the supply of Wisconsin-grown hops, so most hops arrived in bales in the holds of ships traveling west across the Great Lakes.[97] Wisconsin and New York were in constant conversation with each other, with people and products flowing back and forth across these waterways. In the early days, most of the people planting hops were Yankees or from the UK.[98] In all facets except brewing, which was dominated by recent German immigrants, New York played a far more pivotal role in the rise of the Wisconsin hop industry than any other region.

I know for certain that both Best and Blatz regularly purchased hops from New York, Wisconsin, Germany, England, and even California in the 1860s and 1870s.[99] I have found no surviving earlier ledgers for Milwaukee brewers, but given that the 1850 census reported less than 16,000 pounds of hops being harvested the previous year, and given the copious advertisements of hops being sold by the bale in Milwaukee's pharmacies and general stores, many of the early brewers must have relied on a combination of a smaller quantity of local hops and a larger quantity of New York hops. Occasionally the newspaper ads mentioned some Bavarian hops for sale, but New York hops (presumably Cluster and its ilk) made up a significant part of the hop bill for Wisconsin brewers in the 1840s and 1850s. Brewers also sought barley and other grains wherever they could, depending on the opening of railroad lines or the presence of shipping lanes across rivers and the Great Lakes.[100] Druggists and shopkeepers placed ads in the papers to sell the newly arrived hops.[101] In the 1840s, brewers in Milwaukee could stroll over to Cunningham's drug store and pick up enough hops for a decent amount of brewing, and those hops would probably have been from New York. Milwaukee Brewery on Huron street offered "Ale and Beer," and both sold and purchased hops.[102] Only in the mid-1850s did the papers start to report a more robust supply of domestic Wisconsin hops.

Despite a long-standing use of New York hops, the market for Wisconsin hops grew alongside the brewing industry. The international demand for US hops grew in this period as well. In 1854, both the English and the Continental crops fell short, which greatly increased demand for US hops, despite any extra shipping costs.[103] That same year, the Cottingtons grew 4,000 pounds of hops, having quickly established themselves as an important commercial grower in the region.[104] Newspapers reported various successes and occasional failures in the hop industry, but the hop farmers of the 1850s, going about their business relatively quietly, had no idea of the rollercoaster ride that lay ahead.

While the brewing industry grew despite the lack of enough local hops, the availability of local ice was indeed a local advantage as it coincided with the rapid rise in demand for lager, which ages at temperatures hovering just above freezing after its initial fermentation phase. Much of the growth of brewing in this era, in Milwaukee and elsewhere, was shaped by this huge increase in the demand for lager, initially among recent immigrants from Germany and central Europe but quickly shared by far more than these immigrant groups. The names of beer styles change over time, and the precise boundaries of a style like lager can be controversial, to say the least. I will again turn to Hoverson for guidance on ale versus lager: "Broadly speaking, beer is divided into two main categories: ale and lager. Ales are made with top-fermenting yeast and are generally fermented at temperatures around 70 degrees F. Ales tend to be fruitier in both aroma and taste than lagers. Lagers are made with bottom-fermenting yeast and require lower fermentation temperatures, around 50 degrees F." As Hoverson helpfully notes, "within these main categories exist infinite variations."[105] In the nineteenth century, as today, all these beer styles used hops, but they varied in the yeast they used as well as the grains and adjuncts added to the brew.

Lager was becoming more common in Europe, and its popularity continues to this day.[106] Lager had been brewed for hundreds of years without modern refrigeration, thanks to three low-tech solutions: ice, caves, and seasonal brewing.[107] Commercial lager production expanded in 1820s Europe, centered at first in Vienna and Munich, and then the 1840s saw the rise of the lager style known as Pilsener.[108] Given the apparent variation in types of hops purchased even by breweries producing primarily lager, it seems safe to say that the bottom-fermenting yeast (and resultant clear, crisp brew) was the more defining factor in labeling something a lager than the hops added to the recipe. In addition, there would have been less importance with regard to type or region of hop for the bittering hops used at the start of the boil. It is likely that the more expensive and more carefully sourced hops (such as the large purchases of German hops periodically made by Pabst and Blatz, alongside enormous quantities of New York and Wisconsin hops) may have been added toward the end of the boil, where their character would more perceptibly shape the final product.

The popularity of lager in Milwaukee starting in the 1840s had much to do with German immigration.[109] Beer consumption formed an important component of social and economic life in nineteenth-century Milwaukee, and the relatively low alcohol content of lager as well as its lightness lent themselves to sociable consumption. According to historian Alison Efford, "neighborhood bars were primarily male spaces, but at beer gardens women joined men, and children were welcome too. Families, *Vereine* or social clubs, and church groups relaxed at outdoor establishments during the summer months. These sites of German ethnicity dotted the landscape of cities such as Cincinnati, St. Louis, and Milwaukee."[110] Between 1840 and 1880, at least eleven beer gardens existed in Milwaukee, catering primarily to the German immigrant population.[111] These were places for the consumption of beer, alongside coffee and cake, as well as for bowling or ice skating, listening to music, and enjoying the manicured, parklike landscapes.

By the late 1870s, the breweries were getting in on the action and constructing their own beer gardens. Beer also poured into saloons, taverns, and beer halls in Milwaukee and beyond. Early on, the large brewers built adjacent beer halls, and even today it is possible to sit in the charming hall of the Pabst Brewery or its cozy adjoining tavern. The halls were places where other entertainment abounded, including opera and bands, as well as dancing; they drew a typically coed crowd.[112] At times the German thirst for lager was at odds with the temperance movement's rejection of alcohol consumption.[113] By the 1870s, the well-organized brewing industry was vocally advocating for lager as a temperance-friendly beverage, a position not supported by much of the temperance movement: "Discussions of lager's relatively low alcohol content and nutritious ingredients regularly combined with exclamations of German-Americans' sober and orderly habits to assert beer's temperance value, though reformers rarely agreed."[114]

Beer consumption across the country and around the globe was on the rise in the 1860s and 1870s, increasing 140 percent from 1864 to 1873 across the US, and a full 200 percent in Milwaukee. The breweries were ready to meet the challenge.[115] In the early 1860s, Best had produced a mere five thousand barrels, but by 1890, and under its more familiar name of Pabst, it produced more than a million barrels, requiring a million pounds of hops (and 220,000 yards of the iconic blue ribbon tied to each bottle of its "Select" lager).[116] In the early 1860s, the hop farmers of Wisconsin, including Silas Seymour, were eager to take advantage of this growing market.

4

"THE WILD GRASS OF THE MARSHES HAS CHANGED"

Hops on the Move 1861–66

In May 1861, Silas Seymour bought enough rhizomes from his neighbor Jesse Cottington to plant out two acres of hops. This is the first mention of hops in Silas's ledgers, but his remaining ledgers only go back to 1859, so it is possible he grew some earlier than this. However, his interest in hop growing soon increased, as Silas started keeping a separate account book for his hopyard in 1862. No other crop that I know of merited such treatment in his records. From 1862 to 1868, he tallied the finances of his hop growing to see whether it was worth it.[1] For many years, it definitely was, and Silas diligently entered handsome profits on the account book's pages. He carried on with his other agricultural pursuits alongside the hopyard—wheat and corn, sheep and oats, and other crops and livestock common in this time and place.

Silas was neither the first or the most prolific hop farmer in the area, but I know more about his hop cultivation than anyone else's because of the cycles of planting and harvesting that appear in his papers. He tracked the money he earned cutting hop poles and selling hop roots, as well as selling his own hops. He recorded the work of his wife and children in the fields, and the costs of hiring and housing pickers. The ledgers held at the Wisconsin Historical Society Archives reflect the vagaries of the weather, in a time when forecasts were iffy at best, when they were available at all. Other variables affecting his profits included the prices offered by the hop dealers (very much affected by the global trade in hops, even here on this remote Wisconsin farm), the presence of aphids or mildew in his fields or other farmers' fields, and the quality of picking and drying. Although picking was the most labor-intensive part of raising hops, the plants needed various types of tending throughout the year.

In the winter the hop roots slumbered in the frozen ground. Birch, ash, maple, walnut trees were silhouetted against the pale sky above them. The twilight grew just a bit longer on clear days, even though months would pass before the sap would start to run in the birches and maples, and the audible trickle of melting snow would herald a coming change. At night various creatures moved across the fields: possums, rabbits, skunks, if the snowy days were warm enough. When the ground finally began to thaw, farmers and their families and hired hands grubbed up old hop roots to trim them, replanting some, expanding their yards, and selling extras on to others. Later in the season, the farmer, an elder son, or a hired hand would place three poles into each hop hill, women and children would later tie young plants to the poles, and the fields would be manured and plowed. In his hop-yard notebook, Silas recorded the work that his wife Mary Ann did in the hop field, tying the young plants to their poles in June as they began to grow taller. For those not familiar with Wisconsin's brief growing season, the last average frost date is late April, and it can easily snow into April, and even occasionally into May (or, dare I say it, June). For Baraboo, not far from the Seymours' farm, the 2023 growing season was 140 days, and a nineteenth-century source suggests that the growing season in southern and southeastern Wisconsin lasted from 120 to 150 days in the Seymours' time. One recent spring, my own hop plants still slept beneath a blanket of snow as March gave way to April.

The Seymours' profits were modest at first: $300 in 1862, $210 in 1863. Then 1864 saw what must have been a stunning sum: $1,850 netted from the hop business, above and beyond the expenses. In 1864, Sauk County grew 380,238 pounds of hops, as the county began its climb to ascendancy.[2] There was a slight dip in the Seymours' hop profits in 1865, to $1,648, then 1866 brought in $2,176. Profits on the family's hops more than doubled from 1866 to 1867, when the household harvested an impressive 13,249 pounds and netted a rollicking $4,613, even after shelling out hundreds of dollars to pay, feed, and transport thirty-two women for hop picking. I know they were women because Silas lists the entry for the cost of feeding them as boarding "pickers + men," the men being those who were hired to pull hop poles and tend the boxes.

Pickers were essential to the profitability of the hop-growing enterprise, and wives like Mary Ann were essential to the success of the picking because of the quantity of work required to host all those people—they provided the "room and good board" necessary to attract the right quantity and quality of pickers. The Seymours hosted hop pickers over a decade or more, but the thirty-two pickers of 1867 might have been their biggest year. Mary Ann would have been in charge of the work of hosting them. Daughters Ella and Ida would have been around fourteen and twelve years old, respectively, grown enough to be helpful. Ella accomplished all these chores, and picking and tying hops, with more physical challenges than her sister because of having been born with kyphosis, a strong curvature of her spine that continued into adulthood.[3] In a letter from 1854, Silas's mother wrote, "I want to ask how Ellen [Ella] is. I understand she is a feeble child. Give her a kiss from Grandma. I want to see her . . . very much, not excepting the rest of you." Ella herself addressed her body in an essay written late in her life, where she described how, soon after she was born, "it was discovered that I was hopelessly deformed, and the thought of this has lessened the enjoyment of many a pleasure day, but Time, the great healer, has made me less sensitive to the words and looks of strangers."[4] More and more of these strangers would soon enter her house for the annual hop harvest as Ella worked alongside her mother and sister to prepare for their arrival.

At some point in the 1860s, Silas even added an extra kitchen onto his house to make space for the cooking required for the annual hop harvest. That kitchen lasted long past the hop times, as his granddaughter Ruth Seymour Burmester recounted a periodic deep clean of the space:

> The girls [Silas's granddaughters, Ella's nieces] set about cleaning up of the back room, or "summer" kitchen. This was an addition, about 20 feet wide and 30 feet long which had been built onto the northeast side of the house with a connecting door between it and the winter kitchen. It was put up in the late 1860s, the "Hop Times," added onto the house proper so as to provide more room to cook and to feed the hop-pickers, (the workers needed to harvest the hops in the fall). These hop pickers were girls that Grandfather Seymour recruited from Necedah, Mauston, Port Hope, and other small towns in the sandy counties north, where hops could not be grown. They must be fed and sheltered during the hop picking. Bedsteads, a dozen or more of them, old bedsteads which were made for rope springs and strawtick mattresses, that screwed together and had round wooden braces to support head and foot, were stored up in the hop house, some of them hung from the crossbeams nailed to the rafters.[5]

Despite the successes of 1867, the Hop Yard Account Book ended abruptly in June 1868. Silas's other bookkeeping continued, and while he may have tossed the Hop Yard Account Book into the corner in disgust or frustration in the challenging year of 1868, the family continued to plant hops and sell rhizomes into the 1870s.

Since the earliest days of his hop growing, Silas augmented his income by selling rhizomes on to other hop farmers, just as he had once bought rhizomes from Jesse Cottington. According to one history of Sauk County written in the early twentieth century, "The sale of hop roots became an important adjunct to the hop raiser's revenue, as the roots of the older plants needed trimming in, or 'grubbing' in the spring, and as seed roots were very much in demand, these sold for from $15.00 to $25.00 for roots enough to set an acre."[6] In the spring of 1863, Silas was already selling rhizomes to his neighbors, including the ancestors of people who still live in the area today. That year he sold to Linnell, Craker, and Starks—farms all visible on the 1859 map or in the 1870 census, and in street names and tax parcel maps in the vicinity today. Because of the rhizomatic nature of hops, it is possible that some of the hops growing in this part of the world at that time were from the same mother plants, brought to Wisconsin first to Cottington's farm and then spreading through the neighborhood. As discussed in chapter 3, possible descendants of those rhizomes now grow in my own garden.

The ledgers list the many people with whom Silas did business, including one of the few women hop farmers in the area, Mrs. Catherine Welch, an Irish widow with seven children at home all old enough to be helpful with an 800-pound hop harvest in 1869. Silas paid a nearby farmer, Oscar Gregory, to sharpen hop poles. Oscar was married to Agnes Cottington, oldest daughter of Jesse and Rebecca Cottington, the single most influential couple in Sauk County's hop industry at the time. Dellona and Reedsburg can sometimes feel a bit like George Eliot's Middlemarch in the intertwining of families and finances, as well as the careful assessment of the value of agricultural endeavors.

Silas Seymour's ledgers, both the official entries and the marginal calculations, teach us how much of a math problem farming was—the ever-uncertain equation of how to mix enough seeds, sun, and water to pay off debts, feed a family, or even turn a profit. These households were always working with unknown variables—what insects might have made their way west, when a freak hailstorm or early freeze might destroy a crop, or (perhaps the biggest variable of all) when a competing hop market hundreds or thousands of miles away might collapse or rebound. How many hop boxes does a picker need to fill to make the hop-picking jaunt profitable, how much are those hungry pickers going to eat, and how many pies or roasts or eggs or loaves of bread does that translate into in the kitchen of the hop farmer's wife? This work is one edge of American capitalism, rushing to fill the demand of brewers across the country and around the world for hops for the brew kettle. Silas Seymour carefully entered the pennies and nickels he spent on medicine, shoes, books, hop poles, hop sacking, and food and drink for the pickers. The ledgers mark the transformation of sun and soil into a comfortable profit, or the moment when a hop-farming couple might watch their money float away in a flood or dry up to a husk in a drought. Silas's account books also record the effects of hop growing on nearby forests and swamps. Thousands of young saplings became hop poles in the Seymour hopyard alone, and dozens of cords of wood heated the dryer for the hop kiln—five cords of wood in 1863 alone. (A cord is 128 cubic feet, equal to a stack measuring 4 by 4 by 8 feet—imagine five of those stacks!)

Wisconsin's nineteenth-century hop country, including Sauk and neighboring counties, occupied the southern part of the region, which had been scraped bare ten thousand years earlier by continental ice sheets, as well as part of the Driftless Area that had remained out of reach of the voracious glaciers. The hop farms of the nineteenth century clustered in the southwestern part of the state and barely crossed the tension zone, the *S*-shaped ecotone that splits the state into two climatic and ecological regions. To the north and east there are northern mesic and boreal forests, to the south and west are prairie and oak savanna, as well as southern mesic forests.[7] The terminal moraine of Wisconsin's last glacier ran through the eastern part of today's Sauk County, marking the division between the Driftless and the "drifted" sections of the state.[8]

A major source of information for this book was the detailed property maps charting out the terrain of this part of Wisconsin, including work by W. H. Canfield. He is not as famous as his colleague Increase Lapham, but like Lapham, his methodical survey of Sauk County contributed to the stark changes brought by this settlement. One of Canfield's creations was a detailed, even decorative map of Sauk County in 1859, depicting land impacted by the arrival of so many Yankees and European migrant settlers. A vivid color copy of the map hung on my wall as I wrote this book, courtesy of the American Geographical Society Library up the street from my house. This map contains a wealth of information, and a host of secrets and silences. Like any map, it is selective. It would be impossible to include all available information, so the cartographer made choices about what to include and what to omit, choices rooted in the priorities of the US government and these settlers. The map is a fine representation of the surveyor's grid, the section boundaries that, to this day, organize property taxes and deed offices. Certain sections cantilever ever so slightly toward the North Pole, to compensate for the curvature of the earth and the cosmic challenge of laying a grid across a sphere.

Canfield carefully inscribed the names of white settlers, as well as one Ho-Chunk man, across their properties.[9] In fact, at least two Ho-Chunk men were landowning neighbors of Silas Seymour, with a broader understanding of neighbors—at one point Wakąjazi, or Yellow Thunder, lived about ten miles away; Ahuchoga, or Blue Wing, lived about eight miles away. These two men were older than Silas, and they witnessed the violence and loss of previous decades, while also remaining or returning. Well before the hop boom, on June 20, 1851 (two years after Silas Seymour and Wakąjazi filed their claims), Ahuchoga bought the land that he and others had been living on, selling it a decade later. His name is the only clearly Indigenous name I have found on the 1859 plat map of Sauk County, where the mapmaker Canfield scratched at an angle "Indian Ar-hu-choker 120 ac." In 1861 Ahuchoga sold the land to W. W. Henderson, and the residents of that land relocated to "the south bank of the Baraboo River about two miles northwest of Reedsburg, where their lodges could be found in varying numbers until about 1915."[10] Hash marks on the map indicate a "Tamerac" swamp, black alder swamp, and willow swamp, all places where saplings may have been harvested for use as hop poles. The map both enabled and reflected white settlement, the quadrants laid across a deeply unsquare terrain and quickly filling with wheat fields, wooden houses, growing settler families, and, here and there and more and more, hops. This map emphasized and enabled a particular and powerful way of inhabiting the land—individual property ownership divided into townships and quarter sections. Today subterranean networks of hop rhizomes follow the path of the names etched into this map. Canfield captured Silas Seymour's claim in his 1859 map, and I would be surprised if hops don't twine up on the edges of one of the fields on this property. Silas, Mary Ann, Ella, and the other hop farmers and pickers filled this grid with the work of their daily lives.

By the early 1860s, Wisconsin housed almost 160 breweries, a ready market for the increasing quantities of Wisconsin hops.[11] One of the families growing hops in this period had a name that many people today would recognize. In the up-and-coming hop region of Jefferson County (two counties west of Lake Michigan, about halfway between Milwaukee and Madison), one of the farming couples trying their luck in 1861 was the subject of a later book series and a 1970s television show: Charles "Pa" and Caroline "Ma" Ingalls, of *Little House on the Prairie* fame.[12] In the 1860 census, Charles and Caroline were newlyweds living in a household of twelve people, including Charles's parents and siblings. (Their daughter Laura, the eventual author of the book series, wasn't born until 1867, well after her parents' brief foray into the hop trade.) The now-famed Ingalls family farmed hops in Concord, presumably fairly unsuccessfully, since they soon left the area to make a go of it much farther north in Wisconsin (near Pepin, in a log cabin where Laura was born and grew up; it became the setting for *The Little House in the Big Woods*, the first book in her series).

There is a single letter written by Caroline Ingalls that reports on the 1861 hop harvest.[13] Caroline Lake Quiner was born in Brookfield, fifteen miles or so west of downtown Milwaukee. She married Charles Ingalls on February 1, 1860, and the letter reports that they grew hops the following year. Caroline opened her letter with a vivid explanation of her mother's agonizing bout of "scarlet diptheria" and then went on to describe their hop harvest: "Charles is well but he has worked very hard this summer and is about tired out now. We have got our hops picked and pressed. It took three weeks with 20 pickers to pick them. We have sold $82.50 worth and have about as many more to sell as we have sold; but we do not expect to get as much for the remainder as the price is reduced."[14] It was a disappointing and exhausting harvest, and a common experience for many hop farmers—the prices could fluctuate from day to day and week to week during the harvest.

Prices responded to a range of variables—certainly whatever brewers wanted, but also wars or blights reducing sources on which brewers relied could increase demand for local hops. By the same count, a glut in markets familiar to brewers could depress prices everywhere. And the unpredictability of weather, blights, and pests meant that fortunes could turn in the blink of an eye. A promising field could lie in ruin after a hailstorm or even a too-damp night. The botanical qualities of the plant compounded these effects—unlike annuals such as wheat or corn, the perennial rhizomatic hop plants tend to start producing more reliably after three years of being in the ground, which makes it even harder to respond quickly to changes in supply and demand and often led to overproduction in this era as farmers might plant more hops when prices rose, anticipating profits three years down the road, but they were rarely alone in this endeavor.

The rest of Caroline Ingalls's letter was a mix of descriptions of illness and exclamations of familial love. It's unclear to me (as well as the good people of the Concord Historical Society) whether Charles's hop farming took place on his parents' farm or on a separate piece of land, but I did my best to hunt for their hops. The farmer who owns much of the land kindly invited me to scour the margins with him on a scorching August day in 2024. I drove out a narrow country road to his farm, expecting to walk the edges of the fields and thus wearing long pants and long sleeves. But—in retrospect, obviously—the property was much too large to survey solely on foot, especially in that heat and without devoting many hours to the project, so the farmer and I hopped into his all-terrain vehicle and drove through the newly mown hay meadows, alongside woodlots, and past the cattails and hints of glistening water of a nearby swamp. There were pairs of sandhill cranes everywhere I turned, and endless vines of wild grape teased me with their similarity to hop bines. Aside from one round of somewhat delightfully blasting through the tall grasses of one unmown meadow, we kept to the edges so I could scan the trees and bushes for any sign of hops. The farmers' dairy cows huddled beneath a mister in the farmyard, appreciating the cooling effect of the drops of water gathering on their backs.

I was honestly stunned by the beauty of the adjacent land, shimmering wetlands and gently sloping fields of goldenrod and big bluestem. A good-sized river snakes through this farmland, flat and lovely, often hidden behind a stand of trees or a low rise in the land. But sometimes a hop hunt fails to bear fruit. We found nothing that day, and even if we had, it would have been a challenge to determine whether those were truly the descendants of the Ingalls' hops, or a local wild hop, or a cross of hops from other times. The Ingalls family was part of a much larger swing toward hop cultivation, even if few traces of that work remain today. In 1850, Jefferson County had only two hop farmers, harvesting a total of 1,800 pounds of hops. By 1860, the township of Concord alone housed more hop farmers than all of Sauk County that year, and the Ingalls family lived near people who were growing copious quantities of hops—thirteen farmers grew a combined 22,000 pounds of hops that census year.[15] The majority in 1860 were from New York, as was Charles Ingalls.

Charles and Caroline Ingalls had left Concord for Pepin by 1862, and on September 23, 1863, they bought the farm where their daughters Mary and Laura were born.[16] Other Concord hop farmers had greater success and longevity. Isaac Frank of Concord was the most prolific hop grower in Wisconsin in 1859, when he harvested 7,000 pounds of hops. A decade later he was still in business, and harvested 8,000 pounds. People like the Weavers and the Cottingtons planted the roots of hop culture, but thanks to dozens of farmers like the Ingallses and the Franks, the industry took off in ways that would have been difficult to predict. And just a few years after the Ingallses' exhausting harvest, Sauk County eclipsed all other Wisconsin counties.[17]

In the very early 1860s, those banner harvests were yet to come. Year by year individual farmers added hops to their land or increased the quantity of hops they were growing. Many factors influenced those decisions—rising prices for hops, shaped in turn by the heavy taxation of liquor in the Civil War or the fact that a neighbor was growing hops successfully and had some rhizomes for sale. Hop growing was one part of the broader agricultural and colonizing project at work at the time. As early as 1861, a German immigrant recalled the landscape of Sauk County looking entirely different than it had a few years earlier: "The wild grass of the marshes has changed as countless tons of hay have been made there by the settlers."[18] Hay is not hops, but both crops fit into these changed landscapes as one of many attempts to wrest cash out of prairie and forest.

The year 1860 brought a bumper crop of wheat to Wisconsin, but the chinch bug soon arrived and the quality and quantity of harvests decreased.[19] As wheat profits declined, the settlers cast about for horticultural solutions to their cash flow problems, with the help of treatises, pamphlets, reports, and newspapers. Sugar beets, tobacco, sorghum, and other specialty crops slipped into the ledgers and the fields of these farmers as they tried to feed their families and make a profit. Hop rhizomes entered land that had often already been "cleared"—denuded of trees or the deep roots of perennial prairie and oak savanna plants broken by the iron plow. By the 1860s, the finished product—the dried and baled hops destined for brew kettles near and far—could travel along paths of transport and trade already created by the tide of settlers in one direction and wheat and other agricultural commodities in the other direction: blazed trails, plank roads, rivers and Great Lakes, schooners and steamships, and eventually the railroad.

One state agricultural report from this era found that "the [hop] crop of 1860 was so trifling as hardly to deserve mention. But in the year 1864 it amounted to 385,583 pounds."[20] Given the significant increase in prices for hops, it's no wonder that hops caught the eye of farmers hoping to turn a profit. While Wisconsin farmers could expect twenty cents per pound in 1861, by 1865 that amount had in many cases tripled.[21] According to one account, "In 1863 hop growers were getting 7 cents per pound for their hops—a fair price. . . . By 1865 the price had increased to 60 cents per pound. . . . There was some question of the morality of raising hops but with the price at 50 cents per pound it was agreed to be very moral."[22]

Brewers of the day bought hops from Wisconsin farmers and from farmers and hop dealers much farther afield. Even in the early 1860s, Blatz was buying hops from Ella Seymour's neighbor Jesse Cottington, and from the nationwide hop dealing empire of John Eddy and David Wilber, who traded in both Wisconsin and New York hops.[23] In 1865, one newspaper claimed that "the increased culture of the hop is attributable mainly to the great increase in the number of the breweries of this country, which now annually require from 45,000 to 50,000 bales, while 25 years ago they used but 6000."[24] The surviving ledgers of some of Milwaukee's nineteenth-century breweries contain clues about the paths some of these hops followed, although these are incomplete, and at times (especially in the case of Frederick Miller) illegible, even to a trained reader of nineteenth-century penmanship. I found that Miller's early notebooks are not only written in a challenging hand, but they bounce among German, English, and French. I can definitely read German and English, and a bit of French, but not necessarily all on the same page and in a long-ago cursive. When I read through his early daybooks, housed in the archive at today's Molson-Coors/Miller brewery in Milwaukee, I was struck by how personal they felt as objects—leatherbound books small enough to fit in a coat pocket, with a slight curve from having been carried so close to the body.[25] Indeed, throughout the research for this book, I was repeatedly struck by the scale of operations of production and trade that could take place based entirely on handwritten records, and the skills of penmanship and arithmetic.

Other records are a bit more legible. In 1863, as one example, Valentin "Val" Blatz bought hops in every month but August, although with minuscule purchases from April to July. His clerk recorded purchases of Eastern, New York, and Wisconsin hops, ranging from just three cents a pound to twenty-five cents a pound.[26] That same year, he bought $103 of hops from a Cottington, presumably Jesse.[27] Blatz had already started his own small brewery when he married the widow of a competing brewer (and his housemate), Louise Braun, and established the City Brewery with both properties.[28] According to Doug Hoverson, "By 1850, small family businesses had been formed under the names of Best, Krug, and Braun that would eventually become the breweries that brought the city fame: Pabst, Miller, Schlitz, and Blatz."[29] Even though Val Blatz had surely brewed lager in Germany, most of what he and his competitors brewed early on was "top-fermenting rather than lager and had to be consumed quickly," but some sources suggest that Blatz was brewing only lager by 1855.[30] That makes it even more interesting to read his later ledgers, wherein he bought thousands of pounds of German hops *and* hops from New

York, Wisconsin, England, and California.[31] In other words, even at a time when he was brewing primarily lager, he was using all kinds of hops that few people would associate with the central European traditions of lagers. Because the 1850s ledgers do not survive (to the best of my knowledge—perhaps they sit quietly in the attic of a Blatz descendant), I have only been able to closely peruse the 1860s and 1870s ledgers. The pages show Blatz buying profusely from a range of sources, and thus a range of hop varieties.

Many brewers in this period bought hops as needed, although others may have tried to lay in reserves. The international hop trade reports, brewery ledgers, and newspapers from that time all indicate an array of purchases happening nearly year-round, with a clear increase in buying at the time of the new harvest in the fall and an ebb in spring and summer. Each month the hops grew older and older, and they became less and less appealing as they got closer and closer to the new season of hops—although brewers also routinely bought "yearling" or "old olds," hops whose strength had faded in ways that could balance out the strong flavors of fresher hops. Today hops are quickly dried (either with warm or cool air) after harvesting and then generally pelletized, vacuum sealed, and frozen for greater stability and easier brewing, thereby extending the time frame for hops to hold onto their acids and essential oils, as well as easing the brewing process. Another option available for today's brewers is hop extracts, which contain the acids and oils from the hops. Brewing was much more seasonal than it is today, even with technological advances of the later nineteenth century. In 1866, for example, a Milwaukee newspaper announced that "the lager beer brewing season begins about the close of October, and ends about the first of April."[32]

Throughout the 1860s, more and more Wisconsinites started growing hops, whether they knew much about hops or even farming. Many were farmers new to hops, new to the climate and terrain of Wisconsin, and even new to farming. Even among more seasoned hop farmers, there was much debate about the proper use of poles, the style of kiln, and so on.[33] Doing this farming without weather forecasts brought challenges almost unimaginable in the information-heavy environment of the first quarter of the twenty-first century, and most Wisconsin settler farmers lacked the deeper knowledge and memory of seasons and signals held by many of the people living in Wisconsin at the time. As with other branches of farming, hop growers have long sought instruction from outside sources, ranging from *A Perfite Platforme of a Hoppe Garden*, an old English publication from centuries ago, to the Rudd brothers' pamphlet about hop growing in the 1860s.[34] This knowledge came to them through various routes as they converted part of their land into crops that could compete in the local, national, and even international markets. These farmers entered a dynamic, interconnected market, where a blight or a war hundreds or thousands of miles away affected the farmers of Wisconsin. The settler farmers of Wisconsin may have experienced some periods of mostly subsistence farming, but even before the railroad arrived, most were part of larger markets. Great Lakes shipping and expanding railway lines moved goods to and from eastern states, as evidenced in the available port statistics and railway reports. And the hop market had long been international and transatlantic, even before farmers in Wisconsin began planting hops.[35]

With regard to hops, Wisconsin was late to the party. Yes, it supplied local breweries, as we saw with Jesse and Rebecca Cottington's laborious journey with their first hop harvest in the early 1850s, but by the 1860s (and arguably earlier), Wisconsin hop prices and markets were absolutely affected by what was happening in New York, England, and Germany. Brewers had connections to dealers and farmers around the world. These relationships fill the pages of ledgers like those of Blatz and Pabst, where the clerks entered the same names with seasonal regularity, and where the brewers bought all sorts of hops from all sorts of sources, depending on whether they wanted to save money or acquire the very best imported hops, or if they needed a few bales of old hops to balance the pungency of fresher hops. Just as with Silas Seymour's ledgers, the brewery ledgers also reveal social and financial networks and years-long relationships.

New York loomed large in the minds of Wisconsin farmers, as their greatest competition, and New England still played an important role as well. Otsego, Madison, and Schoharie were the biggest hop growing counties of New York in the 1860s. The *Milwaukee Daily Sentinel* reported on these counties, "The ridge of hills lying South of the central railroad, at a distance of from ten to thirty miles, and extending from Schenectady to Chittenango, has proved to be particularly adapted to hop-growing. . . . Portions of Maine, Vermont, New Hampshire and Massachusetts, chiefly lying near the valley of the Connecticut River, constitute the 'New England hop district.'"[36] Fortunes rose and fell, and happenings in one district impacted others. In 1864, for example, New York had heavy rains followed by drought, as well as "clouds of grasshoppers. . . . Under a clear sky and a burning sun the earth became parched and cracked to quite a depth. . . . Hops were in many localities injured, and often destroyed, by an Aphis, or plant louse."[37] When the aphids moved into New York fields, one Wisconsin newspaper nervously asked, "ARE HOPS RUNNING OUT? The comparative failure of the crop in portions of Otsego and other counties, says the Albany (N. Y.) Journal, has led to some fear that hops are running out. For three or four years the vines have been covered with small white insects. They are called lice; are very annoying to pickers, and, in many instances, destroy the bulb, causing the leaves to have black and blasted appearance."[38] Bad news for New York farmers was fabulous news for Wisconsin farmers whose crops could quickly flood into the unmet demand and empty brew kettles. Wisconsin was ready to step in and allay everyone's fears about a hop shortage, for the right price.

The early 1860s saw an increasing acceptance of Wisconsin hops by brewers, who had hesitated to replace familiar New York hops with the less familiar Wisconsin ones. Dealers, brewers, and farmers categorized the hops in ways that reflected contemporaneous understandings of quality, combined with regional rivalries. While this is almost impossible to conceive of in the current era of hop-heavy beers and hop specificity, throughout much of the nineteenth century, there was little sign of the meticulous attention to aroma and flavor that drives so much of the experience of and market for hops today. I found almost no description of variety, names, and aroma or flavor. Purported quality was the main distinction, and in contrast to other regions or in terms of good picking and kilning. As Bonnie Byrd observed in her study of New York hop production during the rise of the American brewing industry, "hop quality was of principle [*sic*] concern for brewers, above even the productivity of the hop fields. Generally speaking hops were divided into five categories: fancy, choice, prime, medium and poor (common). . . . Such evaluations were entirely qualitative, and could vary greatly between individuals—from growers to merchants, and merchants to brewers."[39] These quality ratings broke down further by regions, which competed for reputations as high-quality producers, and underdogs like Wisconsin repeatedly tried to sell people on their product, as in this 1867 newspaper article: "The quality of hops produced in Wisconsin is fully equal, if not superior to that of the Eastern hops. It is even true that Wisconsin hops have been sent East, repacked, and branded as Eastern hops, simply because the reputation (not the actual quality) of those hops, insured better prices than could be obtained for Western brands. This will not be repeated many years, for Wisconsin is not disposed to let her light be hidden under a bushel."[40] Early on in their attempts to break into the hop market, Wisconsin's "growers had to battle against prejudice in selling their hops. . . . Not until 1862 did Wisconsin hops find favor with brewers, except in few instances."[41] But find favor they did.

One of the challenges for Wisconsin growers was to grow, pick, and dry their hops as well as the competition did, and to convince the dealers and brewers that "Wisconsins" could hold their own alongside "States" (the term of the day for New York state hops), Bavarians, and the other hops on the market. Here is where the skill (and happiness) of hop pickers played a central role in hop growers' profits. Poorly picked hops—hops with too many leaves in the bushel, cones left on the bine, or other carelessness—rated as lower quality than well-picked hops, and the prices reflected in part the skill or sloppiness of the pickers. Dealers were also crucial to "the culture of that pungent vegetable" and to translating the quality of a region's hops to brewers and other dealers.[42] In the earlier days in New York, half a dozen dealers conducted much of the hop selling, and those numbers only increased as the demand for beer grew.[43] By the 1860s, there would be multiple firms in a single hop-growing village, such as Waterville or Cooperstown. In this heyday of hop selling, in some cases two types of dealers would pair up. One would be responsible for combing the countryside for hops, assessing quality, and negotiating prices with the farmers, while the other would then sell to the brewers, "visiting the breweries throughout the country and presenting his samples. Most of these firms are in constant communication, directly or indirectly with the European hop-dealers, and export hops to them, or import from them, as the conditions of the market requires. The quotations of prices of hops in Kent and London are received almost daily by these houses during the hop season, and those of the Belgian and French markets weekly."[44] Throughout this book there are research easter eggs, nascent questions that I think could become dissertations or books or articles by others, and this is one! The lives of these dealers have so much to teach us about nineteenth-century commerce and nineteenth-century beer.

Driving all of this work in the fields was the demand from brewers and their customers, and, above all for the farmers, the hope of a good price once the hops were dried and baled.[45] Thanks to a combination of hop dealers and connections to local farmers, brewers' hop purchases came from near and far, the prices varied, and the varieties varied. Only Val Blatz or Fred Miller or Captain (Frederick) Pabst knew their own heart, but their surviving ledgers tell me at the very least that they paid a range of prices for a range of hops. By 1865, Wisconsin was producing enough hops to export out of the port of Milwaukee, a reversal of the twenty-plus years of importing much of the state's brewers' hop needs from out of state (mostly New York).[46] This increase in production meant more and more women in the fields, filling up the hop boxes and clearing the bines. According to an 1864 report to the Milwaukee Chamber of Commerce, "in addition to the large amount of Hops consumed in the manufacture of beer and ale by local brewers, there was shipped from this city during the year 1865 2,864 bales, averaging about 180 pounds to the bale."[47] At this point, Wisconsin was the third largest hop grower in the US.[48] Brewers grew increasingly accustomed to Wisconsin hops, overcoming some of their initial hesitation out of some (unknowable) combination of familiarity and availability. By 1867, *The Janesville Gazette* could proudly proclaim that "the quality of the Wisconsin hop is claimed to be fully equal to that of the eastern hop."[49] The following year, double the amount of hops was shipped from Milwaukee to markets east, at forty-five to fifty-five cents per pound, a price that tempted many more farmers into planting hop rhizomes of their own.[50]

As the valleys of Sauk County and southern Wisconsin filled with ripening hops in late summer, the farmers sought buyers near and far, and they kept abreast of goings-on in distant lands. Even the local paper of Baraboo, Wisconsin, felt obligated to report the current state of the European hop markets to its provincial readers, knowing these markets could have consequences for the bottom line at home: "According to late reports from Europe there will probably be no foreign demand except at figures lower than our growers will be willing to accept. . . . The fact that there are but few good old hops to be had, either in this country or Europe, warrants the expectation that prices will rule tolerably high during the months of September and October. Brewing will commence earlier in the season than usual."[51]

These growing harvests had financial (and olfactory) effects. The harvest of 1866, Sauk County hop farmers saw hearty profits. A self-identified "tourist" observed, "Farmers load their wagons and come to town with hops, returning with from a thousand to fourteen hundred dollars as the price of the load, and the amount of the greenbacks bewilders them. The depot has a very beer-like and hoppy smell, as the weighing, marking, and shipping of the product goes briskly on."[52] This is one of the surprisingly few references I found to the powerful smell of a hop harvest. When I have picked hops, even though I wore gloves, the smell lingered on my skin and in my hair for quite a while. When I bring hop bines for my students to pick in class each September, the funk lingers in the elevator and my office. The hop farmers' houses and crowds of pickers, as well as the depots and train cars, must have given off quite a scent.[53] And that bewildering pile of greenbacks resulted from weeks of hop-scented work by thousands of young women in Wisconsin's hopyards.

Even as more and more hops became available in Wisconsin, brewers continued to buy hops from different locales. In 1866, "the hops used in the manufacture are mostly raised in Sauk and the surrounding counties of this state, although a considerable quantity is imported from New York, and even from Bavaria."[54] In 1866 the *Milwaukee Daily Sentinel* reported twenty-five breweries total in Milwaukee. Even as the dealers increased in number and wealth, there were brief glimmers of caution as well as challenges to the Wisconsin harvest. One paper warned, "it would perhaps not be amiss to guard your readers against a hop mania, which, like oil, sorghum, and politics, sometimes run our Western friends into extremes, resulting in disappointment and financial error."[55] Another writer that same year called on farmers to "be rational and don't build castles in the air."[56] In the winter of 1866, temperatures dropped so low that many farmers feared the cold would damage hop roots. The *Milwaukee Daily Sentinel* reported, "We hear . . . that around Logansville, entire yards have been killed."[57] While some winterkill did occur, in many places the plants bounced back much more readily than expected.[58] However, some fields then fell victim to the ravages of the cutworm.[59] Another looming problem was the need for fertilizing the growing hop acreage. As hop fields expanded, manure became a scarce commodity: "Every stable, cow yard, pig pen, hen coop and corner in Kilbourn City and vicinity are eagerly searched out by the hop raisers, and unlucky is he who has not been on the alert, especially if he has no farm or stock connected with his hop yard, by which to accumulate manure."[60] Hop farmers did what they could to coax this lucrative plant out of the ground and into the kiln at the end of the season, with dollars on their minds.

The potential for profit was so great that confirmed teetotalers and temperance supporters arranged worried meetings in Baraboo to discuss how best to reconcile their distaste for alcoholic beverages with the money to be made from growing hops.[61] At one meeting, a resolution against hop cultivation was proposed—and voted down by the very temperance supporters who had called the meeting. This growing industry meant even more pressure on nearby forests and swamps to supply an ever-increasing number of hop poles. In 1866, the writer of one letter to the editor claimed that "hundreds of thousands of hop-poles are being got out this winter from the woods and marshes near by. Riding over the circumjacent prairies, one-half the farmers that you meet on the road are going after hop-poles and the other half are returning with a load of them. 'Hop-poles' is the cry with these people. With Patrick Henry they exclaim, 'I know not what course others may take, but as for me, give me hop-poles or give me death!'"[62]

The other element in ever-growing demand was young women. The bulk of the tens of thousands of hop pickers in nineteenth-century Wisconsin were young white women. There are hints that many might have been relatively recent Irish, German, or Norwegian immigrants, but most of the sources I have seen described the Wisconsin crews as heterogeneous with regard to birthplace and even class.[63] In an autobiographical novel written by a former hop picker, *The Hop Pickers; Girl Life in the Sixties*, we see young women from wealthy families and families of modest means picking together, as well as stark social divides between the Yankee pickers and the Dutch (or German?) and Irish pickers.[64] In Wisconsin, women found their way into many agricultural fields.[65] Henry David Thoreau even reported, on a trip through the far northwest corner of nearby Illinois in 1861, "women working in fields quite commonly."[66] But the women of the hop fields stand out, in quantity and in coverage in the papers of the day. With small enough acreage and a large enough family of half-grown offspring, a farmer might get away without hiring pickers. As soon as a farmer's harvest grew to any significant size, however, extra hands were going to be needed, and in the height of the boom, this need amounted to far more hands than the local farms and villages could provide. Throughout the region, young white women met that need for these farmers.

Thanks in part to the work of those pickers, many growers became increasingly wealthy: "Many of our hop-growers, too, are making use of their rapidly incoming wealth to build up homes such as a few years ago farmers would hardly have thought of."[67] A farmer identified as J. L. Green in a newspaper blurb grew 17,229 pounds on 7 acres, on which he had planted 5000 hop hills.[68] David W. Small was a major grower in Oconomowoc, planting on six acres in 1866 and harvesting

10,000 pounds by 1869.[69] By 1866, there were so many women heading to the hop fields that hometown papers enumerated the quantities of women and girls missing from their villages, their kitchens, and their dance halls: "As near as we can calculate, twenty loads of girls, of one dozen to the load, from this village and immediate vicinity, have left within the last three days, for the purpose of picking hops in the yards about Reedsburg. The men have now the privilege of running this town to suit themselves."[70] The following year brought even more cartloads of "girls" and left even more men back at home.

Whereas the 1865 hop crop for the state reached well over half a million pounds, the 1867 harvest weighed in at "between six and seven million pounds."[71] Four million pounds of that 1867 harvest were from Sauk County alone.[72] Wisconsin's farmers would go on to harvest a stunning 11 million pounds of hops in 1868.[73] The need for extra hands during this boom quickly became obvious.

5

"THIRTY REGIMENTS IN CALICO"

The Women of the Hop Boom

> Well do I remember how as a child . . . I watched the hop pickers who danced to the tinkling music of the dulcimers in my Uncle John's barn. It was the largest barn on the prairie and every night during the season the pickers from the adjoining farms gathered to take part in the merriment. The huge barn still stands as do the log hop-houses of fantastic shapes, and I never pass them without recalling my awe and admiration of these silk-gowned young women, dressed in their hoop skirts, with their beaux, the young dandies, resplendent with waxed mustaches.[1]

In the summer of 1867, a reported thirty thousand young and predominantly white women entered the hop fields around Kilbourn City, Wisconsin, to pick the cones, one by one, off the sticky bines.[2] They arrived via railroad and wagon, crowding the depot and the roads of the hop-producing counties. For example, "Sauk County's harvest in 1867 equaled one-fifth of the nation's output and the town of Kilbourn was hailed by local enthusiasts as 'the greatest primary hop depot in the United States—perhaps in the world.'"[3] The quantities in question are monumental, especially considering that no aspect of this industry was effectively mechanized. This swift increase had implications for nearby families, young women, and even forests, where saplings hardly stood a chance in the hunt for the millions of slender hop poles necessary for the industry—an estimated 680 to 1,700 poles per acre, each of which was a young tree cut down in a swamp or grove.[4]

The successes of the previous years had encouraged ever more farmers to plant hops. In the spring of 1867, the Kilbourn City railway station alone saw tens of thousands of pounds of hop rhizomes move across its rails. Those roots would be planted in spring and would not produce a saleable crop for another couple of years.[5] Farmers buying up these rhizomes banked on the continuation of these profitable years. Leroy Gates, better known as a broker for hop pickers, also sold hop rhizomes, "English cluster at $8 per acre."[6] The Wisconsin hopyards looked great in August 1867, and Jesse Cottington, in his capacity as a regional hop dealer, offered forty cents a pound. Orders for that season's hops even came directly to Sauk County from England.[7] The *Milwaukee Daily Sentinel* reported on August 6, "The hop itself is in the finest possible degree of thrift that the finest of weather and freshest of vines can produce in any climate. We see on every side hops full an inch long, rank and growing. We verily believe that this year Sauk County hops will be the Star Brand of all markets."[8]

Another force beyond Wisconsin farmers' control was working in their favor. News began to make its way westward that hopyards across the New York hop regions were filling with hop lice, and the plants were turning black overnight at the end of July 1867.[9] When all was said and done, the hop louse cut the New York harvest from seventy thousand to ten thousand bales.[10] What spelled disaster for the farmers of New York's hop belt meant rising fortunes in Wisconsin and strong temptation to plant even more hops. New York's misfortune occurred at precisely the moment that Wisconsin was heading to its largest harvest ever, and when the weather had been good, and the fields relatively free of pests and blight.[11]

What was the secret to these farmers' success in the 1860s? Good hop poles, sure. Some nice alluvial soils, yes. Well-chosen rhizomes and well-dug hop hills, absolutely. And good fortune where weather and hop lice are concerned, naturally. A fair-minded hop dealer and access to an efficient train depot never hurt, and the failure of the

New York crop was certainly key to the riches of 1867. But one element played an outsize role. The young women who journeyed to the fields in their calico dresses to pick the hops by hand in the last days of August and the start of September, and the women who fed and housed them, who made the beds and prepared tempting meals, made beer possible.[12] Without those pickers and their hostesses, there would have been no way to reach such lofty profits. In the nineteenth century, there was no beer without women.[13] The dearth of labor in Wisconsin worked in favor of these young women and their own pursuit of piles of dollar bills and a pleasant excursion.

At various points in the 1860s, these pickers demanded higher wages, changed to another farm if the food wasn't good enough, partied late into the night, danced to their heart's content, stuffed cheeky farmhands into hop sacks, and sang loud songs on packed trains. Much of what we know about this period comes from the same newspapers that the farmers used as their primary source of information. As I read these newspapers, I felt none of the urgency, excitement, fear, or even desperation that the farmers would have felt as they snapped open a fresh paper collected from the general store or the post office. News of hop harvests traveled across the telegraph wires winding along the paths of the railroads, electrical pulses racing along copper cables across oceans and continents, to be received and reported on by the papers. There was a lot of bluster and bother in the newspaper writing on hops in the 1860s, and it can be difficult to distinguish between opinion, boosterism, and factual reporting.

But these old newspapers have left a detailed record of reporters' observations of the annual arrival of the region's hop pickers. The newspaper coverage and published reminiscences of these endeavors are borderline cinematic, with rich portrayals of hopyard flirtations and dining tables laden with "platters heaped with cold chicken and turkey . . . biscuits, pies, cakes, cheese and preserves, with golden lumps of butter, and plates of pickles."[14] The pickers descended on the land, and on the households of untold numbers of farmers' wives preparing for weeks of feeding and housing this throng. Sara Rath reported the following account in her 1979 study of H. H. Bennett, a nineteenth-century photographer who captured images of this time, several of which appear in this book:

> "The railroad companies are utterly unable to furnish cars for the accommodation of the countless throngs who daily find their way to the depots to take cars for the hop fields. . . . Every passenger car is pressed into service and freight and platform cars are fixed up as well as possible for the transportation of the pickers. Every train has the appearance of an excursion train, on some great gala day, loaded down as they are with myriads of bright faced young girls." The "major general" of the army of hop picker was "Leroy Gates, who makes the unsuspecting public believe that he is a Dells pilot. Pilot he is, but not of logs or lumber. . . . He pilots the wearers of calico and crinoline to the fields where the hops do grow. It broadens human feelings to know there are so many lively girls in the world, and beer will be none the worse for a view of the hands which pick the berries, that give it its bittersweet."[15]

As the hops ripened in the field, trains trundled into Kilbourn City and other stations in hop country, laden with women. In Flavia Camp Canfield's autobiographical novel *The Hop Pickers*, the girls being recruited to the hop fields are told by the agent not to pack their crinolines (a.k.a. hoop skirts) because they would take up too much room in the crowded trains and sleeping quarters. Instead he instructs them to pack "gloves, large aprons, heavy shoes, and big sun bonnets" in a "small bundle or satchel," although one of the girls immediately makes plans to "smuggle in a little finery."[16]

In the periodical *Prairie Farmer*, Gates wrote up a flattering description of the experience of hop picking, and of the hop pickers themselves, capturing both their outward appearance and their economic power:

> Hop picking time is when woman reigns in her glory—in compensation for service stands on equal footing with man—is proudly conscious of her importance as she realizes the high value placed on her labour. . . . From all quarters, bankers', farmers', merchants', and every-

> body's daughters, wives, and grand-daughters . . . actuated with the pleasant idea of the romance of the thing, of meeting old friends, of enjoying the hop dances, and "making lots of money," and having a splendid time in general, pack their trunks for several weeks' absence, and depart for the yards, leaving, mistress, mother, and husband to worry and fret over household matters and curse the hop-yards through the painful interval.[17]

Thousands of women set out unaccompanied by family, ostensibly under the protection of the farmers' families. Although crews of women had been picking hops in the area since at least the early 1850s, the mid-1860s saw a huge increase in scale, reaching a crescendo in 1867 and 1868. These women were the available labor force—many men were gone or injured as a result of the Civil War, and other farming men were needed for other farming tasks. The *Milwaukee Daily Sentinel* reported in September 1867, "We have seen this week, going in every direction, *hundreds of loads* of women, with 'Hops' . . . indelibly stamped on their brow . . . A lumber wagon without seats round the edge, like an omnibus is at present a strange thing in these parts."[18] This onslaught of pickers left a visual impact on the countryside. Gates observed, "At this time [fall 1867] the country is alive with a moving army of 25,000 or 30,000 women on their way to the hop fields, making the valleys and woods resound with their merry songs and happy shouts, presenting an animating scene once witnessed never to be forgotten. There is a certain pleasant excitement about hoppicking that almost causes one to forget the fatigue of this laborious work."[19] Certainly for many pickers, "hop picking is not of pleasant memory. It was hard work."[20] But as difficult and uncomfortable as the work could sometimes be, many of the pickers enjoyed their time. The good wages and the dancing were no doubt welcome, as was as the relative power afforded to a group of women who normally may not have had as much say in their wages and their lives.

Belle Cushman Bohn, both a picker and a daughter of hop farmers, wrote that she could "vividly recollect the work and the fun connected with this industry of my girlhood. . . . Men, women, and children flocked to the yards; many an early day schoolteacher spent the summer vacation in this fashion. . . . There was something of adventure and change in being with a crowd out-of-doors, having the best meals served three times a day, and lodging provided for those who lived many miles away . . . although some said they were out for their health, I noticed they always took the pay too."[21] There is ample photographic evidence of children in the hop fields, but I have not seen many references to them as paid members of the workforce, and I lean toward the assumption that they would have either been of the household or neighbors, or accompanying parents engaged in hop picking. In other words, unlike, say, industrial textile mills, children were not employed on the same scale because this was a migrant labor force that relied on people who could travel independently, and also where the strength and speed of an adult picker was likely preferable to that of a child.[22]

There is much anecdotal evidence that, especially at the peak of Wisconsin's hop growing, Yankees picked alongside immigrants, and working-class women picked alongside better-off women who were in the fields not just for the money but also for the adventure.[23] According to the *Milwaukee Daily Sentinel*, "Almost everybody picks hops . . . [including] merchants' wives, and professional men's daughters. Few indeed are the Flora McFlimseys in Sauk County who are not at present scratching their hands with hop-vines, and picking up an appetite and two boxes a day of the light basis of lager beer simultaneously. Women all say there is a fascinating excitement about it, which is enjoyable by anybody of sound mind."[24] This cross-class participation in seasonal agricultural labor is surely not unheard-of, but it does strike me as somewhat unusual.[25] One observer for the newspaper reported, "All are upon a common platform in the hop yard—the wife of the rich merchant or retired gentleman, who seeks this employment for the purpose of recruiting her health and earning a couple of dollars a day, is on a level with the poor seamstress who has been stitch, stitch, stitching her life away in a miserable garret, barely earning sufficient bread to support herself, and an invalid mother. Here all alike are jovial and gay."[26]

The women's labor was in such demand that they could at times be quite assertive about wages, meals, and musicians. Over the years, there are many instances of hop pickers demanding better wages and working and living conditions, in Wisconsin and beyond. Sometimes such efforts succeeded, as in the case of Chinese workers at Haggin Ranch in California in 1884, and other times they failed, as in the Wheatland Hop Riot, or when Portuguese, Chinese, and white workers walked out of the 100° hop fields in 1894 to demand higher wages but were quickly replaced by hundreds of strikebreakers.[27]

Picking in 1860s Wisconsin could be lucrative, bringing in $2.50 a day for those who picked swiftly and well.[28] There were at times disputes over pay.[29] For example, there was an 1866 "meeting of ladies . . . held at the Court House in this village on Monday afternoon, to take action in regard to the prices to be paid for hop-picking. Some thirty or forty ladies were present. It was resolved that they would under no circumstances accept less than fifty cents per box and board, with a proviso that if the price paid for hops exceeds fifty cents per pound, the price of picking per box be advanced to the market value," although as Laura Paine notes in her study of the hops era, it is somewhat unclear whether they succeeded.[30] In Canfield's fictionalized autobiography, the Dutch and Irish pickers threaten to strike because the price of hops has increased but their wages have not. Upon hearing rumors of the strike, one of the Yankees exclaims, "A strike! . . . Why, girls can't have a strike!"[31]

Waves of hop pickers traveled from larger towns and cities such as Milwaukee, Janesville, and Monroe, as well as points in between.[32] The *Milwaukee Daily Sentinel* reported on September 7, 1867, "One hundred girls have gone from Beaver Dam to Sauk county, all to pick hops for two or three dollars a day. Forty have gone from Waupun."[33] Two weeks later, the paper reported that "seven hundred hop pickers arrived at Kilbourn City lately on one train from Beaver Dam and other points."[34] There is little sense in the materials on Wisconsin that the hop pickers were hoping to escape anything but boredom or a lack of cash. In the hop fields of Kent, England, by contrast, there was a much greater sense both of hop picking as an escape from the dirt and crowds of London and of concerns about the poor living conditions (and many temptations and dangers) of the hop pickers. The Wisconsin communities of Beaver Dam, Waupun, and even Milwaukee had nowhere near the pollution and overcrowding of London. At the same time, some descriptions in the US did speak of the good effects on health and well-being: "In the older hop areas of New York and Wisconsin, the emphasis was on the healthful aspects of hop picking. Hiring agents told city dwellers that work in the hop yard was as beneficial a change as a sojourn by the sea. Pale seamstresses and nervous housewives were assured that they would be restored to radiant health through hop-picking."[35]

As the industry expanded, pickers became both more important and harder to find. Brokers stepped in to connect urban and rural pickers with specific farms. Just as there were dealers who facilitated the movement of hops from farm to market (for a healthy markup), in the boom times there were men like Leroy Gates who facilitated the movement of young women into the fields to pick hops, at times charging a dollar per picker. Gates had come to Wisconsin in 1849 with his parents Schuyler and Mary Ann, sleeping beneath the boughs of an oak for their first couple of months in the state.[36] By the 1860s, Gates "had become deeply involved with a neighbor, Anson Rood, in supplying the local hop yards with 'lively girl hop pickers.' This was no small undertaking for them and the other contractors, for by 1867 the industry needed 15,000 pickers and arrangements had to be made for special trains from Milwaukee and elsewhere, each carrying over a thousand pickers."[37] Brokers set out across the Fox River Valley, Madison, and Milwaukee to recruit the thousands of pickers.[38] Some growers dispensed with the recruiters and secured their own pickers from the towns or places where they had long-standing connections, as Silas Seymour did, in hiring girls and young women from "the sandy counties north," and towns such as Necedah, Mauston, and Port Hope.[39]

The newspapermen were not all thrilled about the large lady labor force. One complained, "There is scarcely women enough left in town for necessary courting purposes, and to run the culinary departments. Tea-parties, rag-bees, washing and ironing, pastry cooking and dancing parties are respectively postponed until after hop picking [because] there are more [hop pickers] wanted than can be spared without 'breaking up families,' and raising the devil generally in usually quiet and respectable homes."[40] A side effect of the decent picking wages was the temporary loss of the many domestic workers employed in households across the area, as many women who worked in these positions set off for the more profitable hop fields once a year. As the *Baraboo Republic* reported, hop-picking time was "the gala time of the year . . . to which housekeepers and housemaids alike look forward, the one with anxiety, the other with the most joyous anticipations. . . . It is the universal hegira of the maids of the kitchen; no wages can induce Bridget or Mary to do housework during the three or four weeks when their services are in demand by the hop-growers."[41] This enticement to the hop fields meant weeks without household help every harvest season: "Housekeeps were terribly put to it for kitchen help, for the faces of nearly all the waiting maids were set hopyardward."[42] The wives of the area were reported to be "panic stricken—there is scarcely a housekeeper in town whose hired help is not going with the crowd. Never before did we appreciate so fully the power of 'hired girl tyranny.'"[43] The desperation for household help led many people to place urgent classified ads in the papers: "Wanted, a good girl to do general housework, one who knows how to cook, wash and iron. To one who can bring good references, the highest wages will be paid, especially till after hop-picking."[44] Schools also found their desks empty at hop-picking time, and at times they adjusted their schedules accordingly.[45]

POLE PULLERS AND BOX TENDERS

Men were scarce here during the Civil War years (1861–65), and not all of them returned from the battlefields.[46] Wisconsin sent around ninety thousand Union soldiers and officers to war, and more than twelve thousand of those never returned; among those who did, surely few returned unscathed in body or soul.[47] Even during the war, and certainly after, men played important roles in the hop fields, but not on the same scale as the women. The hop fields had fairly strict gendered divisions of labor. Women and girls tended to pick, and men *pulled pole* and *tended box*. That is, they lifted the hop poles out of the ground, shrouded in hop bines, and laid them across the picking boxes where four women would then pick the hops, dropping them into the boxes; the box tenders transferred the picked hops into sacks, to then be carried to the kilns: "The menfolk cut the vine, pulled out the poles and carried the vine, still clinging to the pole, to a big box . . . and laid the pole and vine across the top of the box."[48] This is a far more rustic system than the large-scale mechanized picking and trellis systems of today. In the 1860s, "large boxes, eight feet long and four feet wide, and divided into four compartments were placed at intervals in the yard. Each compartment had a capacity of seven bushels of hops. Four pickers and a 'box tender' were assigned to each box. The box tender cut the vines at the top and bottom of each pole, pulled it out of the ground and carried it to the box where the pickers would strip the hops from the vines."[49] The boxes, poles, and box tender are all visible in one of Bennett's photographs (figure 5.1).

Male journalists were clearly taken with the scenes of dozens, hundreds, thousands of young women entering the countryside. The workers in the fields stood out to passersby, distinct from the mostly male bodies that usually populated those spaces, and in much smaller numbers. As the harvest approached, villages and fields filled with "girls [who] wore rough work gowns and sunbonnets. They lugged baskets and parcels."[50] A lot of male journalists (and one female journalist) spilled a lot of ink waxing rhapsodic about the women and girls in the fields. For example: "Hops! Hops! Hops! This is the cry through all this section of country. We eat hops, we smell hops, we drink hops, and we talk hops from 'early dawn to dewy eve,' and at the still hour of midnight we dream of hops for our pillow, and of the nimble hop-pickers as our guardian angels."[51] They marveled at both the quantity and quality of the pickers.

Journalists and others expressed concern about the virtue or safety of the pickers, or both, but pickers welcomed the break from the routine and the possibility for social interaction, even as many found the

FIGURE 5.1. Hop picking. Original photo caption: "Slightly elevated view of hop pickers in hop yard, in the vicinity of Mirror Lake." Photo by H. H. Bennett, Delton, Sauk County, date unknown. Wisconsin Historical Society, W012OC4.

work exhausting. In both Wisconsin and New York, "Hops picking allowed young men and women to interact in the fields with far less adult supervision than before. . . . Young men aspired to become box tenders as the job brought them into close contact with female pickers whom they could impress with the sheer physical strength required for the task. . . . Combined with hops dances and camp meetings, the harvest offered new ways for the young to meet, court, and marry."[52] The men played a range of supporting roles as the women stood at the hop boxes for hours on end:

> Pickers were paid by the box for hops cleanly picked from the vines and prices for picking were 50 cents and sometimes more, per box. . . . A man, termed 'pole-puller,' was allowed for every two stands,—it being his duty to keep pickers supplied with vines upon the poles ready for picking, and later to strip the poles of the denuded vines and place them in large, round, upright stacks. As boxes were filled, hops were emptied into sacks and carted to the hop-house for drying. After being cured they were pressed into large bales and covered with canvas, when the crop was ready for the market.[53]

Imagine how fragrant this work was! (Or pungent, or overwhelming, depending on your feeling about the smell of fresh hops.)

One pole puller and Union army veteran, John Rooney, met (or at least supervised) his future wife in the hopyards after returning from the war.[54] He worked as a pole puller, supervising many pickers, including his "three sisters and . . . present wife who picked five boxes a day, during the season of 1866." Several years before that productive encounter, on a brief visit home from the war, in 1863, he had toured the countryside: "I had at that time two sisters picking hops for Samuel Bliven, two miles southeast of the Village of Loganville who were getting 16 cents a box for picking."[55] At a local hopyard, that of

> Andrew Kyle and Lyman Twist, south of Loganville . . . while many of the pickers had husbands, brothers and friends then in the south, they were a jolly lot of women and girls and the hop dance was quite frequent. I got home from the war on the 12th of July, 1865, and immediately after getting home, James Kyle, a son of Andrew Kyle [who grew four acres of hops in Sauk County], called on me and engaged me to pull hop pole for them when the hops were ripe. . . . He then picked up all lose hops and placed them in the picker's box. This was a critical transaction for the box tender, because if he happened to forget and put

> a few more hops in one box than he did in another he was sure of either a tear or a frown. The box tender also emptied the boxes into the burlap sacks that held two boxes of the hop and, if a careful man, he would place them on a bunch of vines so they would not heat and color.[56]

Pole pulling after the war paid off for Rooney and the soon-to-be Mrs. Rooney (Sarah Maria Lamb), and by the time the 1870 census taker came by, they had a little baby.[57]

Sometimes a box tender who failed to perform would get more than a tear or a frown from the throng of young women around him:

> Mob law—If the box-tender does not properly attend to his business—gets careless, and after a few warnings continues to permit the poles to strike the cross pole and jostle down the hops, which pickers abhor above all things, mob punishment is generally the result. One of the pickers, with a roguish, knowing look, silently leaves, as she has often done before, ostensibly to make a visiting tour to the other boxes; but, alas! Soon she returns with an army of crinoline [or rather, women wearing the hoop skirts popular at the time], and the disobedient masculine is seized and plunged head foremost into a hop-sack, the sack tied securely, and then picked up and 'toted' and dragged about over the ground, at a fearful rate, the mobbish party the meanwhile laughing, screaming, and yelling like devils. . . . When once seized, for a fellow to try to extricate himself . . . is worse than useless; for he is a "goner," which I can testify to from experience.[58]

The flirtations at the hop boxes were just setting the scene for the vibrant nightlife of the hop-picking times.[59]

DANCES, ROMANCES, AND WAXED MUSTACHES

> Young men and maidens got busy. More than one baby lay on a blanket and kicked away happy hours while the nimble fingers of father and mother rapidly filled the boxes.[60]

> Years after the hop growing faded from the scene, people remembered hop picking time. Women recalled picking hops until their fingers bled, yet spending evenings singing and stepping to the lively music of nightly barn dances.[61]

Despite working all day long in the heat or the cold, arms scratched up from the irritating hop bines, sunburned and tired, many of these thousands of young women were ready to party at the end of the day. I have done a bit of hop picking myself, in my own garden and, once, on a commercial hop farm in Wisconsin. I sat outside with some relatives of the farmer, picking the straggler hops off the bines that weren't picked clean by the cantankerous machine they had bought from a farmer in New York. We sat on plastic chairs pulling bines out of a purple plastic paddling pool and dropping the cones into plastic bins. It was hot work, and our hands sweated in our rubber gloves. At one point one of the older women brought us some very welcome Gatorade. It was also slow work—there always seemed to be one more cone on the scratchy bine. In nineteenth-century Wisconsin, there were attempts to develop mechanized picking, but they did not take off at the time—and rubber gloves had yet to be invented.[62] By the time I got home that night, the last thing I was ready to do was dance the night away, but then I was a bit older than most of this historical hop-picking force.

For young women who had few opportunities to travel or (especially those in small towns or on farms) to meet new people, the sociability of the hop harvest was a powerful draw, alongside the pay. The harvest was "a time of feasting and merrymaking. Each night when darkness put an end to labor, the well-used fiddle was fetched from its case, and to its merry strains, under the mellow autumn moon the unwearied tripped the jovial steps of the hop dance."[63] Ah, youth! Hop profits were already being transformed into very nice houses, and people made architectural adjustments to new and existing homes specifically for the hop-picking time, including a Mr. Kipp's house in Reedsburg: "The old gentleman talks of finishing up a hall in it, 36 feet in length, for dancing purposes at hoppicking times! Such gallantry should secure him pickers enough, even when scarcest."[64] These parties, and the facilities to host them, factored into the farmer's calculation of his profits, as ways to attract enough pickers to get the harvest to market each year. Consider the following newspaper op-ed from a writer with the cutesy byline of Willie Hopper:

> There are 15,000 women, girls and children picking *hops* in the region . . . and I think five thousand and a half of these are good looking *girls* from twelve to twenty years old. There's a paradise for No. 1 young men. . . . It is worth a trip to Hopland, to see a hundred pickers in a yard. . . . Health, happiness, songs and fun only serve to make the fingers nimbler; and after hopping all day, of course these sprightly girls must "wind off" by a union *hop*, in the early hours of the night. No wonder the girls want to come from Milwaukee, Watertown, Beaver Dam, and all other places where the fame and fun of hop-picking have reached; and lucky are the young men who get the position of box tenders in such a crowd.[65]

The pickers sought their dance partners among the pole pullers and box tenders, as well as other young men who found their way to the hop dance from surrounding farms and towns, drawn by the multitude of sociable young women: "Every evening a dance was put on in the hop house or elsewhere, while fiddlers played tunes. . . . Someone would call out the square dance, and the dancing continued until about 9:30 p.m. Growers vied with one another in providing entertainment, while boys came from the surrounding towns and neighborhoods, and many lasting romances had their start during the hop picking season."[66]

While these pickers were there solely to meet the demands of the beer industry, I have not seen a single mention of beer or other alcohol consumption by the pickers or at the dances. That doesn't mean there wasn't a keg or a whiskey jug nearby, but the imbibing of alcohol in any form did not appear in the records I have seen of the Wisconsin hop harvest (unlike England, Germany, or California, where there are more references to alcohol consumption, including hard cider). In New York, especially as farmers turned to more itinerant pickers for their harvests, and pickers who did not reside under the farmer's roof, the consumption of alcohol by hop pickers was actively discouraged because of fears (whether warranted or not) that alcohol consumption among these people from outside the community would lead to risky or damaging behavior.[67] The raw material hop had a long journey (across both time and space) before it would become consumable. Hop picking would have been thirsty work. People of the day drank water when there was good well water or spring water to be had, sometimes mixed with ginger or transformed into lemonade, either with actual lemons or with citric acid. I have also been told that barley water may have quenched the thirsts of the day as well.[68]

Dancing, music, and the proximity of fellow young people were the primary intoxicants—at least the ones that appear in the historical record. During the day, "the girls all vie[d] with each other to see who will pick the most while in the field, and in the evening to see who will look prettiest" by the light of candles and lanterns.[69] Flavia Canfield wrote of a dance that began as "four quadrilles dancing with 'might and main' to the music of three fiddles and a bass viol," becoming so frenzied that at least one dancer emerged from the throng with her clothes torn and her hair undone.[70] These dances must have been a relatively rare opportunity to meet strangers, especially for the people coming to the hop fields from small towns and other farms. Dances were not at all uncommon in the day, but the scale and cross-pollination of hop dances was novel, and it had lasting effects on people's lives.[71] Belle Cushman Bohn's 1935 magazine article on hop culture stated, "Some old couples today remember that their acquaintance began at a hop-picking dance."[72]

In nineteenth-century Winnebago County, one hop-farming family "would get the Norwegian girls from Winchester to pick hops. They had a big hop house. . . . Every night the Norwegian girls would want to dance, and Harry Allen's brother used to tell how even when he was only six years old, he would have to go and dance quadrilles with the girls [because] they just didn't have enough boys! Harry's mother had to cook for that whole gang!"[73] Thurine Oleson, who picked hops in Winnebago County in the 1880s, well after the boom, reminisced fondly, "Every single evening there was a dance in the hop house. Since they dried the hops upstairs, not on the first floor of the hop house, the lower floor was empty. All the light we had was lanterns hanging around, but we didn't care. We could see to dance, and the fiddler played by ear. The dance would probably not last more than two or three hours."[74] She found that the Yankees and well-off Norwegians often looked down on the Norwegian women who worked outside the home, whether as hop pickers or housekeepers.

One reporter went to great lengths to detail the final picking party of the 1868 season: "Gaiety, fun, and frolic reign supreme; conventional restraint and codfish etiquette are thrown aside. If you are tickled, laugh as loud and long as you please, and no one will whisper 'how vulgar.'" He was not describing the regular weekday picking dances, but rather the closing event of the picking season, "the great hoppenfest [which] takes place when the labors of the year are over, the hops all picked, dried and baled for market."[75] His account was based on attending the dance at E. F. Lewis's substantial hop farm in Columbia County, adjacent to Sauk County. Lewis must have fared better than other 1868 farmers, as we will see in chapter 6. As reported in the *Wisconsin State Register*, "The girls were, of course, the chief attraction. Oh what a swarm of them—hearty, healthy, bouncing lassies. No paint and putty about them. They were girls as is girls. When you put your arm around one of 'em you felt as though you had something. . . . But the best of all was their numerousness. The parlor was full, and the hall was full, and the kitchen and dining-room all full." The party wrapped up at 4:00 a.m., after an 11:00 p.m. supper. The reporter concluded, "So long as lager is a beverage, so long as hops will grow, and pretty girls will pick them, so long will hoppenfests be with us a cherished institution. And to you seventy-five girl-hoppists we depose thusly: You were the slickest, tidiest, neatest, best looking, best behaved lot of girls we ever saw at a hop dance."[76] With reporters like these in the crowd, and in a cultural context where female chastity supposedly reigned supreme, it is unsurprising that the families of the hop pickers relied on the farmers' wives to intervene when things threatened to go too far.

HOSTING

> Hop-picking time at the Houston farm was a gala event for the young folk of the neighborhood. They were paid so much a measure for the hops picked, and all were permitted to enjoy the wonderful meals prepared by Mrs. Houston. Later in the evening they would gather around the grand piano . . . and sing ballads and folks songs. . . . The Houston home was a large and commodious one, which included among other conveniences, some eighty built-in bunks, each of which the occupant was able to raise and lower by means of ropes. The Houstons were firm believers in Spiritualism and held frequent séances in one of the large rooms on the farm.[77]

These large-scale hop harvests brought a unique form of labor in scale and type: not just the thousands of pickers but also hosting so extreme that sometimes farmers built whole new kitchens and dormitories to accommodate the workload of a once-a-year event. In Bohn's recollection, "At mealtime a bell was rung; the yards were emptied quickly. . . . The farmer had a steady job getting supplies from town; the cost of it all was enormous."[78] The wives, daughters, mothers, and sisters of hop farmers performed prodigious amounts of labor to host the annual onslaught of hop pickers. Many women hosting hop pickers were already familiar with the challenges of feeding extra mouths and having strangers under their roof. The annual work of threshing, for example, often brought together a hungry labor force, requiring extra food preparation for the shared midday meal, as Clara Allen of Winnebago County reminisced: "When the threshers came . . . we women fixed a thanksgiving dinner every day for a week."[79] Women settlers were caring for nonfamily to varying degrees and in rhythms of seasons: "It matter little whether the mother's house was situated on a well-traveled road, or on a scarcely discernible trail which wound through tall grasses, brightly flowered meadow patches, and dark forests. Almost without exception she became an innkeeper."[80] Caring for hop pickers fit into that larger picture: "Unlike the pickers on the West Coast who were required to provide their own food and shelter, the hand-pickers in New York and Wisconsin were housed and fed by the hop growers."[81] As the next harvest season approached, newspapers exhorted the hosts and hostesses to get ready: "Everything should be in readiness for picking, hop-house and kiln in repair, dry wood and brimstone [sulfur, used to preserve the color of the hops] on hand, hop-boxes in repair and at their places, pole-starters and vine-cutters secured, sacks for conveying hops from the kiln made, a good supply and variety of provision for the table, extension dining tables, extra beds, and house ready to turn into a temporary hotel at a moment's warning."[82]

Along with the work of feeding, housing, and managing the crowd of hop pickers at harvest time, many hop farmers' wives engaged in years of literal reproductive labor as they were conceiving, gestating, lactating, and raising the offspring who would become the household's own hop pickers. Early on in the primarily Yankee and European settlement of Wisconsin, it was almost impossible to hire domestic help, although by 1870, the population census records many households with both farm laborers and domestic servants living under their roof. But even then, there were not always enough young women around, and few grandmothers or "spinster" aunts.[83] One historical account of the Wisconsin frontier published in the mid-twentieth century concluded:

> It is plain that a husband and wife were an economic necessity to each other; their children in turn filled the role of helpers and were well worth their frugal keep in return for their assistance in the work of the home, the fields, and the forests. . . . If death took the mother, who would cook, sew, spin and weave, process the meat, mold the candles, boil the soap, [take] care of the children, and do the thousand tasks that were her burden? Bachelors were generally in a sad plight, and the records indicate that they found it expedient to hustle around and improve their status since frying salt pork and baking bread were not compatible with cutting-back the forests.[84]

Thus, it was fairly easy for a young single woman to get married in the early years and then soon find herself becoming a mother. Indeed, the aforementioned historical account declared, "Unimpeachable proof of the fecundity of the frontier mother is contained in the federal manuscript census records. Parents were commonly credited with ten or twelve children, and if the total reached fifteen, in about as many years, it still seemed credible."[85] Another account, this one published in the early twenty-first century, mentions a settler woman who, while working in the fields, "always wore an apron to wrap up the baby in case she gave birth. . . . [She] would eventually birth ten children with similar lack of fuss. She also helped neighbor women birth their children and was often paid in kind. She took in boarders—loggers and families without a place to stay."[86] One of my husband's Wisconsin grandmothers had a similar experience with childbirth, coming in from the fields to the farmhouse kitchen, when (according to family legend) she kicked off one boot and then "out came Wayne," one of my husband's many uncles.

Even the arrival of assistance for the backbreaking agricultural work could actually bring more work for the wife: "In warmer seasons there was the company of neighbors who came to assist with picking hops, husking corn, or harvesting or threshing wheat. But to the mother of the family, with extra mouths to feed, these occasions generally meant more work than recreation."[87] The labor of hop growing was possible because of legions of women scrubbing plates, stuffing straw into fabric cases to make mattresses, pickling vegetables, and tending their laying hens—and not just female labor at harvest time, a combination of year-round labor and the intensive work of the hop harvest. Hops don't get picked without the dishes being washed, tables groaning with food cooked up on the woodstove, and bed linens laundered. People were hosting dozens of pickers, which created a spectacular amount of sheets and other linens to wash after a three-week harvest. This work of hospitality was so important because of the scarcity of hop pickers, especially in the 1860s, and the urgency of getting the picking crew into the fields at the right moment. Good food, comfortable beds, and amusing dances all helped guarantee that the pickers would return the following year, or that they would at least speak highly of that farm to their younger sisters and acquaintances back home.

At the height of the demand for their labor, pickers expected hop farmers' wives not only to meet the minimal needs for food and shelter but also to outhost the competing hop farmers in the region. Such a criterion must have included the farmstead's provision of bathing facilities and some kind of system to allow such a large number of houseguests—dozens or even hundreds more than the usual household inhabitants—to relieve themselves, such as toilets, latrines, or outhouses. A big change in the volume of human waste took place in these counties for a few weeks in the hottest, muggiest, buggiest time of the year, and it would have to have been handled somehow. Yet I have seen no mention of the human waste problem in Wisconsin hopyards, with the possible exception of Silas Seymour's expansive privy, or outhouse—which contained three adult-size seats and one child-size seat and was the pride of the neighborhood. "None of our neighbors," wrote Ruth Burmester, Silas's granddaughter, "the Peltons, the Horkans, had one as fine as this. . . . One always took a lighted lantern going to the Privy after dark in winter, or in bad weather, and took someone along for company. . . . Weeds grew up . . . around the Privy, taller than a man, and around icehouse, smokehouse, even at the doorstep: burdock, hemp, mustard, pigweed, lamb's quarters."[88] At one point there was a rat infestation in the privy, which sounds . . . terrifying. I do wonder if the generous dimensions of the privy date back to the time of hosting dozens of hop pickers.

In nineteenth-century England, similar concentrations of pickers sometimes contributed to deadly outbreaks of illness, no surprise given the temporary but elevated pressures put on the streams and rivers suddenly serving as sewers, laundries, and a water supply for hundreds of hop pickers.[89] One farmer, a Mr. Ellis, had frequent outbreaks, especially when the pickers chose to drink water rather than the beer he supplied to them: "I am sorry to say we have lost more than I can bear to think of. Unless I give it to them they never buy or drink beer: they drink water . . . and sometimes a fellow will come along with bad fish and then we get the cholera."[90] Though I do wonder which of these outbreaks was cholera proper and which was dysentery or "summer complaint," 1832 and 1849 did see outbreaks of actual cholera among hop pickers. While the information on sanitary options in hop fields is scant for nineteenth-century Wisconsin, more evidence is available for England, Oregon, and California, as well as later time periods, including makeshift latrines with canvas covers in twentieth-century English hopyards.[91] According to an article in an early twentieth-century medical journal, "In the picturesque graveyard of East Farleigh is a monument over the grave of 40 pickers who died of cholera many years ago. The foul latrines were on the banks of the Medway and polluted the river; they were opposite the old Water Works which were closed many years ago after the classic Maidstone epidemic of typhoid."[92] In Wheatland, California, scene of the infamous Wheatland Hop Riot of 1913, "nine shallow, doorless privies serviced the camp, but they were completely inadequate for the huge crowd."[93]

I am mildly amazed that the only mention I have seen with even a hint of a link between hop pickers and outhouses was Silas Seymour's generous three-and-a-half-seater, even though tens of thousands of people working the hop fields were generating tens of thousands of people's worth of human waste in a usually much more sparsely populated space that, unlike a city, had no existing infrastructure for handling such a sudden increase in the amount of waste. Cities had systems in place and had a similar volume of waste year-round. Keeping rural hop pickers both healthy and happy increased the likelihood of a profitable hop crop. The laundry, cleaning, and cooking that Ella Seymour described in her diary (as well as the outhouse described in her niece's book) all contributed to the success of the hop harvest in a given year, and in subsequent seasons as well. The stakes were high—good hosting meant good pickers, and better returns on the investment in hop growing.

RISKS AND REWARDS

Part of the appeal of hop picking for young women was the opportunity for freedom, a change of scenery, good income, and the chance to meet young men from somewhere else. Sleeping in the farmer's house under the watchful eye of the farmer's wife gave the young women an air of Victorian respectability and some protection from unwanted attention or violence, as did the economic importance of pickers having a positive experience so that they would return in subsequent years—but a balance probably needed to be struck between protecting the young women and letting them have enough fun to want to come back to the same farm the following year. Here and there people expressed concerns about possible risks in the relationships between young men and women, and there is no doubt that a range of flirtations and liaisons took place.[94]

Some of those so-called risks were only in the eyes of those overly concerned with young women's behavior. Hop farmers were cautioned by one newspaperman, Alanson Holly, "Besides the healthful work involved, there is the social enjoyment which may be pleasant and profitable, if the company being kept is intelligent and pure. If the company kept by the girls is corrupt it will prove to be of a ruinous character. You employers of these innocent girls have great responsibilities. . . . The girls will be divided into groups of from 20 to 100 each, and you employers are under a moral obligation which you cannot avoid, to stand in the place of parents and guardians and look to the welfare of these young visitors."[95] These arrangements reflected the notions of sexuality and morality of the day—placing young women under the supervision of the farmer's wife, but that supervision was surely neither consistent nor total.[96] Far beyond Wisconsin—in California, England, or Germany, hop harvests have had a reputation for activities ranging from festivity to exploitation and the looming danger of assault in insecure sleeping quarters, and most of those settings involved self-provisioning rather than moving in with the farmer's family for the duration of the harvest.[97]

Yet another newspaperman warned, "May there be no clouds of

sorrow to darken the bright dreams of these girls, many of whom are beyond parental restraint, and for the first time without the counsel and guidance of a watchful mother. They seemed happy and gay, and on the still evening breeze the joyful laugh and sweet strain of music wafted across the beautiful river and was born away into the deep forests beyond its rock-bound shores."[98] This is the river in today's Wisconsin Dells, where you can watch a water ski show or take raucous amphibious boat rides along those rock-bound shores. That same writer acknowledged, "A gay time, good pay, and a release from the dull routine of every-day life, are the inducements presented to the thronging multitude of girls."[99] But this departure from home exposed them to certain risks, he cautioned. He expressed concern about the "virtue" (more precisely, the virginity, sexual abstemiousness, and perhaps safety) of these young women and admonished the hop farmers, "You have . . . a great responsibility. There are to be, for the next three or four weeks, between 20,000 and 30,000 young girls picking hops in this region, most of them from outside and of course they will be beyond the reach of immediate parental or guardian indulgence. . . . Most of these will be intelligent, pure-minded girls, who love fun and undoubtedly ought to have it; but who will have little idea of any dangers to which they may be subjected."[100]

Although many pickers would have had romance on their minds, including physical manifestations thereof, the other end of this spectrum would have been sexual assault—that is, some of these women surely chose to engage in a range of physical experiences with the young people around them, and just as surely there were risks of rape and other forms of sexual assault in these relatively unsupervised circumstances. Housing the pickers in the home of the farmer could mean that the farmer's family stood between these young women and potential sexual attackers *or* partners, but there was also no guarantee that they were safe from the family or each other. Providing good food and entertaining dances along with beds that were comfortable and safe (as opposed to some of the sleeping situations in Kent and other hop fields, where pickers slept away from the main house, either in tents, barracks, or crowded cottages, and the safety or solitude of the sleeper could not be guaranteed) could have been a bonus, although some young women surely bristled at too much supervision.[101] One final exhortation came from that previous Wisconsin newspaperman: "Now we hold that every man of you and his wife, who employ 10 or 20 or 30 or 100 of these [young women hop pickers], [must] see that none of those under your charge are subjected to evil influences. Unless you do this, corruption will come, and on you the blame will rest."[102] Paying these women well, giving them good food and entertainment, and striking the right balance between liberty and protection—all played a role in ensuring the labor forces that would power the hop boom.

PRICES AND PROFITS

As the last hops were dried and pressed in September 1867, the pickers boarded wagons and trains and headed for home. The young men of one town even arranged a dance to welcome home the dearly missed hop pickers at the end of the harvest: "The hop picking season is nearly over, and every day brings back long trains of girls who have concluded their labors for the present year. . . . The gallant young men of the city have already got up a dance in honor of the returned hop pickers, just as we used to get up demonstrations in honor of our returning soldiers. . . . Great are the hop pickers, and welcome are Katy and Mary."[103] Meanwhile, the hop farmers began to count their earnings. In the harvest season of 1867, one historian recounted, "the price soared so high that every grower began to dream of the crop of 1868 as the one out of which he would reap a fortune and retire."[104] A few reporters here and there displayed hints of concern, but many newspapers were bullish about this market.[105] One report in March 1868 asserted with great and mislaid confidence, "In view of present indications *it would seem impossible* [emphasis added] for the price to fall below a remunerative point in this section for several years to come . . . [in part because of] the enormous increase in the consumption of malt liquors, the production of 1860 amounting to 3,239,545 barrels; of 1866, 7,916,575 barrels, while the estimate for 1868 is placed at 10,000,000 barrels, or an increase of 300 per cent since 1860."[106] Yet the prospect of ten *million* barrels of beer being brewed in the coming year could understandably be grounds for such optimism.

In the autumn of 1867, the Wisconsin hop market grew so hot that hop dealers became "night riders"—collecting contracted hops in the dark of night to prevent farmers from breaking their contracts or "getting excited."[107] John Rooney, the Civil War veteran and later beau of a young hop picker whom we encountered earlier in this chapter, told one newspaper that he "rode three nights with A.L. Harris buying hops. I got $10 a night for myself and horse. One night we bought 10 lots of hops. All but two of the growers we had to wake up to show their hops." Imagine just minding your own business in the middle of the night in your nightshirt and nightcap in the middle of nowhere in Sauk County, Wisconsin, and suddenly two gents on horseback appear at your door! "The last lot we bought of John Hackett," Rooney said, and by then it was surely very late at night.[108]

As noted in chapter 4, some growers had a pang of guilt about growing a plant solely used for a beverage they vehemently opposed. But that plant's potential profits were often balm enough for a guilty conscience, even in Quaker settlements.[109] According to one history of Sauk County, "Preachers and temperance men even went into hop raising, quieting their consciences with the [largely fictitious] rationalization that the hops would be used for tanning [leather]. In fact a meeting was held in the county courthouse one evening to discuss the matter. 'The arguments were many and the house was filled. The argument of big profits . . . seemed to be sufficient for most of them.'"[110] In 1867, as prices were skyrocketing, the *Milwaukee Daily Sentinel* reported, "the citizens of Baraboo are holding a series of discussions on the question: 'Is it morally right to raise hops for the general market?'"[111] Temperance supporters wavered in the face of the profits to be made on hops. Some people in the temperance movement supported beer as a lesser evil when compared with whiskey, rum, or gin.[112] But the Methodists unequivocally disapproved of hops and tried to dissuade farmers from planting them.[113] Those attempts fizzled, based on the monumental harvest of 1867.

The financial results of that harvest began to be visible in the streets of Sauk County. Belle Cushman Bohn, who picked hops as a young woman, later recalled that soon after the Civil War, as the hop profits began to pile up in Sauk County, "new homes were built and furnished; silk dresses, furs, paisley shawls, and pianos were bought for the wife and daughters; fine horses and carriages were kept in the stable and coach house; farm machinery was purchased."[114] Sauk County must have fairly glittered with all of this newfound wealth. Early twentieth-century historian Frederick Merk reported, "The magnificent profits realized by hop growers were usually as royally spent. If one may credit the tales still told in Sauk and adjoining counties, farmers' daughters rustled in silks and satins, purchased pianos and visited foreign courts, while sons exchanged overalls for broadcloth and sported blooded horses and fancy phaetons."[115] One source even credits the hop boom for a particular architectural style among the descendants of Swiss immigrants: "As a result of this flourishing economy, the generation that arrived as children in the 1840s, now with children of their own, built new houses or expanded older settlement-period dwellings. . . . Expansion was done by adding a wing or ell extending to the right from the lateral side of a rectangular house, resulting in a gabled-ell house form and a new arrangement of interior space."[116]

Farmers in remote Wisconsin were in active deals with far-off markets, including through dozens of New York hop dealers who descended on the county.[117] Dealers eased the movement of hops from the countryside to market and to the city, and they were an integral part of turning the rural landscape into money. In breweries, warehouses, country farmhouses, dusty fields, and train stations, they assigned monetary value to bale after bale of hops. Bohn recounted, "After the hops at each yard had been baled, the hop buyers were as plentiful as politicians before election. Finally the bales were sold and carried away, many going to England."[118] Hop dealers visited farms, chatted with farmers, and moved themselves, as well as hops and money, in and out of people's properties and houses. Laura Paine reported in her study of the hops era, "Bales were brought there [Kilbourn City, today's Wisconsin Dells] from much of the state to be shipped by rail to and from there to the east coast, some being exported overseas. There was a well-established trade network involving not only the settled areas of the United States, but also European markets."[119] In early October 1867, eighty-two bales of hops left the port of Milwaukee on the SS *Detroit*.[120] This ship was a wooden steamer that ran between Grand Haven, Michigan, and Milwaukee, linking up rail lines on either side of Lake Michigan, a potentially faster route than the rail lines running south of Lake Michigan and through Chicago.[121] Less than two weeks after that October shipment, the *Detroit* loaded up with eastbound hops once more.[122] Like so many ships carrying hop farmers or hops, the *Detroit* eventually foundered in a gale—in 1872, while carrying a load of lumber—and was destroyed after drifting onto the Michigan shore.[123]

Improvements in transportation facilitated the dealers' work and the farmers' sales. Railway lines and steamships allowed farmers and dealers to overcome the mud, the ruts, and the distance. Track workers assembled these transportation lines with breathtaking swiftness and extended the tentacular reach of the railroad into the countryside.[124] The Kilbourn City railway station was the beating heart of the hop boom in the 1860s. It was reached by the La Crosse line of the Chicago, Milwaukee, St. Paul Railway, a path along which the hops fed into other places, along with wheat, barley, and other field crops.[125] Speed and safety increased and enabled the profitability of the hop boom, but the casualties were still colossal. In 1869, 97 ships were wrecked on the Great Lakes, in the midst of a single four-day gale.[126] In 1871, a quarter of the vessels on the lakes experienced "sinkings, collisions, groundings, [or] explosions."[127] Thousands of vessels that carried the settlers and the hops for their beer (among other cargo) now lie at the bottom of a Great Lake.[128] In the 1860s, sidewheel steamers plied the waters along the western shore of Lake Michigan, and a busy fleet of schooners, sidewheel steamers, and propeller steamers crisscrossed the blue and gray waters of the Great Lakes, laden with wheat and hops.[129]

By September 1867, hop growers along the La Crosse railroad line were pulling in $1,000 per acre.[130] Some growers had direct connections to breweries and brought their hops to market without relying on dealers. One farmer, a Mr. L. Hawk, took his own hops straight to Chicago, where he sold them to Lill & Diversey for an impressive sixty-two cents a pound. Hawk was one of the first to harvest that year, and I can imagine that the brewers at Lill & Diversey (and their customers) were itching for the new hop crop.[131] Around the same time, a Mr. M. S. Gibson sold directly to the Falk Brewery in Milwaukee, for a substantial sixty cents a pound. At that point in the year, brewers would have been using up hops from the 1866 harvest and eager to start fresh. Many Sauk County farmers were selling to some of the biggest breweries in the Midwest and selling directly to the English markets as well. And by October 1867, many more farmers were getting sixty cents a pound for their hops.[132]

This rise in prices changed the Seymour family's house (with the addition of a summer kitchen), their property (with the addition of a hop house and hop fields), and their cash flow. The same thing happened over and over, neighbor by neighbor, county by county, as Wisconsin farmers strove to capitalize on the voracious demand for hopped beer within and beyond the borders of their state. Silas Seymour's children observed these changes: "In the boom days of the Hop Craze, 1865, 1866, 1867, he, Merton and sisters, Ella and Ida, had watched the steady stream of travel up and down the North Road to Kilbourn (now Wisconsin Dells). . . . On the road passed loads of grain, dressed hogs, iron from the Ironton furnace, people riding and walking, herds of fattened pigs and cattle, and (in season) endless wagon loads of baled hops. One day he and Ella counted 114 loads of them."[133] The thirst for Cluster hops and their cousins rapidly transformed stretches of southern Wisconsin. After the pickers had gone home, after the dealers had moved through the stacks of bales in barnyards and depots, after the hops themselves had trundled off to breweries around the state and the globe, the farmers could tally their earnings. Those who had borrowed to plant their own hopyards could pay down their debts, and others, like Silas, who had been growing before the full-blown hop frenzy reigned, could contentedly count their money in that prosperous autumn of 1867. The plentiful cash changing hands that fall inspired even more farmers to take up the cultivation of hops. As winter came on, farmers and foresters could set out into the quiet snowy woods on the hunt for ever more saplings for hop poles.

Every time I drove from Milwaukee to Madison, for a deep dive into the archives of the Wisconsin Historical Society, I tried to imagine the spectral presence of fields full of calico-clad women and the thickets of hop poles bristling with ripe cones. The image is always just out of sight, masked by the very solid fact of the fields of corn and soy that dominate the landscape today, with the occasional woodlot, subdivision, or discount mall. Here and there is an oak old enough to have witnessed the images I conjure in my mind's eye, a whole other way of working the land, one nearly unimaginable as I speed along the interstate.

SIDEBAR: HOP POLES

Every photograph I have seen of a nineteenth-century Wisconsin hop field captures not only a crowd of young women but also dozens or even hundreds of hop poles. This brisk hop industry required thousands upon thousands of slim young saplings to be used as hop poles, which often came from neighboring swamps and forests.[134] Baraboo hop farmer Howard Potter had seven thousand tamarack poles at some point in the 1860s.[135] Imagine the impact on a nearby tamarack swamp! Silas Seymour traded in hop poles throughout the 1860s. The photographer H. H. Bennett, who took several of the nineteenth-century photos in this book (see figures P.1 in the prologue and 5.2 in this chapter), even augmented his own income by sharpening hop poles.[136] Settlers processed forests and swamps into a range of products, chopping down trees for fences, firewood, housing, and even roads, and planting new woodlots. Timber was an enormous part of the story of Yankee and European settlement of Wisconsin.[137]

Even though growers could reuse poles from one year to the next, when the number of hop plants grew so significantly each year, the demand for young saplings continued to increase each year as well. While these farmers filled former prairies and bottomlands with hops and hop houses alongside their barns and wheat fields, they clear-cut tamarack and ash swamps. Other hop-growing regions solved this problem in other ways. In England, some growers imported hop poles form Norway, while others planted groves of future hop poles on "the western and southwestern sides of our homesteads and hop-gardens. By cutting one-half the breadth of these belts at a time, a continual lew or shelter belt is kept up."[138] In Kent, England, farmers grew their own future hop poles on existing trees that were coppiced (very heavily pruned) in ways that encouraged the growth of new shoots that would be big enough to serve as hop poles within a few years.[139] Some Wisconsin farmers did harvest saplings from previously felled forests, as when "a large quantity of young hickory has sprung up on the bluffs in the southern part of [Sauk] county, which is largely sold for hop poles."[140]

Anyone with access to swamps and forests, legally or illegally, could make a go of profiting from this form of lumbering, as "the cutting of hop-poles furnished profitable employment to many during the great hop excitement from 1865 to 1872."[141] Tamaracks took on a near-mythical quality in so many of these accounts, as the perfect balance of affordability and longevity. Cedar saplings had even more longevity but could be prohibitively expensive. Tamaracks became fundamental to hop cultivation, as the straight, narrow trunks of younger tamaracks made excellent hop poles, and the wood resisted rot much better than softer trees such as pine or birch. Fortunately for the hop farmers, in much of Wisconsin, tamarack swamps were close at hand. So many settlers could gaze upon a stand of tamaracks or other trees as a financial calculation—the value of the trees as housing material or hop poles: "During the winter men cut down trees which were two or three inches in diameter at the base and about sixteen feet long. Poplar poles which lasted two or three years were used extensively. Oak poles brought from $15.00 to $18.00 a thousand. Tamarack was the most durable and used where available."[142] In 1867 alone, Wisconsin's 2,500 acres of hops may have required as many as 1.7 million hop poles.[143] One estimate saw hop poles costing $60 to $100 per thousand and suggested using 2,000 poles per acre.[144] Another estimate advised 8,000 tamarack poles for 5 acres of hopyard.[145] Yet another recommended 9,000 tamarack poles for 5 acres (3 to a hill), or 1,800 poles per acre.[146] Howard Potter of Baraboo used 7,000 tamarack poles (at a cost of $630) for 9,320 pounds of hops.[147] If he was average in his ratio of poles to pounds of hops, then we can calculate that each pound of hops required 1.3 hop poles. That would have meant 9 million hop poles in 1867 and 14.3 million hop poles in 1868 in the hop fields of Wisconsin.

Some of these poles arrived on wagons, while others came along rivers, at least part of the way: "Messrs. Martin and Prickett are running a drive of nearly four thousand hop poles down the river. It is a new business and we hope to see them succeed in it.—Shawano County Journal."[148] The harvesting of hop poles transformed previously undervalued swamps into sources of additional profit: "There is now, since the fall of snow, a grand rally to supply the growing demand. Those with teams . . . are rushing for the swamps, and will supply themselves. There are large tamarack swamps on both sides of the St. Paul & Minnesota railroad track, between Tomah and Lisbon. These poles are mostly transported by rail. Of the other large swamps, one covering large tracts, in the vicinity of the head waters of Yellow river, is the most prominent."[149]

As usual, the newspapers could be counted on for vivid portrayals of the goings-on:

> But the great article of traffic just now is hop-poles, hop-poles, hop-poles! Every freight car and everybody's conversation is laden with them. . . . The number billed from New Lisbon station thus far since January 1st is 89,100 . . . [and] about a like amount has been shipped from Tomah, making in the vicinity of 180,000 thus far. The season is only about half over, and therefore we may safely calculate that what will yet be shipped together with the large quantities hauled by teams, will swell the aggregate to half a million poles, as the product of this pole-ar region of Juneau and Monroe counties for the winter of 1867. By far the greater portion

> of these poles go to the famous hop-growing districts of Sauk and Columbia counties, though some go to Watertown and vicinity. The poles cost one cent apiece on the ground, another cent to cut, and from one to two more to haul and load. The speculators have no trouble in getting six cents apiece for them on board the cars, and many are driving a very profitable business at the traffic.[150]

The *Milwaukee Daily Sentinel* published a guide to hop poles, including the preferred tree species—poplar, gray pine, white ash, spruce, hickory, red oak, white tamarack, red tamarack, ironwood, and red cedar. Poplar would only survive one or two years in the hop fields, while red tamarack would last twelve to twenty-six years, and red cedar twenty-five to thirty-five years.[151] A new farmer might not know this but could quickly be informed by neighbors with more experience and by the various cultivation guides published in newspapers and pamphlets. Some farmers couldn't afford to be choosy, and for some "any kind of pole, from 2½ to 4 inches in diameter at the butt and from 16 to 20 feet in length, is the proper size. . . . By reason of its lightness and fine proportions, the tamarack pole is the best. Tamarack, cedar, iron-wood and white oak for hop poles are the most durable."[152]

Even if a large percentage of the 1867 poles were being reused in 1868, given the explosive growth in those years, many of the poles had to be new from one year to the next because the farmers were new. I assume that even more poles were used than mentioned here—the figures in the census represent hop yields, not the number of rhizomes or hop hills planted, so they don't reflect failed hills, blighted hills, or fields left unpicked as a result of the drop in prices (not so much an issue in 1867, but a much bigger issue in 1868).

As the local forests emptied of young trees, saplings poured in from other regions: "The scores of thousands of hop poles that have been shipped to this station [Kilbourn City] during the winter from Baraboo and vicinity, and other localities, would astonish one unacquainted with the traffic." These poles could have diameters up to four inches at the base and reach heights of sixteen to twenty feet, although this newspaper source declares that "3 inches in diameter at the butt and 17 feet long is preferable in every respect."[153] While there was a robust Wisconsin trade in hop poles, other forested regions got in on the game, particularly as the hop-growing country began to exhaust its sapling supply. In September 1867, the scow *Mary Emilia* brought "cedar hop poles from nine miles above Thunder Bay Island light to Buffalo."[154] Two months later, as farmers geared up for the banner harvest of 1868, fire swept through areas of Sauk County on the west side of the Wisconsin River that had been a source of hop poles, further increasing the need to reach beyond the region.[155] The long-distance trade in hop poles thus expanded in this period. When the hop industry later declined, hop poles became firewood and construction materials. In 1918, long after the end of Wisconsin's hop trade, one reporter wrote, "I venture to say that some old tamarack hop poles are yet doing service as auxiliaries in fence building upon Fairfield farms."[156] Perhaps, more than a century after that commentary, some of those long-lived tamaracks may yet hold up fences in hop country.

PART 3

DEATH KNELL

6

"THE GREAT AVENUE FOR LOSING MONEY"

1868

In January 1868, the pickers had long returned to their homes and the hop rhizomes slumbered in the frozen earth. Farmers had counted the money they made in the fall.[1] Women enjoyed their new silks and furs bought with hop earnings, precocious children played shiny new pianos, and fine-looking horses pulled jolly sleighs through the snowy countryside. Many hop-growing households felt flush, and they prepared to keep on planting and harvesting hops in the coming season. The year 1867 brought fantastic profits to those with the foresight to plant hops two or three years earlier, and many people were planning an even bigger harvest for 1868. The hop houses of Wisconsin stood ready. Stacks of hop poles waited in barns and fields, and people also bundled up against the cold and headed into the quiet frozen forests to harvest whatever usable saplings they could find for the ever-expanding hop fields. Farmers took advantage of the leafless forests and good sleighing weather to lay in a stock of hop poles for what they hoped would be an even more lucrative harvest in 1868. In Adams County, just north of Sauk County, one newspaper reported, "the tamarack swamps in the northern part of the county are filled with anxious seekers after hop-poles. At the present price of poles, some of these lands are very valuable, and many entries are being made. Considerable stealing is also going on, and it will not be at all surprising if the State Land Commissioners should send a clerk from Madison to pounce upon the trespassers on State lands."[2] That same season, another paper noted, "20,000 hop poles have already passed through Waupaca since snow came," Waupaca being a region more known for its timber than its hops.[3]

Many settlers had previously deemed the tamarack lands largely worthless but began to buy them up much more rapidly because of the rising demand for hop poles.[4] Whereas some hop pole suppliers went the legal route and bought up land at the state land office, others simply made their way onto government land, much of which was being used by Ho-Chunk communities for hunting and harvesting, and made off with hop poles. Not all of them got away with it, and one government agent confiscated the poles and sold them for the government coffers.[5] According to one newspaper correspondent, "The hop-growers have improved the fine sleighing here during the past winter, in obtaining a supply of poles for the increased crop—and as a result, many an honest man has 'come to grief' in having his hard earnings in the woods confiscated by the State Agent, and their hop poles are advertised for sale by thousands, in favor of the state."[6]

In February 1868, the hop dealer and columnist Emmet Wells reported that everybody in the hop market wanted Wisconsin hops—all the more reason to scour the landscape for more hop poles and set about planning to plant even more acres of hops.[7] The failure of New York's 1867 hop harvest had introduced an even larger number of brewers to the quality of Wisconsin hops. "The inquiry [from brewers] has been chiefly for Wisconsins, but on account of their extreme scarcity the better grades of Bavarians have been taken. Common and Medium qualities of American are still entirely neglected."[8] For any self-respecting brewer today, the thought of using Bavarian hops as an easy substitute for Wisconsin Cluster simply because they were actually on the market is at least a stretch, although there are overlaps in their profiles ("spicy" and "floral" appear in the descriptions of both Cluster and Hallertau hops).[9] At this moment in the season, brewers could choose from New York State, Eastern (Vermont and other eastern states), Wisconsins, Michigans, Yearlings, "Old Olds," and Foreign (Canadians, Bavarians, or Belgians). Within these regions were varying quantities of a hierarchy of qualities: common, fair, good, prime, choice, and fancy.[10]

Wells grew cautious at the end of March 1868, as he learned of Wisconsin farmers feverishly setting up their hop poles in anticipation of their largest crop ever. He cast doubt on whether the previous two years could really be representative of the industry, and in early April he warned that Wisconsin might also be visited by the insect that "caused almost a total destruction of the crop in Michigan last season, and such as has impeded hop culture to a fearful extent in New York State during the past seven years."[11] At that point the hop market was still very quiet, not uncommon for the springtime. In May, Wells wrote, "Literally nothing is doing. . . . As there yet remains a brewing season of only four months before the advent of the new crop, it is not very probable anything can now influence the market."[12] That is, many brewers had the hops they needed, and anyone buying hops now was buying the previous year's harvest.

Hop shoots began to emerge from the newly thawed earth. Farmers' wives and daughters moved through the fields, tying the young shoots to the poles that had been placed in the hills by the farmer, an elder son, or a hired hand. The bines grew tall in June, wrapping clockwise around their poles. As they reached toward the sun, Wells reported that "much interest is now attached to the Wisconsin crop. If the blight does not extend in that State, and if the yield per acre, equals that of last season, the present heavy increase of bearing acreage will undoubtedly bring the yield of the coming season up to 60,000 or 70,000 bales; or *over two-thirds the consumption of the country*. . . . The vine is further ahead, and the prospects generally better than in any other state."[13]

The growing season of 1868 started out well. Newspapers crowed about the health and scale of Wisconsin's hopyards. "O, powerful weed! how grand ye grow! . . . For two years and more, almost every citizen of this town has profited mightily . . . It took some 3000 acres of land, and 20,000 girls (many of whom were women and boys), to produce and pick this 500 car-loads of beer-basis. And this year . . . more than 6000 acres are to be cultivated within a range of country directly tributary to Kilbourn City [Wisconsin Dells]. And that will require more than 40,000 pickers, most of whom must come from abroad (outside of the county, not outside of the country), and naturally pass through Kilbourn."[14] It shouldn't be too surprising that the papers offered astronomical predictions for the 1868 harvest, a nearly sevenfold predicted growth in acreage, from 888 acres picked in 1866 to a predicted 5,588 in 1868.[15] While Wisconsin's hop yards were thriving, Wells reported, "from Central New York, particularly from Oneida and Madison, our reports this week have been very unfavorable. The insect has made its appearance in many yards, and growers, whose old yards give no promise of fair yield, are ploughing them up. . . . Old yards in Chenango County are reported almost a complete failure," while a hailstorm damaged many new yards.[16]

In fact, the picture was not completely rosy in Wisconsin. A farmer in Portage found a hop louse in June 1868.[17] Another hop farmer, identified as E. F. Lewis, wrote disgruntledly to the *Wisconsin State Register*, which had mentioned the hop louse being in his hopyards. He was annoyed because that unwelcome newspaper coverage made it seem as though he was the only one with that problem, but he said he had seen the louse in many other hopyards "and found them much more plenty than in mine."[18] The louse might disappear completely, or it might lurk and then swiftly bring down an entire crop. Even in my own small hop-growing endeavors, some years the hop plants in the garden fill with aphids and yield little, other years no aphids appear at all, and one time the aphids arrived but were soon followed by ladybug larvae, which ate all the aphids and rescued our crop. The *Milwaukee Daily Sentinel* explained, "Hops may thrive finely up to the 15th or 25th of August, when the bur is fully developed, and then be destroyed in a week as though by the evil one, it behooves every hop-grower to be fully prepared to commence picking at a moment's warning—even by the 20th of August, if necessary, whether the hops are sufficiently ripe or not. Immature hops will sell for first quality, while lousy hops are of but little value."[19]

Every week, any farmer reading the papers was well aware of the prices of German, Belgian, English, and New York hops, thanks to

Wells's reports. At the end of June, Wells could announce that the market was still calm. The brewers were in the driver's seat with regard to price, and choosy given the advanced age of all of the hops on the market. On the Fourth of July, Wells noted, "Brewers will only buy when 'bargains' are offered them. Choice [New York] State and Wisconsins are in somewhat better request, and desirable parcels meet with ready sale at our highest quotations."[20] A week later, Wells reported that the young yards in New York as well as the English and European yards all looked good. That was bad news for Wisconsin farmers, who might not have realized it yet.[21] The *Baraboo Republic* found Wells's reports "unworthy of publication," rejecting his mentions of trouble in their readers' hopyards, happily proclaiming that "if the present favorable condition of things continues, we shall harvest fully double our crop of last year [in Wisconsin]."[22] The summer of 1868 saw extreme heat and drought in Wisconsin, which may have actually helped slow the growth of hop lice in the fields.[23] "Our advices from Wisconsin, though yet somewhat conflicting, still favor the opinion that the hop crop in that state will be an early and large one."[24] Estimates ranged from 60,000 bales to 100,000 bales—which could be good news, or bad news. "Should their anticipations be realized, and the crops in other states turn out large, we hope they will be fully prepared for the inevitable crash which must follow. Bearing in mind the fact, that the consumption of hops in this country is less than 90,000 bales, it is easy to foresee the result. . . . The great uncertainty of the hop crop renders most opinions or predictions of little or no value."[25] And who knew what the louse would do, from one day to the next. "The crop in New York never looked more promising than it did on the 20th of August last. In less than five days the lice nearly destroyed it. 70,000 bales was considered a low estimate for this state in the early part of August [1867]. She did not produce over 10,000 bales of good."[26]

As hop fever still ran high among many farmers, others sounded notes of caution, such as this one quoted in the *Wisconsin State Register* on August 8: "But I'm taking even 'betses' that the mad infatuation—equaling gold-mining, oil-welling, land-grabbing, or any other mania which betimes turns men's heads topsey-turvey—will have in a great degree ceased two months from now. Were the yield and quality to be this year equal to the last year's hereaway, there would be fifty per cent more hops to be picked *this year*, in Wisconsin *alone*, than will be wanted to supply every brewery in the United States for the next year. . . . *And more hops were planted last spring, for next year's picking, than are to be picked this fall!*"[27] Also on August 8, with the new harvest just weeks away, Wells reported that the New York hopyards looked pretty good and that the brewers were buying the old hops still, "the chief inquiry being for Wisconsins; but, as none of this favorite variety was to be had, the best grades of [New York] 'State' were taken. There is always more or less demand for old hops throughout the season, as many brewers are in the habit of buying them to mix with new."[28]

The previous month, in preparation for the harvest, local shops had been "thronged with hop-growers, in quest of stoves, pipe, lumber for hop-houses, sacking, bedsteads and other articles of household furniture, for the accommodation of the pickers."[29] By the end of August, the pickers began to head toward the fields. Some rode freight and platform cars because there weren't enough passenger cars to fit the "myriads of bright-faced, young girls clad in neat attire and bearing light, expectant hearts to the fields of labor."[30] These pickers departed for the fields fully expecting to receive fifty cents a box.[31] Both the pickers and the hops just kept coming. Even with aphids beginning to infect some of the hopyards, the sheer volume of rhizomes planted in the previous years meant that an epic harvest was barreling toward the bright-faced pickers, and toward the market. Hops would soon begin to fill the kilns and pile up at train depots and in warehouses. By the time the pickers completed their work later in September, and despite reportedly lower yields, 11 *million* pounds of Wisconsin hops would stand at the ready in their burlap sacks, headed for market.[32]

On September 1, 1868, one *Milwaukee Daily Sentinel* columnist estimated that, whereas fifteen thousand pickers had been needed in Sauk County alone in 1867, fifty thousand would be needed in 1868 based on how many hops had been planted.[33] Thirty thousand were expected in the counties adjacent to Kilbourn City, and many thousands more fanned out across the other hop-growing regions.[34] In 1867, Wisconsin farmers had grown an estimated 35,000 bales, and a year later an estimated *60,000* bales.[35] Even without the return of the New York market, they might have sealed their own fates two or three years before, when planting out that many hop plants. One prescient reporter exclaimed in May 1868, "Whillikens! . . . in two years from now more than nine-tenths of the ten millions of hop poles now within a range of twenty miles from here, will be used for firewood, fencing and the like." This reporter spoke from experience, having witnessed a hop crash in New England twenty years before: "The only hope a western [or Wisconsin] grower can possibly have of prosperity in the herb is, that the crop will fail everywhere else—in foreign lands, and down east, and south, and that *this* region may be louseless, and supply the breweries of the world."[36] Not the best strategy, but popular nonetheless.

PICKING IN 1868

As the industry boomed, many families continued to use their own children as hop pickers, and many also had a male farmhand or two in residence. But the demand for pickers increased swiftly. The harvest of 1867 had brought an impressive result for many modest farmers of the hop-growing counties, encouraging others to plant their own hop hills, setting up 1868 to be a uniquely large harvest. This meant a giant scramble for pickers as the hops began to ripen, and an unprecedented flood of pickers into the fields. As the 1868 harvest season approached, many growers' biggest concern at this point was finding enough hop pickers. *The Watertown News* reported:

> We are told that there is every reason to believe that the hop crop will be fully up to the average in this County. . . . As the breadth of ground set out is much greater than ever before, we have reason to expect a corresponding increase in the aggregate yield. It is feared that there will be no little difficulty experienced in getting hands to secure the crop as agents are busy engaging all who will go for the hop picking

> in Sauk and Monroe Counties. A fine opportunity will soon be offered for all who wish to earn from two to four dollars per day at a "light and pleasant employment."[37]

Newspapers spilled much ink on the topic, sometimes even quoting each other, as with this early September report in the *Baraboo Republic*: "The Green Bay *Advocate* gives the following as a digest of the local exchanges: Prairie chickens; more prairie chickens; prairie chickens. Hops; more hops; hop lice; hop-picking; hop-sacks; hop-driers; hops; girls for hop-picking; more girls; 20,000 more girls; girls."[38]

The papers filled with predictions and solicitations. One from May claimed, "Twelve hundred girls will be needed in and around Sparta to pick hops next fall."[39] The *Wisconsin State Journal* ran an ad in early July 1868: "500 girls wanted to pick hops. Come soon so as to secure good places. Enquire of A. M. Daggett, at the store of M.L. Daggett, Main St."[40] Later in July, Leroy Gates and his partner Anson Rood sought

> the services of 6,000 Girls, Women and Men to pick hops in Sauk, Juneau, Adams and Columbia Counties the coming hop harvest. . . . The pickers fares will be paid from Watertown Station to the yards; also have the Proprietors of the yards, entered into an agreement to pay one fourth of the return fare after the picking is over. Thrifty, first-class yards have been selected, where will be found pleasant homes and convenient accommodations for lodging, as well as plentiful supplies of wholsome [*sic*] and substantial food. Those wishing to take an excursion into the hop districts of this section and enjoy a season of healthful exercise, coupled with money making—one that will replenish the purse, renew the health and refresh the mind—will find this an excellent opportunity.[41]

They then list many references, including several clergy members, to vouch for the wholesomeness of the hosts and hostesses. Fields soon grew crowded with pickers, anticipating a bumper crop and bumper profits. At the beginning of September, the trains carried "smiling girls and sober matrons, bound for the hop yards of Columbia, Sauk, and Adams counties."[42] One train was so laden with hop pickers that the engine struggled up a hill on the way into Kilbourn City, but they made it only an hour late and "by the light of a very early moon."[43] As the train pulled into the Kilbourn City depot, "as far as the eye could penetrate, in every direction, there was a solid mass of upturned faces, and [a] variety of costumes, as shown by the flickering lights thrown from numerous lanterns. . . . There were probably on the grounds, on our arrival, not less than 4,000 hop-pickers, mostly females."[44] On a single day in September 1868, twenty-five railcars left Milwaukee full of pickers for Sauk and neighboring counties.[45]

The demand for pickers had broad impacts, keeping young people out of school and leaving homes without their domestic servants. According to one report, "During the summer term, the percentage of attendance at the schools was very low. Up to about the middle of the term the attendance was good. But after that, all the larger scholars, and many of the smaller ones, were kept at home to work in the hop fields. This state of things will exist as long as the people are engaged in hop raising."[46] Even the local baseball teams had to reschedule their championship games "on account of having lost so many out of their first nines by the seductive allurements of the hop-fields."[47] Sara Rath, biographer of the photographer H. H. Bennett, described how (according to newspapers of the era) "one day in early September of 1868, two thousand women with umbrellas, satchels, baskets, bandboxes, bundles, and babies poured out of a twenty-six-coach train. There were twenty-five hundred pickers on the next day's train. They were paid about two dollars per day (fifty cents per box) plus board. . . . Late that summer there were from twenty-five thousand to thirty thousand women in the hopyards. Harvest season was a time for feasting, dancing, and fabulous profits."[48]

While the farmer's wife and elder daughters did most of the work of hosting all of these pickers, local businesses did step in at times. Bakeries and restaurants offered to deliver bread and serve meals to the crowds of pickers. In September 1868—the year of the largest picking force in Wisconsin's history—Pfannstiehl's Bakery provided helpful services, for a price: "To Hop Growers. Pfannstiehl's Bakery. For the accommodation of hop growers near to town I have made arrangements to deliver at their houses daily upon order during the hop picking season, fresh baked bread, cakes, pies, &c., at low prices, thus saving them the labor of baking and lightening the labors of the women during the busy season. . . . I will also be prepared to furnish meals to farmers passing through town with loads of hop pickers on such short notice as to save them from all delay, and at low rates."[49] This ad reveals the urgent drumbeat of the harvest—the sooner the pickers got to the fields, the sooner the cones would come off the bines and into the kiln, safe from aphids, mildew, and weather, and ready for the depots and the dealers.

In September 1868, the papers reached new heights of hyperbole, turning to military metaphor to express the scope of the labor force entering the hopyards:

> The Army of Hop Pickers. Women's Rights Triumphant—Thirty Regiments in Calico—30,000 Rallying to the Poles—Great Excitement in Kilbourn City—2,500 Hop Pickers on a Train—900 Wagons Captured—Kilbourn City Surrendered. Probably in all the history of hop picking, since yeast and lager were invented, there has been nothing to compare with the scenes that have been going on in this region, and in Kilbourn City especially, for the last six or eight days. For two or three weeks the hop growers have been gathering their supplies; and the merchants and traders of this place, Baraboo and Reedsburg have been on the jump waiting on their customers. The first of last week the pickers began to come in; and this week there must be at least 30,000 lively at work, picking the hops of the region that ships them at this depot. . . . Wagon loads of from 8 to 15 each have been almost constantly passing through town for the last eight days, generally coming from the north and east. . . . Of the 10,000 that pass through this village, about 8,000 come on the railroad from the east and stop here.[50]

One important exception to the overall predominance of white women pickers comes from several references to very large crews of

Indigenous, presumably Ho-Chunk, hop pickers in 1868. For example, "The railroad station at Kilbourn saw the arrival of thousands of young women in the late 1860s who came for the hop harvest. . . . The enterprising Leroy Gates recruited thousands of young women to come by train to Kilbourn and help local Indians pick the hop blossoms from the vines that grew on long tamarack poles."[51] To date I have located one such farm for sure and a possible second. In the second case, in the fall of 1868, one paper reported that "over a hundred Indians near La Crosse are engaged to pick hops."[52] I would make the educated guess that this was the farm of James McKinley, who harvested 28,000 pounds of hops in 1869. He had moved to Wisconsin in 1850, originally from Pennsylvania, with his Irish parents. At one point in his hop-growing endeavors he had "thirty-two acres set to hops, and the annual yield is between 30,000 and 35,000 pounds."[53] The confirmed farm employing Indigenous hop pickers was owned by a forty-six-year-old Prussian immigrant, Herman Greve, married to a woman named Marie and father to at least four children. Greve hired two hundred Indigenous people in Sparta to pick hops in 1868.[54] While I can easily find the names of Greve and his family in census records, I have so far been unable to track any names of the *two hundred* Indigenous hop pickers he hired.[55]

It is no surprise that Greve hired hundreds of people to pick hops. His farm reported a harvest of 53,400 pounds of hops in 1869, making him one of the largest hop growers in the history of Wisconsin (and in the country at the time). Given the location of the farm in Sparta, it is fair to assume that this was a large contingent of Ho-Chunk neighbors working in the hop fields.[56] While the newspapers covered the white women pickers with column after column of effusive praise and exclamation, the references to Indigenous workers disclose almost no details at all, despite their obvious importance to many farmers' profits and livelihood. Thus some of the ghosts of the hop yards are much harder to discern than others. The outlines of Ella and Ida Seymour glow more visibly through the archives than the two hundred unnamed Ho-Chunk pickers at Greve's farm, but I continue my search for more detail on the Ho-Chunk experience of hop picking in Wisconsin. As noted in chapter 3, in both New York and on the Pacific Coast, it was fairly common to hire Indigenous families, who would self-provision rather than stay in the farmer's house, and far more extensive records of Indigenous hop pickers exist on the Pacific Coast in particular, in part because these labor practices continued well into the twentieth century.[57]

Overall, however, Wisconsin farmers held fast to their habit of hiring young white women. At one point, so many pickers were arriving on two trains one evening, that there were

> acres of two and four horse wagons about the depot, and the music and fun of the merry drivers. . . . But as the two trains came thundering along, and as they stretched themselves away beyond and away back of the depot and stopped, excitement was on tip-toe. And when 2000 pickers began to pour out of every door of those 28 cars the scene beat all other western shows. Cheering, laughing, singing, shouting! Admirable confusion—no disorder. Sections of tens, platoons of twenties, companies of forties, all officered, moving in every possible direction; corporals guiding their squads; captains giving orders to their companies; marching and countermarching . . . forming camp and breaking camp; armed and equipped with umbrellas, parasols, satchels, baskets, band boxes, bags, bundles, babies! Teamsters shouting for their loads . . . We can't do justice to the subject.[58]

This was a Saturday—on Monday, even more women arrived on the two trains. "Truly, Hops are King, and in this region 30,000 Queens are waiting on the old fellow."[59]

BUMPER CROPS AND TRYING TIMES

And so it was that in early September 1868, the biggest hop-picking labor force to ever enter Wisconsin's hop country was just getting settled on their straw ticks, just getting to know their box tenders and pole pullers, and maybe hadn't even had the chance to dance a quadrille in a hop house.[60] The farmers' wives had finished their preparations, and the pickers were just starting to consume the generous provisions that had been laid in reserve. Hops were ripening in the field. There was no turning back. As the fields filled with pickers and the "gala time" began, a bumper crop of Wisconsin hops soaked up its last few days of sunshine. In at least one county, the bines were "vigorous and healthy, the burr is large, and the lupuline rich and abundant."[61] A wave of hops was rising. Massive, inexorable, they were the literal fruit of decisions made months and years earlier, given that hops don't hit their stride until their second or third year of growth.[62]

That same season, to the delight of brewers everywhere, a glorious bumper crop began to ripen in New York as well, recovered from the previous year's aphid infestation.[63] As early as July, signs of an extraordinarily large harvest began to appear in hop country: "Ale and porter brewers are mostly holding back to get the late crops. Growers must be prepared for the inevitable crash which will follow if the Wisconsin crop reaches 60,000 to 70,000 bales in 1868," or 12 to 14 million pounds.[64] Hop dealers traversed the United States and reported the return of a strong crop in New York in that month, while also realizing the final yields could still change in an instant. In July, the bines had begun to set bur, and it was possible to get some sense of what the final harvest might be like—pending any unforeseen hailstorms, fly infestations, or blight. According to one history of Reedsburg:

> Some of the Reedsburg hop dealers visited New York and other eastern cities in July 1868 and after a careful review of the situation, on their return, advised caution on the part of merchants and growers, but so completely had the "wish been father to the thought" that the insane belief in permanent high prices had so bewitched the minds of the people, that they would listen to no advice or words of caution, but at once raised a clamor that the hop dealers were in league with outside purchasers and brewers, to keep them out of the market for the purpose of forcing down the prices.[65]

These sentiments ran so deep among the hop farmers of Loganville, a village south of Reedsburg, that a dealer who predicted a price drop to twenty cents a pound would apparently "get the unkindly attention of the mob."[66] This was no joke, as mobs were very much afoot in this part of the world. Indeed, the first farmer to bring hops to market that fall was a former sheriff named E. F. Lewis, who had a few years before successfully faced down a mob and prevented the lynching of a man accused of murder.[67] Said sheriff was a prolific hop farmer later in his life, and his hops were among the first to reach the market in the first days of September 1868.[68] At that point in the season, Lewis—the same farmer who hosted the "hoppenfest" described in chapter 5—was paying good wages to his pickers. The *Wisconsin State Register* reported, "Good, smart, faithful girls, working in good fields, have told us that one box (50 cents per box, is the price paid) is a good, fair day's work, and Mr. Karch, who keeps the books in Mr. Lewis' yard, where some 75 girls are picking, informed us that perhaps a box and a half would be a fair average."[69] Even as rumors of a pending oversupply circulated, and reports of lice emerged here and there in Wisconsin yards, still the fields filled with pickers.[70] As late as September 12, a German-language newspaper in Minnesota still extolled the wisdom of planting hops in Wisconsin and lauded the banner harvest that was just about to come in.[71]

But within days, for the hop farmers of Wisconsin, the worst outcome imaginable was well underway: "The crop turned out well everywhere [including New York], in this state [Wisconsin] was a very large one, and the actual decline in prices far exceeded the worst apprehensions of those interested in the Hop trade or culture."[72] As the pickers toiled in the fields, ate the farmers' food, and danced to the fiddler's tune, the depots filled with bales of hops and began to inundate the markets in New York and Wisconsin alike. Prices began to free-fall. Some farmers held back their baled hops and waited to see whether the European crop was short, in which case the growers could ask for higher prices. An early September newspaper article advised, "Probably one week more will settle the matter as to the destruction of the crop in this country; and whether fair prices or very low will prevail. In the meantime, keep cool and wait."[73]

Two weeks later, in the space of two days, prices dropped from the range of thirty to thirty-five cents a pound down to twenty to twenty-five cents a pound.[74] By September 12, the market for hops in New York had become "dull and drooping," with prices at fifteen to twenty-five cents a pound for the very best quality. Another week later, even that price would seem like a dream. One reporter wrote, "In Kilbourn, yesterday, I saw many bales of prime hops sell at 15 cents. Poor were unsaleable. . . . I can hardly believe a strictly prime hop will continue to sell thus. In Kilbourn at 6 p.m. some bales were unsold for want of funds."[75] And by the end of the season, hop farmers were getting just a few pennies per pound: "The [Wisconsin] crop had to be sacrificed at three to five cents per pound [down from fifty to sixty cents per pound at its high point in 1867], with no demand whatever for a considerable portion of it."[76] Prices sagged as low as 2½ cents per pound.[77] By September 16, the *Wisconsin State Journal* (figure 6.1) was ringing the death knell of the industry: "The days of profitable hop culture in Wisconsin . . . are over."[78]

Wisconsinites felt the free fall of prices on farms and in homes, in general stores and lumberyards. As the prices plummeted, farmers tried to back out of the generous wages they had originally promised to the pickers, sometimes resulting in violence: "In one case the pickers were Germans, from Watertown . . . there being two or three men among their number. As the employer attempted to leave without paying them, they caught his horses by the bits, and a general fight ensued. The employer had got the help of another Irishman . . . who mangled two of the Germans' heads badly with a piece of board. Our citizens interfered, and the hop-grower paid the pickers the usual price."[79] In another incident, "the pickers, mostly women and girls, gathered about [the employer who was refusing to pay], and declared they would stay around him until he paid in full, and they were backed by about thirty or forty of our citizens, some of whom occasionally intimated that he could never get out of town with a whole hide if

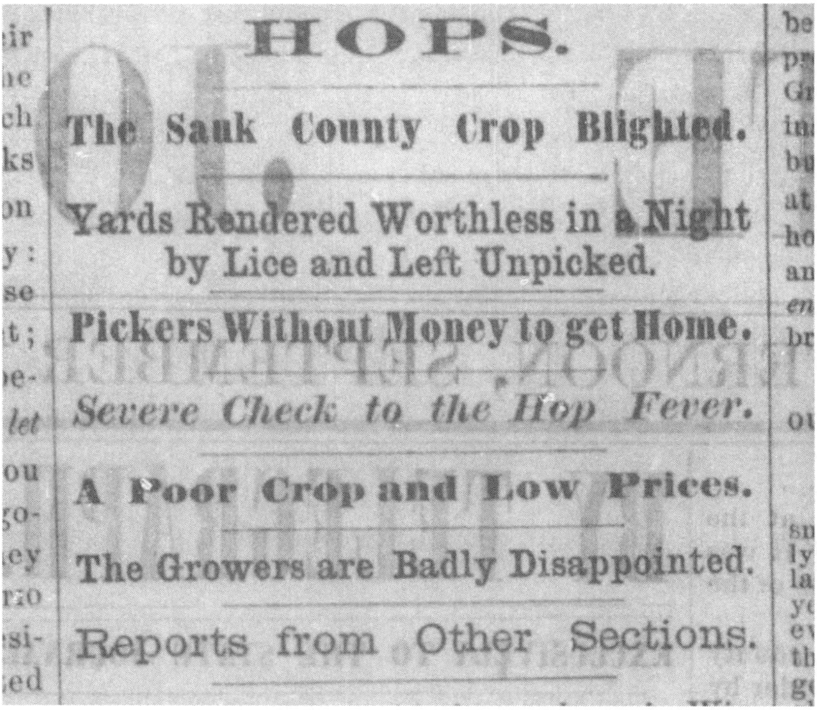

HOPS.

The Sauk County Crop Blighted.

Yards Rendered Worthless in a Night by Lice and Left Unpicked.

Pickers Without Money to get Home.

Severe Check to the Hop Fever.

A Poor Crop and Low Prices.

The Growers are Badly Disappointed.

Reports from Other Sections.

FIGURE 6.1. Dire news in the *Wisconsin State Journal*, September 16, 1868.

he didn't pay. After being picked [on] for about an hour in that way, and seeing no escape, he came down handsomely and paid the whole amount."[80] Many families had come to depend on this extra income, so many pickers did all they could to secure their wages as the effects of the crash began to spread far beyond the provincial hopyard.[81]

Compounding the price drop, the aphid began to spread in Wisconsin, so that some hop yards were damaged, resulting in an incongruous mix of crop failure and overproduction. Farmers scrambled to cover their expenses in the absence of any interested buyers, and this lack of funds directly impacted pickers hard at work in the fields. The *Wisconsin State Journal* reported, "All cannot borrow even at the heavy rates mentioned, and money must be obtained, especially as some have their houses full of strangers (pickers) who live 100 to 500 miles away *without even funds to pay their return railfare.* It is a trying time, but a few days must bridge this crisis by borrowing, credit, selling stock or grain or putting hops to sale at going prices."[82] The farmers had houses crowded with pickers, while the hops withered on the vine or headed toward warehouses where they would idle for months or years. Pickers who so joyfully arrived days or weeks before found themselves with empty pockets: "A number of persons who went from this vicinity [Watertown] last September to Sauk County for the purpose of picking hops were obliged to come home without their pay."[83] Many of the pickers who, days before, had streamed happily into the county now found themselves stranded without wages or train fare as the hopyards crumbled beneath the weight of the blight, in some cases, or the free-falling prices, in others.

Some farmers desperately tried to sell their hops directly to English dealers or breweries to try to cover expenses, or even salvage a profit, with limited success: "A party who worked for a man living near Kilbourn City, learned last week that he had shipped a large quantity to Liverpool, and they at once guarnished the Milwaukee & St. Paul R.R., upon which they had been shipped, and the owner will doubtless be obliged to settle the bill for picking the hops before they will be allowed to go aboard. The hop raisers of course have had a hard time this year, but the pickers earned their money."[84] The crash impacted the shopkeepers who had sold on credit and the farmers who had bet everything they had on this fragile crop.[85] The demand for hop stoves and other tools of hop production such as pole sharpeners and pole-setting tools was so intense that it made abundant business for a local foundry, near today's Wisconsin Dells in Delton. When the hop industry crashed, the foundry dissolved as well.[86]

Each pound of hops or penny reported in the census and the newspapers was a farmer's bank account, a dewy morning full of promise or ruin, scrambling hop lice, and thousands of young women picking hops, expecting to be fed and paid. Prices dropped as the weeks passed, even as some farmers held their hops back in the hope that the prices would rebound. Most who had done so soon realized their mistake and settled into deep regret—and debt.[87] The rest of that season was spent in various attempts to salvage even a fraction of what farmers had invested in their hop crop.

Farmers who had borrowed heavily and planted many acres of hops suffered far more than those who were more diversified. We can see how diversification offered some protection in Silas Seymour's case. Although he never again saw the fantastic profits of 1867, he continued to grow hops into the 1870s, including enough hops to require the hiring of outside pickers. He adjusted the size of his hop fields and continued to engage in dairying, wheat farming, and other agricultural work. In Silas's township of Dellona (a tiny fraction of Sauk County), in 1869, the year after the crash, there were thirty-eight hop farmers, harvesting a total of 52,400 pounds of hops. The average harvest was 1,380 pounds, a smallish but respectable commercial crop. That year Silas Seymour reported a harvest of 2,140 pounds of hops to the census taker for the 1870 Census of Agriculture, above the average but far less than a few years before, when he had harvested more than 13,000 pounds.[88] That places him squarely in the realm of commercial hop growing and means he may have taken some loss that year but, because he was diversified, not enough to have lost everything. And even with such a turn toward hops, staple crops still dominated acreage and harvests. In 1869, Wisconsin's farmers grew 25 million bushels of wheat and 20 million bushels of oats.[89]

The troubles of 1868 had started small and were by no means uniform. Conditions and profitability varied from one hopyard or county to the next.[90] Some fields were already blighted, but others had their best showing yet. A cataclysmic mixture of overproduction, lower quality (attributable to the hop louse and possibly some weather challenges), and the success of the 1868 New York hop crop led to this downfall.[91] The town of Portage, not far from Kilbourn City, reported extensive hop louse infestation, while nearby Adams County concluded its picking season on September 19, with better yields and quality than expected. The aptly named William S. Grubb, a Baraboo hop dealer, wrote in September 1868, "the glorious days of early September, with its frosty nights and bright windy days, withheld the 'destroyer's hand,' and the great hop harvest of 1868 was inaugurated under favorable auspices; but the 6th of September was ushered in by a foggy morn; with a hot sun at noon and showery evening, followed by six days of hot, foggy, showery, reeking weather, and splendid yards perished in a night from lice and mould."[92] John Rooney, the gent who courted his future wife hop picking in Sauk County (as described in chapter 5), went into the hop business at an early age and an inauspicious moment. In 1867, he and his business partner made $1,100 profit, and a year later they lost $3,000—could have been worse, and for many it was.[93] While many farmers had planted a few acres of hops alongside their other crops, some growers had put large numbers of acres into hops, borrowing heavily to plant hopyards, and some people in other lines of work saw hop farmers getting rich and planted a few acres of their own.

During these volatile weeks of August and September 1868, some fields even went unpicked—something that would have been unthinkable the year before at fifty to sixty cents a pound.[94] Many farmers soon grubbed up some or all of their hops. In 1868, E. F. Lewis of hoppenfest fame had space for *fifty* pickers and eighteen acres of hops. In anticipation of the 1868 harvest, he had even added on to his house, including a huge dining room. He set up fifty-five "good beds, all on good bedsteads," and hired fiddlers for the evening dances.[95] But by the 1869 harvest, he reported a yield of only 3,800 pounds of hops, an amount that could have possibly been picked just by his older children and the three laborers and domestics living in his household. He had probably ripped up many of his acres of hops and drastically cut back his outlay of expenses for the hop harvest. Similarly, in 1866, Isaac Frank of Jefferson County (not far from where the Ingalls family had tried their hand at hops a few years earlier, as described in chapter 4) hired sixty pickers for his substantial crop.[96] By 1869, he was harvesting only 8,000 pounds, surely with a much smaller labor force.

"CRAMMED, JAMMED FULL OF HOPS, CELLAR TO GARRET"

Brewing carried on, unscathed by the bottom dropping out of the Wisconsin hop market. Spring 1868 had brought unusually "cool and unseasonable weather," which left the brewers with too much lager on hand.[97] Just a few months later, the reverse happened: "The past few weeks of excessive hot weather has caused an unprecedented demand for lager beer, and local brewers, whose business suffered in April and May by reason of the cool and unseasonable weather, are now reaping a rich harvest. Many of them not anticipating such a favorable season, now find their stocks of beer reduced, and are beginning to brew. In ordinary seasons the lager brewing does not begin much before the latter part of September."[98] The previous season's lesser hops had few buyers in this kind of market, and the brewers were eagerly anticipating the new harvest: "Low and medium grades of all kinds are a complete drag in the market. Lager brewers cannot use them, while ale and porter brewers are holding off for the new crop, many of them having hops enough on hand to carry them through till October."[99]

By 1868, the international supply of hops was so plentiful, and so supple, that the brewers could immediately adapt, week by week, and decide what prices they wanted to pay, whose hops they would purchase, to buy on demand rather than stockpile. This flexibility was possible because hop markets were already translocal and transnational, managed by hop dealers who moved about the world with relative ease, mobile gentlemen ready to negotiate with farmers and brewers, riding the rails with samples of hops and fistfuls of cash. That is, before and after the Wisconsin boom, brewers across Milwaukee and elsewhere had well-established networks of dealers and growers, varying their buying from local farmers to German dealers in the same season, even in the same week. The ledgers of Pabst and Blatz vividly depict these networks, the seasonal swell of hop purchasing from many sources, just down the road or clear across the Atlantic. For brewers, the crash of 1868 simply meant that their hop expenses dropped significantly, while farmers and pickers stood with empty pockets and worrisome account books. The Phillip Best Brewing Company, for example, sold 300 barrels of beer in 1842, 3,677 barrels in 1863, and 25,000 barrels in 1868; "In the production of this 'sea of lager,' eighty thousand bushels of malt, and three hundred bales of hops, averaging two hundred pounds to the bale, were consumed."[100] In 1880, Best brewed a phenomenal 275,000 barrels, using 550,000 pounds of hops (!!).[101]

Blatz brewed 150 barrels in 1851, 16,000 barrels in 1868, 125,000 barrels in 1880, and 245,000 barrels by 1884.[102] Blatz bought hops from "Germany and the East."[103] By 1884 Schlitz was brewing 345,000 barrels a year.[104] Soon thereafter, Schlitz was using around a million pounds of hops a year, shipped primarily from New York and the West Coast.[105] In the late 1860s, that sea of lager had not yet reached its full potential, but the brewers and their bookkeepers surely had few complaints about the bottom dropping out of the Wisconsin hop market.

Despite the louse and the early departure of many pickers, the 1868 harvest in Wisconsin was *one hundred* times as big a harvest as that of 1860.[106] The volatility of the hop market continued long after the end of the harvest. In the fall of 1868, many growers attempted to unload all the hops they could. Although the harvest was complete by mid-September, hop sales continued through the following months, as happened every year. Hops continued to cross the Great Lakes and even the Atlantic in search of a market. The steamship *City of Fremont* carried eighty-three bales of Wisconsin hops to Grand Haven, Michigan, in October.[107] The sidewheel steamer *Alpena*, the *City of Fremont*, the *Manitowoc*, the *Detroit*, and the *Orion* all kept shipping hops from Wisconsin to Michigan deep into October and on through November, even into December, a riskier venture with each passing week as the weather worsened.[108] At this point, "some brewers still [had] hops on hand from the previous fall, when they paid as much as 65 cents a pound."[109] By December, Emmet Wells reported that only the "finest qualities" were selling and that many brewers were holding out for the prices to go even lower. "Were the lowest point now reached, brewers who have been holding off for lower prices would lay in their supplies for the season. Speculators at the slaughtering price of ten cents per pound! This we call no market at all; and growers who continue forwarding their hops to New York, until stocks become reduced, must do so at their own expense, and for the benefit of insurance companies and parties who receive storage. Every hop house in [New York] . . . is crammed, jammed full of hops, cellar to garret."[110]

As winter approached, the news continued to be good for brewers and bad for Wisconsin's hop farmers, especially those who had borrowed against their hop crop or failed to hedge their bets by balancing their hop crop with other agricultural endeavors, or both. "Large quantities of hops are being shipped from Waupaca county direct to New York, on owners' account," one newspaper reported, and other farmers shipped straight from Kilbourn City to London.[111] In early December 1868, the small town of Ironton, in Sauk County, sent 985 bales of hops directly to Liverpool, with some of the growers traveling along with their hops.[112] Two of the local farmers, Samuel Livesley and Jack Jessop, "took a shipment to England."[113] At Kilbourn City, it was reported that by early December "there is no hop market—no one even taking them to forward on commission, and the railroads refusing to receive them as freight unless charges are paid in advance. In short, the hop crop isn't of as much account, in the commercial world in this section, as the bees-wax crop."[114]

Because the hops were relatively stable once dried and baled, though still declining enough for there to be a noticeable difference between this year's hops and the previous year's hops, farmers could choose to hold some back in hopes of better prices as the weeks or months passed. Wisconsin's failure happened in part because its farmers were in direct competition with farmers across the country and around the world.[115] On November 25, 1868, Emmet Wells wrote:

> Our Western [that is, Wisconsin] friends could not have made a more fatal mistake than they have, by rushing their hops into this market at one time, and in such large quantities. . . . Chicago and Milwaukee commission houses are said to be full of hops, while there is no sale for them. New York commission concerns are filling up—many already overflowing and there is nothing but a slight demand for home consumption. The question naturally arises, what is to become of all the Hops? Will England take them? Our London letter given below almost suggests an answer in the negative. . . . Those who have hops on hand had better keep them at home, for a spell, at least, until the demand improves.[116]

That week thirty bales of German hops arrived in New York Harbor, and eight hundred bales of US hops came ashore on the docks of Liverpool and London.[117]

The international market ebbed and flowed with gluts and blights. Wisconsin growers were well aware of the "stiff competition . . . from Canadian farms and . . . Michigan, as well as constant threat of imports of hops from England."[118] The reputation of Wisconsin hops had certainly spread, but that could not insulate them from this shock to the market or the effects of the louse.[119] Growers holding their hops back in hopes of prices rebounding risked getting aced out of the English market by German hops.[120]

In 1868, predictions had the English brewers buying up 25,000 bales of US hops and 45,000 bales of European hops—in other words, it was not at all uncommon for English brewers to have both American and European hops in their brews.[121] My research on hops in Wisconsin confirms what others have found: that hop growing and other agricultural pursuits were quite often decidedly international and global, even in times and places that many people think of as remote and inaccessible.[122] Farmers in Wisconsin avidly read the newspapers for any scraps of information about the hop harvests in New York, Germany, and England, and badgered English relatives for any intel on the season's harvest, to aid in their own decision-making about when to sell and what prices to settle for.[123] Likewise, the hops grown in Wisconsin were sold just down the road, and shipped to Milwaukee and beyond, the prices and destinations shaped by global instances of blight, war, changes in beer drinkers' habits, brewers' preferences, and other factors. Hops left the New York ports for Liverpool, London, Cuba, China, Brazil, and points in between.[124] The 1868 Wisconsin harvest was bountiful—but not nearly enough brewers wanted enough of it. The New York blight that had so increased hop prices had ended, and brewers turned their attention back toward New York hops, in a market glutted with millions of bales of hops, reflecting the work of tens of thousands of young women.

7

EVEN OUT AND FADE AWAY

1869 and Beyond

In September 1869, dealers sent an early bale of the newest American hops aboard the steamer *Scotia* to London, receiving a cable back from the Borough, the neighborhood of London south of the Thames where the hop factors conducted their business, to confirm its arrival.[1] They were hoping to spark English interest in US hops for the coming season. The dealers, farmers, and brewers conducted all these calculations and tracking of shipments by hand: no Excel spreadsheets, no emails, no bookkeeping software or electronic bills of lading. And the hops traveled on the high seas aboard steamships and schooners. The *Scotia* was the last paddleboat on the Atlantic, eventually being converted to screws rather than paddles and turning to the laying of ocean cables rather than carrying passengers and light cargo as technological change continued apace. Like many of the vessels that carried nineteenth-century hops and hop farmers, the *Scotia* now lies at the bottom of the sea, in this case on a reef near Guam.[2] Unlike most of the vessels that transported hops, the *Scotia* also appeared in Jules Verne's *20,000 Leagues Under the Sea* and carried Theodore Roosevelt's family across the Atlantic.

As the *Scotia* made its way across the sea, the farmers of Wisconsin grappled with the unusual harvest of 1869 and waited for news of hop harvests across Europe and the United States. The 1869 harvest was one of the strangest hop harvests in Wisconsin history. Many farmers had grubbed up their fields after the disastrous year of 1868, but many others let the hops ride, having already invested in the rhizomes and hopeful there might be improvements in the 1869 prices. This is also the harvest year for which I have the most precise numbers because this was a census year—that is, in the summer of 1870, the census takers for the decennial Census of Agriculture asked farmers about their harvests of the year ending in June 1870, which included the hop harvest of August and September 1869. In 1869, each grower of hops in Wisconsin must have asked themself whether this would continue to be a worthy endeavor. Some had already abandoned the trade, some had lost their farms, and many were reducing their acreage, in part to lower the costs associated with hosting and compensating pickers.

By the time the 1869 harvest had been tallied, there were just over 1,200 people listed as growing hops in Sauk County, and still (despite the 1868 crash) 3,609 hop growers in all of the state—up from a mere 369 ten years earlier. The number of hop farmers in Sauk County increased a hundredfold in the space of a decade, and the state as a whole saw nearly the same level of expansion. In 1859, Wisconsin produced 135,587 pounds of hops. In 1869 that figure was more than 4.6 million pounds.[3] Along with overproduction, blights, and falling prices, another risk appearing on the horizon was the fact that the demand for beer, while increasing, could not keep pace with the rate at which farmers were setting out hopyards. A *Milwaukee Daily Sentinel* correspondent quipped, "Although a large class of our population keep themselves constantly lager-logged, yet as it requires but a comparatively small quantity of hops to flavor an ocean of the Too-tonic beverage . . . the demand for the delicious embitterment is absolutely limited. Two or three years of high prices are sufficient to double the supply of hops, but to double the demand for lager in the same time would be about as difficult as to double the capacity of a thirty-one gallon cask."[4] There was no alternative market or use for a surplus of hops: "The fact is, hop culture is greatly overdone, both in this country and in Europe, therefore, the best plan we can now devise, in order to restore a healthy trade and bring about higher prices, is to 'plow up,' otherwise, 'drink more beer.'"[5]

By January 1869, in English and European markets there was "no demand for American [hops]."[6] As the 1869 growing season began a few months later, a large crop of 1868 hops still sat in warehouses and barns.[7] Yet the collapse in prices could do little to stem the 1869 crop. Because hop plants take two to three years to produce a full crop, the plants ripening in the summer of '69 had been planted in 1866 or 1867, at the very least. The brisk, if not remunerative, global trade continued apace. The older hops leftover from 1868 fetched prices of three to five cents a pound—a stark loss compared to recent years of fifty to sixty cents a pound. According to the *Milwaukee Daily Sentinel*, "The reports we are now receiving from Wisconsin, leads us to the conclusion that about one-third of the yards picked last fall, are likely to be plowed up: that is to say, a yard of 30 acres is to be reduced to 20. . . . Many yards will be entirely plowed up, while many others will not be destroyed at all. Growers who can work their yards without being dependent upon outside labor, will do so."[8] In other words, the crowds of tens of thousands of young women heading to the fields were unlikely to reappear. Newly built summer kitchens might stand empty, the extra bedsteads and mattresses to remain stored away in attics and barns.

Many farmers had a less reliable strategy: they kept their hopyards planted in full and continued to hope that their neighbors would plow up *their* hopyards: "The *Baraboo Republic* says every hop-grower believes that every other hop-grower will abandon the business, so he will stick to it and make money."[9] The numbers recorded in the 1870 census are a combination of momentum and hope (or unfounded optimism), and probably not a small amount of bitterness. One newspaper reporter wrote, "This year . . . the man who would offer any [hop rhizomes] for sale to a Sauk countyzen [a.k.a. a citizen of Sauk County—this is the reporter's made-up word] would get his eye punched for the insult," though Howard H. Potter (who grew hops on four acres on the outskirts of Baraboo) reported selling hops to brewers around the country, including one in Missouri.[10] Many farmers grubbed up their fields as soon as the ground thawed in the spring of 1869, while others started the season fully expecting to harvest a normal commercial crop but tore out the roots later in the season as hop lice made their way through the fields.[11]

Oversupply continued to be a real risk given the sheer quantity of hops that had been planted. By mid-July around Kilbourn City, according to area newspapers, "we hear of some [farmers] who are even now pulling up the poles they had set, plowing up the roots and sowing the ground to buckwheat." Other farmers left their hops unpicked in September, as dealers were quoting prices that would not cover the cost of transporting and hiring pickers.[12] One newspaper correspondent reported:

> A remarkable change has come over the farmers all through the valley of the Lemonweir [River, northwest of Kilbourn City] since my last visit here one year ago. Then every farmer was half crazy with the flush of excitement over the enormous hop crop which was then being secured, and every yard was vocal with the music, mirth and glee of the happy hop-pickers, and the high prices paid induced thousands of girls to leave comfortable homes and "rough it" in the hop fields for a few weeks . . . enjoying a jolly good time. . . . But as the season closed, prices waned, until, in fact, no market opened for the large crop raised, and many a poor girl returned to her home wiser and sadder. . . . Where thousands of pickers found profitable employment last year, hundreds will answer the purpose this year. Everything looks gloomy and sad among growers and pickers alike now.[13]

Thus the change in fortune was felt not only by reporters and farmers but also by the young women who had hoped to make money in the hopyards that fall.

The 1870 Census of Agriculture leaves a fairly precise snapshot of those sad and gloomy farmers, as well as their more successful compatriots. More information is available about the 1869 harvest than any of the preceding nine years. That census year captures a region reeling from the previous year's failure and plotting its future with a range of strategies. For the farmers recorded by the census enumerators in the summer of 1869, this census may have captured their final go at a hop harvest, or their longer-term adaptation to the changing market. In the 1870 census, around 94 percent of hop-growing households in Wisconsin in 1870 were home to someone whom Ancestry.com lists as a presumed spouse.[14] This is also the first census year (that I know of) for Wisconsin that lists hop growers who were not white, and with a substantial complement (over 2 percent) of solitary women farmers. The vast majority of the four thousand hop farmers listed in the agricultural census were white men, European or Yankee, but a few dozen women end up listed as hop farmers, as well as one Indigenous man that I am aware of, David Fowler of Calumet County, and one Black man, Jermiah Jackson.[15]

Jeremiah Jackson was husband to Martha Jackson and father of Cassius and Caroline Jackson, who were ages nine and seven, respectively, in 1870.[16] In 1869, on a farm in Sparta, in Monroe County, he grew 600 pounds of hops, a quantity the household may have been able to pick without hiring extra help, although it would have been a challenge. Jackson's farm was two townships west of Adrian, a township known to have a community of Black farmers in the nineteenth century.[17] These farmers are an important correction to my initial assumption that all hop farmers would have been white, either Yankees from the East Coast or European immigrants. Between 1850 and 1860, the recorded Black population of Wisconsin rose from 630 to nearly 1,200 people.[18] The work of both Christy Clark-Pujara and Anna-Lisa Cox highlights the variability in safety, access to political power, and connection to the surrounding community for Black settlers in the Midwest. As Cox notes, while in many cases in the Midwest in this era, Black and white settlers married one another, at the same time, "by the 1850s nothing was as dangerous to these mixed families as other white people. Nothing about this violence was fated; nothing natural forced whites to rise up to destructive hatred," and this violence extended to other Black residents of the area as well.[19] The Jacksons may have lived in relative safety and community, or in a more solitary or threatened way. To date the archives are silent on the conditions of their lives. And, as Clark-Pujara writes, "the experiences of Black people in the Midwest, like everywhere else in America, were profoundly impacted by the institution of slavery and its legacies."[20] Indeed, the Fourteenth Amendment to the Constitution, which gave citizenship to formerly enslaved people and mandated equal protection under the law, was passed in 1866 and ratified in 1868—that is, the political and economic position of families like the Jacksons, and the path that led them to raising a Wisconsin hop crop, differed profoundly from the paths of most of the other farmers.

The same fact applies to the small number of Black people in the 1870 census who I am confident engaged in some amount of hop work as well. The population census contains the names of a handful of Black Wisconsin residents who, based on living in a hop-growing household, may have picked or otherwise tended hops. I have never seen "hop picker" listed as an occupation in the Wisconsin census (in contrast with the California census). In addition to Martha Jackson, who I assume engaged in hop tying and hop picking just as Mary Ann Seymour did, the only other Black woman I have so far discovered near a hopyard is Nancy Alcorn.[21] She and her husband William and their three-year-old daughter Bertha lived in the same house as a fifty-four-year-old white woman from New York, Mary Lusted, who was listed as the farmer in the Census of Agriculture for Jefferson County in 1870. The household reported 750 pounds of hops in the 1870 census, which meant that it was by no means among the biggest producers in the county, but there would be little doubt that the Alcorns played a role in this household's hop production. Indeed, 750 pounds is an amount that could have been picked by the household, perhaps with a little additional help. For anyone unfamiliar with Ancestry.com, when you search a name, the site offers up a list of additional sources on the right-hand side of the page for a given person. Usually there are other census records, birth certificates, obituaries, and the like, but to date there is not a single additional document for anyone in this household. In other words, tracing the Alcorn family backward and forward in time poses a much greater challenge than I found with so many other hop-growing households.

There were also several Black teenagers and unmarried (that I know of) Black men living in larger households, including sixteen-year-old

Ben Van Dyke, born around 1854 in Kentucky, who appeared in the census as a farm laborer living in the household of a white couple named Alexander and Mary Arnold, along with a fourteen-year-old Swedish servant girl named Hilda Ross, in Trempealeau in far western Wisconsin. This farm produced 8,000 pounds that year, and Arnold was a successful and influential farmer for many decades. Arnold had been a Union officer in Kentucky, so it is possible that is where he met Van Dyke. Black seventeen-year-old John Brinkley, born in Virginia, lived in a large household of seemingly unrelated people in Columbia County, Wisconsin, in 1870, along with Morton Brown, also listed as Black and also born in Virginia, nearly ten years before John. The white head of that household, Ira Ford, had been a captain in the Union army and had been taken prisoner by the Confederate army and kept in prisons in Jackson, Mississippi; Montgomery, Alabama; and Macon and Madison, Georgia. As with Arnold, it is possible that Ford had met Brinkley and Brown during the Civil War. This household harvested 2,800 pounds of hops in 1869, a considerable amount but possibly manageable by the existing household members.

There was also John Walkins, born in South Carolina in 1837, listed as "Mulatto," and in 1870 living in the household of William and Mahala Rayner, their five surviving children, a sixteen-year-old German domestic named Paulina Schultz, and a forty-two-year-old boarder named Jane Mead, all of whom were listed as white. The Rayners' farm in Milford, in Jefferson County, harvested 1,100 pounds of hops in 1869. George H. Dade, a Black farm laborer born in Virginia in 1840, lived with Stephen R. Sweet in Newport, Columbia County. This household was quite heterogeneous with regard to age and familial relations—Stephen was seventy, the woman in the household was thirty-six, perhaps a daughter, and among the three children there was a three-year-old in the house with the last name Sweet, and a twelve-year-old and a ten-year-old with a different last name. All but Dade were listed as white. John Glessner, a Black man born 1845 in Virginia, was listed as "living in family" with a thirty-seven-year-old white man named Charles Gallett and his wife, Lydia; three children who were six years, four years, and five months old; and an elder family member, all white.

All these Black residents of 1870 Wisconsin probably assisted in the hop harvest, picking hops, pulling hop poles, or hosting a crew of hired hop pickers, given that they all lived in households that reported hop harvests to the 1870 census enumerators. It is also quite possible that there were more Black Wisconsin residents involved in hops—here I am only able to find the people whom the census recorded as living and working in households where I know hops were grown. The experience of these hop pickers may have more closely resembled Ella Seymour's, as they were picking hops at home, and differed from the experiences of many of the young white women detailed in chapter 5. But these biographies differ starkly from everyone else's in this book. All but Nancy Alcorn (born in New York) and Bertha Alcorn (born ca. 1867) were born in a time and place where slavery was legal, and may have been enslaved until as recently as five years before this census.[22] The archival record is (so far) silent on the experiences of these laborers in these households—whether these were comfortable or exploitative situations, a place of peace and safety or new forms of danger.

WOMEN FARMERS

Based on my analysis of the 1870 census in Wisconsin, the census taker listed ninety white women and one Indigenous woman as sole proprietors of farms with a hop crop in 1869. Thirty-three of these women lived in Sauk County—eleven born in New York, nine born in Germany, six born in England, and the rest from other European countries or other US states.[23] The Wisconsin census rarely assigned the occupation of "farmer" to a woman in 1870, so often these women were listed as "keeping house," but they were the head of a household that grew a measurable quantity of hops—thus, they were hop farmers. For the 1870 Census of Agriculture, I found that 2.5 percent of Wisconsin's hop growers were women, compared with the 1860 census figure of 1.08 percent. Two of the women farmers lived near each other, as their names were adjacent in the agricultural census: Caroline Albert and Laura Wilkinson. Albert's husband had died four years before the census, "of slow consumption."[24] She lived on the farm with her grown son, Augustus Albert, who was married in 1872. Margaret Chris was the youngest of the women farmers, at age twenty-nine; she was a Norwegian immigrant with a seven-year-old daughter named Emma. They were living in the household of a German farming family when the 1870 census was taken. The oldest woman hop farmer in 1870 was supposedly ninety-five, Norwegian-born Mary Thompson. Her household grew 200 pounds of hops that year. This statistic also reminds us to think about what "farming" entails: Owning the land? Profiting from the crops? Doing the physical labor? To the best of my knowledge, not one of these ninety-one women farmers had a living husband.

Nancy Humphrey, for example, grew hops in 1869, after her husband and two daughters died of typhoid fever in 1864. The cluster of family gravestones rests in a tiny cemetery just behind a farmhouse off a country road. I missed the turnoff because it looked like someone's driveway, but on my second pass through I realized I could take a (public) dirt road up alongside the house, the road opening onto a deep green hillside cemetery. I found Nancy's husband and daughters, but not Nancy herself. Some headstones had fallen face down onto the ground after decades of frost and heat, however; perhaps one of those was hers. Some sources credit "Mrs. Humphrey" with the creation of a namesake seedling, including the following history of Reedsburg from 1875:

> To propagate a new variety of hop, is a most difficult matter, on the account of the necessity of combining so many different qualities. A new variety has accidently presented itself at Reedsburg, named by Samuel Ramsey, a hop dealer, the Humphrey Seedling, in honor of Mrs. Humphry [*sic*], who brought it to Reedsburg. Mrs. Humphrey came to her present farm some twenty-six years ago, and planted the seed in Walworth County, Wisconsin, from which this new variety sprung. On coming to Reedsburg, she brought a root with her, and planted it by

> her door, and used the hops for domestic purposes for fifteen years, not knowing the difference from the common kind, excepting the fact of its being from ten days to two weeks earlier. This new variety combines in itself, all the elements of a very choice hop, besides being as ready to pick 20th of August, as common kind is 1st of September. The vine is hardy, a vigorous grower, arming out from top to bottom, has not been as subject to depredations of insects as common variety. The hop itself is small, of very fine and silky texture, in compact clusters, slightly Bavarian in flavor, aroma existing somewhat in other parts of the hop plant than in lupuline, similar to Bavarian—strength exceedingly good and flavor very fine. . . . They are much sought after, and give satisfaction above common kind to dealer and brewer.[25]

An 1894 source credits a Mr. Humphrey in Waterville, New York with the creation of the Humphrey seedling.[26] Yet a 1909 volume on hops brings the origin back to Wisconsin, and presumably to Nancy: "About a week earlier in ripening is Humphrey's Seedling, originated by chance in Wisconsin, which is being grown quite extensively. It is a good grower, but sometimes yields lighter weight hops than Cluster, lice are very partial to it and the yield is sometimes cut by a hot, dry spell coming just as the hops are in burr."[27] I corresponded with hop expert Stan Hieronymus as we tried to determine which sources might be most accurate. Although our findings have so far been inconclusive, the level of detail in the 1875 account is compelling, as it is the closest to the actual events in question.

The 1870 census lists all but one of these women hop farmers as "white," the sole exception being Mary Walsworth, whom the census categorized as "Indian" and whom other sources identify as Menominee.[28] She raised 1,000 pounds of hops in 1869, a substantial commercial harvest. Mary Walsworth, Nancy Humphrey, and the other women farmers suffered the vagaries of the post-1867 harvests as well, and likely even more women farmers had been growing even more hops before the 1869 harvest but had, like so many others, grubbed up their hop fields and either ended or scaled back production to focus on more lucrative crops.

INTO THE 1870S

By November 1869, prices were improving a little in Sauk County, where dealers paid twenty to twenty-three cents a pound for 1869 hops, in part attributable to global shortfalls, but nothing close to the glory days of 1867: "It is said to be an incontrovertible fact that the world was never so short of good hops as now; England has produced only one-third of a crop, and Germany, which until now has been able to export 125,000 to 150,000 bales per annum is an importer, and has sent heavy orders for hops to New York city. . . . American brewers have been laying back on old hops hoping to beat down prices, but the season for brewing stock beer is at hand, and they must buy."[29]

The real end to commercial Wisconsin hops came later, as the 1870s saw continued hop production, with fluctuations in prices and harvest, but nothing like the near-vertical free fall of 1868. By 1870, Jefferson County—once a dominant hop-growing county—already had half as much acreage as it had at its high point.[30] People who had diversified their crops or their careers fared better than those who had bet all on hops. Many of those people had other occupations, and the census is full of pharmacists and other tradesmen planting hops: "One of my uncles went broke in the shambles of the low-price seasons, but happily for him, it was a sideline to his regular vocation as a grist miller."[31] Many German farmers of Sauk County fared better than others because they had planted more measured quantities of hops.[32] Farmers with livestock were in a better position to give their hop plants the fertilizer the plants craved.

Price volatility continued in the 1870s, and the established patterns of hiring outside hop pickers continued as well, just not to the same degree as they had in 1866–68: "Some lots have been refused on account of mildew and poor drying, and others have been sold at rates that would hardly pay for picking. Many farmers are entirely discouraged, and will never raise another hop."[33] Newspapermen, dealers, and farmers scanned the fields to try to predict whether money would be lost or made, and the rollercoaster continued. The year 1871 saw failures in England and Germany, to the benefit of farmers in Wisconsin and New York.[34] Navigating these twists and turns had to have been nerve-wracking. By 1871, fully half the Wisconsin hop fields had been plowed under.[35] This contraction in acreage helped calm prices, as did various failures in England and continental Europe. As one observer noted, "The prices were stabilized at ten cents a pound in 1871, and some [farmers] continued to raise hops for a time, but the day of lighting cigars with ten dollar bills was past."[36]

When prices rebounded a bit, as happened in 1873, many observers advised caution, as did the *Reedsburg Free Press*: "We would, in conclusion, again advise our Wisconsin growers not to get excited, seeing hops are again selling for 50 [cents per pound] in our market. Remember the disaster of 1868, increase your acreage only as increased consumption would appear to warrant. . . . Pay no attention to the bablerdash . . . about quality, which we assure you is entirely satisfactory to Brewers; cultivate your yards carefully; allow your hops to ripen on the pole; pick cleanly; dry carefully; bale neatly; and sell early."[37]

As hard as the 1870s were for many hop growers, the Weaver family found ways to prosper, despite (or at times because of) the ups and downs of the hop market, as several of its members became hop dealers. They dealt not only in the Wisconsin hops of their neighbors but eventually in New York and West Coast hops as well. James Weaver's son Richard planted his crops in what is now the Sussex Heights neighborhood, north of Main Street. Richard and James joined to form a hop dealership in 1860, although James retired a few years later.[38] Clerks recorded the Weaver name throughout the ledgers of Blatz and Best/Pabst. Richard eventually became a millionaire through his hop dealing. These kinds of riches were a distant dream (if also a goal) in the late 1830s. But by 1879, "Mr. Richard Weaver, accompanied by his wife, went to the Pacific Slope, visiting San Francisco, Oakland, Sacramento, Placerville, the mining camps, Portland, Salem, Eugene City, and making a trip the entire length of the Willamette Valley. The object of the trip was to purchase hops. Mr. Weaver bought some fifteen car loads at a cost of $28,000, being the first to ship from that section direct to the breweries at Milwaukee."[39] Richard Weaver later had the good fortune to learn of hop crop failures in the eastern US and Europe via telegraph in 1882. He immediately bought "all he could of the Wisconsin, Missouri and Washington state hops for 15 cents a pound, and when the world realized the crop failure, he had the majority of what was available. Richard had a small corner on the world supply and sold it at $1 a pound making a reported $600,000 in 90 days."[40]

Even though "a large proportion of the yards were plowed under in 1870," pickers continued to head to the fields at harvest time, catching the eye of local journalists, just not in the same numbers.[41] In August 1870, one newspaper reported, "loads of hop-pickers are daily passing through the city [of Watertown] on their way to the hop-growing region northwest of us. They are mostly bright young girls, full of fun and vivacity."[42] In September 1872, another paper reported that the hop fields were "alive with calico dresses all over the county. The crop is reported excellent. The weather has been favorable, and we have heard no complaints of mildew nor the hop louse."[43] Likewise, "The Sparta *Republican* says hop yards in that vicinity present an animated appearance this week, as each can boast of a congregation of women of sufficient magnitude to form a respectable sized woman's rights convention. . . . The Mauston *Star* says in almost every yard the pickers are busy."[44]

While many of the pickers continued to be white women, Ho-Chunk pickers continued to work the hop fields as well. In 1873, the *Milwaukee Sentinel* reporter Frank Moore wrote of Ho-Chunk residents' mix of highly successful hunting, trapping, and fishing, with money earned from "picking hops, picking huckleberries and picking cranberries."[45] Elsewhere Moore reported that "each September they [the Wisconsin Ho-Chunk] engaged in picking hops and cranberries. Some of them also worked as lumbermen where they were doing well."[46] A few months after Ella Seymour began to keep her diary, the US government made what turned out to be its final effort (after four decades of attempts) to forcibly remove her Ho-Chunk neighbors from their homes. As described in Stephen Kantrowitz's twenty-first-century history, "At the end of [1873] US soldiers ventured into the frozen Wisconsin woods to capture and expel the state's remaining Ho-Chunk bands. . . . Troops surrounded their winter encampments, took hundreds of people prisoner, drove them to nearby railheads, and deported them to a reservation in eastern Nebraska. Like every prior forced removal, this one brought suffering and death to hundreds of Ho-Chunk people. These losses remain seared into the memory of today's Ho-Chunk communities. But just as with every previous attempt to exile them, Ho-Chunks refused, resisted, and returned."[47]

As the Ho-Chunk leader Spoon Decorah explained in an account published by the State Historical Society of Wisconsin in 1895, "Life on the reservation is hard. The [Ho-Chunk] in Wisconsin do not want to go there. They want to die on their own land. They like best the streams and woods where their fathers and uncles have always hunted and trapped."[48] In 1873, many of these streams ran alongside acres of hop fields, among many other crops, and many of the young trees in these woods had been felled by farmers and other lumbermen for use in the hop fields.[49] The US Army imprisoned Ho-Chunk people against their will in the hop house of Herman Greve, the hop farmer mentioned in chapter 6 who had employed hundreds of Ho-Chunk hop pickers.[50] Adam King theorizes that one reason behind this comparatively late attempt at forcing Ho-Chunk people off of their land, after many years of economic and social interdependence of Ho-Chunk and settler communities, was the growing interest among a handful of investors in the profitability of Ho-Chunk cranberry bogs.[51] These events took place side by side—the army forcing Ho-Chunk families onto trains and into a hop house, not far from where Ella wrote her diary, and the annual activity in fields and barns where pickers cheerfully gathered.

Along with their custom of hiring young white women, New York farmers had at times hired Indigenous pickers: "Farmers welcome[d] [Haudenosaunee] from the Onondaga Reservation as pickers because they brought their own provisions, kept to themselves, and worked for low wages, but they made up a very limited portion of the available workforce. Beginning in the 1870s, male and female hoboes collected in large numbers during haying season and stayed through the hops harvest."[52] So in the 1870s, the labor force in New York was changing, with many more itinerant laborers whom many farmers were less willing to bring into their homes.[53] These workers did not receive the same level of hospitality the young white women had enjoyed: "Sometimes farmers housed workers in dormitories away from the farmhouse if they distrusted the urban folks, and hoboes were left to fend for themselves. Farmers rarely served alcohol or beer to their workers, offering water or lemonade instead." In other words, the role of the family home in hop picking shifted in New York—less hosting, fewer dances—with the rise of migrant labor.[54]

The archival sources I found captured only a fraction of hop pickers, whether Indigenous or not, in part because they were so rarely listed as hop pickers. These records differ from many I found in the California census, where I came across pages full of people whom the enumerator listed as hop pickers. Mainly I have seen this identification for Chinese men living in boardinghouses or bunkhouses, as on a page of the 1870 population census where the census taker worked his way through the entire boardinghouse writing down names and occupations on August 29, a moment when everyone he asked was engaged in hop picking.[55] For many people, hop picking fit into the much larger and longer span of a given individual's career and life course—a youthful adventure or an urgent part of the patchwork of making ends meet, and much less of an occupational identity than, say, "farmer" or "domestic," at least in the eyes of the census takers. The demographics of hop picking changed depending on era and location. As the West Coast became an increasingly serious contender in the global hop market, growers in the states of California, Oregon, and Washington relied on a far more heterogeneous picking force than Wisconsin did. The West Coast hop industry in the nineteenth and early twentieth centuries depended on the labor of Indigenous families, Anglo families, Chinese men, Japanese men, and at times Filipino men, as well as some crews of young white women, and later Italian and Portuguese pickers (sometimes families, sometimes solitary men). As noted in chapter 3, out West pickers often lived in barracks or boardinghouses, or they camped near the fields and provisioned themselves, and many moved from crop to crop—a very different pattern from Wisconsin's merchants' daughters, maidservants, and seamstresses heading to the hop fields for a few weeks a year.[56]

ELLA AT WORK

Silas Seymour still found hops profitable enough to bring in outside pickers in the early 1870s. At this point Ella was fully involved in her household's hop-picking endeavors, as both a picker and a hostess. As brief as Ella's diary entries were, they contain a rare glimpse inside the house and inside the daily life of hop pickers, and especially the work of hosting, as well as hints at the intimacy of having so many people under one roof. Ella's diary contains multitudes—rich lists of fruits gathered from the forest and visitors to their tidy home, and the wild swings between scorching heat and frigid temperatures that make up Wisconsin weather to this day. She mentioned Silas stacking wheat, in quite a rush before the hop harvest started. Ella's diary implied that the Seymour family's pickers were young and female. Three days after the pickers arrived in 1873, Ella wrote that "many of the girls are half sick, and Ma is nearly tired out, Pa . . . got a man to pull poles." On August 30, it "rained so as to prevent the girls from picking some of the time." On September 1, the work continued: "We had a busy day . . . us girls went down to the hopyard after we finished the supper dishes." It wasn't *all* work for Ella, however—on September 2, someone taught her a new way to braid her hair, and "when I went upstairs, the girls [the hop pickers] went into ecstasies over the length of my hair." This passage also suggests that the pickers slept in the upstairs bedrooms, fitted out with all the bedsteads that Ella's family had assembled before Silas headed to the station to pick up all the girls.

A few days later, Ella and her sister Ida's work on the hop harvest continued: "Ida picked hops this A.M., Ida & I in the P.M. The yard was finished about five oclock. I got about 1½ boxes." Whenever they weren't helping their mother with chores inside the house, they were out picking, contributing the work of their bodies to Silas's efforts to squeeze every possible penny out of his hopyard. On September 6, as we saw in the prologue, "the pickers started for home early, so all the hurry and bustle is ended for the season. P.M. The beds are down the floors are mopped, & we can breathe more freely. Windows cleaned also." The next day it was nearly "cold enough for a frost."

That is how Wisconsin rolls—some autumns linger on, others give way so quickly to winter that it makes our heads spin. I have made several excursions to Ella country, albeit without actually setting foot on the property or disturbing the current owners. These visits happened in the summer or early fall, and each time I found the landscape so beautiful. By September, stretches of this state become burnished, golden in ways they aren't in July, almost finished with the whirlwind of reproduction that is the short Midwestern summer. Some of what I see is what it would have looked like to the hop pickers. They may have had glorious sunshine, cool overcast days, sudden changes of temperature, and swarms of mosquitoes or gnats. On one September visit, a frost had been unimaginable even a week earlier. But that September day, driving past the drying prairie grasses, the glowing goldenrod, the trees just glossed with a tiny bit of yellow, the change of season was indeed imaginable.

Returning to Ella's story in 1873, as a chill fell over the land, on September 9, Silas found out what that year's hop harvest would bring him—forty-five cents per pound, an impressive amount. With this good news on everybody's mind, Ella and her mother and sister spent the day ironing and putting down carpet. Note that Silas found out the price before he had even pressed the hops—Ella recorded the pressing finishing up on September 18. On September 21, their neighbor "A. Cottington" (I assume Amos, the son of Jesse and Rebecca) "called to look at the hops." The hops picked on the Seymour farm traveled first to the drying house, then to the railroad depot, and then presumably eastward along the network of railroad tracks to Milwaukee, or other towns and cities.

In May 1874, Ella made the first reference to hops of the new growing season: "Mr. Vant is here shearing sheep today. Ida is tying hops. They are not all polled yet." Perhaps a bit ironically, Ella and Ida attended a Fourth of July picnic that year where they signed a temperance pledge. Week after week that summer they picked quart upon quart of blackberries, and around August 25, preparations began in earnest for the hop pickers' arrival: "Ma, with Ida's and Walter's help cleaned the kitchen chamber, ready for hop picking." Meanwhile, Silas was sowing his winter wheat. On August 31, he left to pick up the hop pickers, and the next day the "hop pickers came just dusk." On September 2, Ida picked hops, and the next day Ella picked 1½ boxes. On September 4, Ella wrote, "I was going to do better picking hops today, but it rained so I had to come to the house about two oclock." The next day she and Ida picked from two o'clock in the afternoon until sunset. On September 6, "one of our last years hop pickers was here today. Twas Katie O. Conel. Some of the girls went to Reedsburg." By September 10, "we got done picking hops last night just supper time. Lon started this A.M to take the pickers home. I picked just seven boxes." Once again, within days of concluding hop picking, the temperature dropped to nearly a frost. While I can't say for certain which brewery bought up Ella's seven boxes of hops, I know her father sold to the Cottingtons (father and son), and that the Cottingtons sold to Valentin Blatz's brewery as early as 1863. The dealers in her neighborhood conducted business with Best Brewery, the predecessor to Pabst, and with Valentin Blatz in Ella's lifetime. Some of Ella's hops may have passed into kettles still lurking in the city of Milwaukee or through narrow lanes flanked by buildings made of Milwaukee's characteristic pale yellow brick, known as Cream City brick, or boarded a ship or a train headed out of state.

In late September 1874, the hop fields grew quiet. Hop picking and its attendant chores were the work of a few weeks at the end of the summer, one brief moment in a cycle of tending plants that closely follows the orbit of the earth around the sun. In so many households, there was such an intimacy to hop picking. All these strangers were given beds inside the house, with little privacy, and ate either at the family table or, as in the case of the Seymours, in the kitchen extension built especially for this purpose. Some of these elements are what made it fun for many of the pickers. These few weeks may have felt like an extended sleepover, a chance to socialize with peers and away from the possibly watchful eyes of parents. The profitability of the hop endeavor rests on these small domestic interactions. The small gets us to the big. These figures in the census or the hop reports in newspapers translated into millions of hop cones, each picked by hand from the lengthy bines, and thousands of straw ticks, pillowcases, and dinner plates. Far-off beer drinkers shaped the rhythms of these families and the land around them.

Ella's diary records the weaving of the work of the hop harvest into the broader rhythms of daily life. The diary recounts an array of visitors throughout the year, some overnight and some just for the day or the afternoon, some more welcome than others. Ella and Ida and their parents went visiting as well, and both Ella and Ida pursued their teaching certificates. In Ida's case, this pursuit ended in tragedy (we'll get to that in chapter 8), and Ella's diary provides an unceasing account of illness. Family members frequently fell ill, sometimes gravely, at other times more mildly, suffering from a toothache or insomnia. Sometimes they had unspecified ailments; other times they contracted familiar diseases such as mumps. Ida and brother Merton had mumps in February 1874 but fared well. That same cold month, Ella wrote with horror of the sudden death of a neighbor, age-mate, and presumably friend, Agnes Montross Pelton, a young newlywed: "Just one year ago she stood a happy bride in the home [the Seymours'] that now awaits her coming in such a different manner. Feb. 21 Elvira B. & I watched with the corpse, a thing I never did before in my life. . . . [She] was dressed in her bridal dress."[57] It's possible that Ella had known Agnes all her life, as they were about the same age, and the Montross farm (of Agnes's parents) was one of the closest farms to the Seymours.' It's possible that mumps was raging in the village and is what took this young bride, although the fatality rate of mumps is very low, compared with so many of the other diseases circulating at the time.

Sorrow and joy run through the pages of Ella's diary. One of her seasonal joys was clearly fresh fruit and garden vegetables, objects that receive much ink on the pages of her diary. Over the course of the time Ella kept her diary, she picked raspberries, currants, string beans, green corn, transcendants (a type of crabapple), wild strawberries, green peas, cultivated strawberries, asparagus, blackberries, sweet corn, onions, apples, potatoes, and cabbages, among other fruits and vegetables—some in their garden, some in the nearby forest. This family loved their fruit! For thirty years they wrote letters and diaries about fruit, gorged themselves when favorites were in season, shared seeds, gathered from the forests, and accepted gifts of peaches and quince. On top of other chores, Ella's diary and other documents describe the women of the family sewing and knitting constantly, using wool from their own sheep and spun by their mother.[58] Ella's diary offers a glimpse of the ways her family had changed the landscape they inhabited—the hop fields, wheat fields, vegetable garden, pastures, even the house built from timbers drawn out of nearby forests. Silas and his family didn't just inhabit a landscape, they made a landscape with the labor of their bodies and the labor of hired hands.

BREWING AND GROWING

During the time when Ella kept her diary, many of the breweries of Milwaukee and other cities were experiencing ongoing growth and continuing to use hops from different places, not only from several dealers in and around Kilbourn City but also a farmer in Greenfield (very close to Milwaukee) and several New York dealers, one named Simon Uhlmann, plus another dealer in Cooperstown.[59] In 1873, many Wisconsin hopyards failed to yield as a result of widespread winterkill after a heavy winter.[60] The harm to the fields helped contribute to higher prices for the farmers whose crops survived.[61] In an 1873 letter to his cousin, James Weaver wrote from Waukesha County, "You must tell Henry that our hops in this state are badly winter killed that his old yard and hops are a going to be pruty well use up this year in this country so we look for a good price this year agine if there his a good crop as the Germans beat the English."[62]

In 1874, the *Wisconsin State Journal,* in a statement as overconfident as it was incorrect, proclaimed that "it is safe to say that hop culture will not decline in this region."[63] This is the period when hop grower David Small left a comparatively detailed record of his hop growing, noting the dates of picking and the size of harvest, although interestingly without mention of who did the picking.[64] In 1875, Wisconsin and New York were still producing 75 to 80 percent of the US crop.[65]

Other states had a go at hop cultivation, even Kansas, Kentucky, and Missouri.[66] With the intensity of competition, the importance of clean picking and efficient drying only increased. The dealer Richard Weaver chided farmers about properly picking and drying their hops, as they were competing with the clean-picked hops of England and Germany. Sometimes, however, clean picking was irrelevant, as when a rare August frost "fatally ruin[ed]" the crop in Clark County, Wisconsin, in 1875.[67]

In the early 1870s, Schlitz was brewing more than 50,000 barrels each year. Founder Joseph Schlitz died in a shipwreck in 1875, at which point his step-nephews the Uihleins took over.[68] By 1868, the future Pabst was the largest brewer in Milwaukee and remained in that position until the end of the century (Phillip Best Brewing Company did not become Pabst until 1889).[69] In 1874, the brewery that would later become Pabst brewed 100,000 barrels of beer, which would have required at the very least 100,000 pounds of hops.[70] Schlitz brewed a mere 250 barrels in 1850 (at which point the brewery was known as Krug), 49,623 barrels in 1873, and half a million barrels by 1886—just remarkable rates of growth.[71] These quantities of beer demanded an immense workforce, including the brewers themselves as well as the maltsters, coopers, teamsters, engineers, and chemists, all of whom busied themselves with turning the raw materials into barrels of beer. Like its sister cities across the Midwest, Milwaukee in its taverns and beer gardens served keg after keg to thirsty customers. German families gathered in the beer gardens of the city.[72] Workers gathered in the taverns after their shifts in the tanneries and mills. Taverns such as Puddlers Hall, built in 1872 as a union hall and drinking spot for the "puddlers" who worked the nearby blast furnaces, were ready customers for the barrels of beer sent out across the city from local breweries.[73]

The surviving brewers' ledgers and newspaper reports on hop markets give ample evidence of brewers buying from Wisconsin, New York, England, and Bavaria, in varying quantities.[74] Even when there was a glut of Wisconsin hops, brewers continued to buy from both Wisconsin and far-off places. They balanced any additional cost of something like freight with the fact that the prices of faraway hops—even with ocean freight on an Atlantic journey, and the risk that a bale might be damaged by seawater (an event recorded in the ledgers)—might, in a given week or month, be better than the prices of Wisconsin hops, or the hops might be of better quality, or both.[75] In the last ten days of 1873, Valentin Blatz spent $10,000 (in gold) on a single shipment of hops bought through the Scharrer and Sons hop dealers on the Nuremberg hop market, and also spent $1,000 on hops from two farmers in Wisconsin.[76] In March 1874, Blatz bought 103 bales of hops from the small Bavarian town of Spalt, spending more than $13,000 in gold. That same year, he bought hops from Portage, Wisconsin, from New York, and from the hop market in Nuremberg. He also purchased two bales of hops from a neighbor of the Weavers, Alfred Frost, in Sussex, Wisconsin.

The ledgers reflect both flexibility and variation, as the global quality of the hop market and the entrenched networks of dealers and shipping routes gave brewers many options in response to gluts or shortages, as well as changes in demand from their own customers. And although there were times when brewers laid in hops for much of the year's brewing needs, there is also plentiful evidence that they would, at times, wait out the market, holding out for lower prices on hops they wanted but maybe didn't need quite yet. Transport costs did not necessarily prevent brewers from seeking out hops in distant markets, including those in Germany and England. Aside from the fact that a barrel of beer needs only 1–2 pounds of hops (so the sizes of shipments for a given brewery were just a fraction of the barley, corn, wheat, and rice they needed with respect to weight), brewers absolutely had preferences for specific hops, and the fluctuation in prices was so wild from one year (or even month or week) to the next that transport costs were at times a minuscule component of the cost. The costs often had to do with (presumed) quality. The remaining ledgers of the Milwaukee breweries indicate brewers using multiple sources of hops in any given year—some hop growers in Sauk County providing local varieties; Waukesha County dealers selling hops from all over; Frederick Miller contracting with one particular farmer; Valentin Blatz buying from the Cottington household as well as from John

Eddy and David Wilber.[77] Ledgers listed hops from Germany, from New York, eventually from California, and from Wisconsin. And US hops continued to find their way to ports and breweries around the world.

It may be surprising that New York hops (usually Cluster or a close relative) could apparently be swapped out for Wisconsin, English, or German hops, but based on the ledgers and the newspaper reporting, that is, at times, exactly what happened. It is entirely likely that Valentin Blatz's purchase of so many bales of Bavarian hops ended up in particular beers, and at particular points in the brew (at the end of the boil rather than the beginning), and I am not at all suggesting that brewers were indifferent to the origins or varieties of their hops. But the use of a range of hops from a range of places, even at breweries that were primarily brewing lager, is undeniable. Freight prices were just one consideration among many, and certainly Val Blatz was willing to pay a premium for Bavarian hops while also buying up large quantities of Wisconsin and New York hops *simultaneously*. From the outside, without access to their explanations of the process, I would think they were making their hop purchasing decisions based on an ever-changing balance of variables: price, but also quality (quite distinct from much of today's understanding of hop quality), region, age (new or old, yearlings or even two-year-olds), and sometimes variety—although through the 1870s hop variety name rarely appears in newspaper coverage or in the ledgers, but the city or state where the hops were grown appears frequently, and Val Blatz went out of his way to buy hops from Spalt and Nuremberg along with New York and Wisconsin hops.

By the late 1870s, much of Wisconsin's hop industry was shrinking, and consolidating, to the point that many counties that once grew hops didn't have a single hopyard, and to the point that some farmers once again left hops unpicked in the field because the picking would have cost more than the hops were worth.[78] In Richland County, also a once dominant hop-growing county, the commissioner of agriculture reported that "the yards will be nearly plowed up in 1879; the crop of 1878 was a total failure; prices below cost of production." The in-

FIGURE 7.1. Hop pickers. Original photo caption: "Hop harvesters, mostly female, stand with hops, probably on the farm of Knudt Heimdal. Many of the harvesters have hop wreaths on their heads. Two men with hats lie in front of the group. The brim of the man on the left is decorated with hops. Note the shadow of Andreas Larsen Dahl in the foreground." Created in 1879 by Andreas Larsen Dahl. Deerfield, Dane County, Wisconsin. Wisconsin Historical Society, W011O6Z.

dustry experienced lice, storms, "an unknown worm," winterkill, and other issues; and exports of hops dropped in correspondingly drastic fashion.[79] But according to Laura Paine's examination of the hops era, "Some [farmers], however, continued raising [hops], a few even planting new yards in the 1870s. One such gambler was Knudt Heimdal, a Deerfield farmer who set out a yard in 1874 and reportedly lost money on every crop except his first. He was still raising hops in 1879, when photographer Andreas Dahl captured his harvest on film" (figure 7.1).[80]

In 1879, Wisconsin harvested almost 2 million pounds of hops—it was still the second largest hop-producing state (behind New York, at 21.6 million pounds), despite all the setbacks, but this yield is less than half the harvest of 1869. And California was breathing down Wisconsin's neck at that point, harvesting 1.4 million pounds.[81] By the beginning of the twentieth century, Wisconsin's contribution to the global hop trade had faded into insignificance, even if folks did grow hops here and there, such as at Pabst Farms. As late as 1908, Pabst proudly grew a small portion of its own hops, and the newspapers proudly (and very incorrectly) proclaimed a resurgence in Wisconsin hop cultivation.[82]

This shift in Wisconsin hop growing is visible in the ledgers of Milwaukee's great breweries. By the mid-1880s, for example, Schlitz was buying "about 1,000,000 pounds of hops . . . annually from New York State and the Pacific coast."[83] The ledgers from what would become the Pabst Brewery list purchases of hops from many dealers in New York, as well as dealers in Nuremberg, the location of the main Bavarian hop market.[84] The ebb of Wisconsin's hop culture had no discernible effect on Wisconsin beer production because brewers had long bought hops from multiple sources and had existing links of farmers and dealers to supply them with the hops they needed. The quantities of hops consumed in Milwaukee and Wisconsin brewing continued to rise, but they came from a combination of the older fields of New York and the flourishing new fields of the West Coast, plus imports from England and Germany, even if brewers continued to buy from local farmers as well. Wisconsin was not the only hop-growing region experiencing an ultimately permanent decline in hop production. By the end of the nineteenth century, not only had Wisconsin lost out to the West Coast, but once mighty New York was losing ground to the Pacific Slope.[85] In 1870, Wisconsin brewed 189,664 barrels of beer.[86] By 1876, when the hop boom was becoming a distant memory, Wisconsin brewed 450,508 barrels.[87] In other words, the brewers of the state found plenty of hops with which to brew even with ever fewer Wisconsin hops on the market. Lager brewers at this time also went to great expense and effort to acquire ice. In 1873, Val Blatz spent more than

$6,000 on the ice necessary to his operations.[88] As one recent history of Milwaukee explains, "Until mechanical refrigeration became practical in the 1880s, a reliable source of ice was needed to keep all that beer cool during fermentation, prevent it from spoiling in storage, and allow producers to ship their product by rail."[89] Milwaukee brewers acquired ice from smaller lakes to the west, as well as the Milwaukee River above North Avenue and the nearby Menomonee Valley.[90] In 1880, the breweries of Milwaukee went through 335,000 tons of ice.[91]

The women of Wisconsin's hop industry were essential—until they weren't. The brewers of Milwaukee and beyond did not bat an eyelash at the fall of Wisconsin hops. They had well-established routes to getting other hops. The breweries of Milwaukee ascended into regional, national, and even global success in the 1880s, just as the Wisconsin hop industry was heading into its final ebb. People were buying lager from Milwaukee around the globe.[92]

In many cases, hop farmers began to move on, either slipping off in search of wage labor or turning their farms (if they hadn't lost them in the bust) to sugar beets or tobacco and, eventually and with more success, dairy cattle. "Some of the families who invested so heavily in hops were able to recoup some of their losses by digging and selling the roots of ginseng," as well as by capitalizing on the rise of dairying and the success of milk, butter, and cheese.[93] The failure of hops drove even more farmers to the relative stability of dairy farming, later strengthened by the establishment of land grant university research and agricultural extension programs, although that stability has now come to an end for many farmers in Wisconsin.[94]

That story repeats itself over and over in agriculture. The conundrum of wresting sustenance and money from the interaction of sun, water, soil, and the genetic instructions encoded in seeds and rhizomes comes up again and again. As stalwart as any current agricultural landscape may feel, in many cases, change is on the horizon.

Nineteenth-century hops can instruct us in the taken-for-grantedness of the commodity crops and food plants that surround us. In Wisconsin, the hop industry vanished almost entirely. A few hop houses still stand, and abandoned rhizomes sprout on the edges of fields and streams. A few growers have recently worked to create supplies of local hops in Michigan, New York, and Wisconsin locally-grown hops.[95] But the old hop fields gave way to later eras of agriculture—dairying, corn, and soybeans, depending on the location and microclimate. Each of these fluctuations in markets—competition, oversupply, shifts in consumer demands and tastes—leads to tangible change in the countryside, swapping out wheat for hops or grubbing up hop plants as the prices tumble in the wake of a glut and investing in more dairy cows. Even though hops ultimately faded from Wisconsin, they built on what came before and provided the foundation for what came after. We can witness cycles of boom and bust in all kinds of crops and places, including rubber in the Amazon, cotton in the 1860s across multiple countries, and coffee and cinchona in Sri Lanka. The individual farmers in this book, as well as large-scale enterprises and empires, all seek profitability out of a given landscape and respond to crises with a given crop by abandoning it, doubling down, or seeking additional alternatives to plant alongside. Today's landscape is built on layers of failure and success, experimentation and sticking with tried-and-true approaches.

HOP HOUSES

The boom times left their mark in many ways: the harvesting of tamarack and other saplings to serve as the all-important hop poles, the influx of cash that translated into new barns and even elegant homes (plus well-dressed daughters and shiny carriages), and the annual arrival of first thousands, then tens of thousands of young women to harvest the hops, and the reverse flow of hops back out along the roads and rails and lakes. Another striking effect of the hop boom: the hop houses constructed to dry the hops as quickly as possible after harvest. Hop houses dotted this landscape, yet now they are almost en-

FIGURE 7.2. The former Joseph Spaulding hop house. Photographer unknown, Oak Grove, Dodge County, Wisconsin, 1993. Reference Number 93420, State Historic Preservation Office at the Wisconsin Historical Society.

tirely gone. Unlike the sturdier English versions, most Wisconsin hop houses were made of wood. Some burned to the ground, while others that survived were either dismantled when the hop boom ended or converted into barns or other uses (figure 7.2).[96] According to one history of Sauk County, "The most expensive part of the hopgrower's outfit was the hop-house, affording room for storage and the drying kiln, the heat for which was furnished by huge cast iron heaters, denominated 'hop stoves.' Many of these buildings were quite elaborate, and some of them even pretentious in style and finish. These old hop-houses are yet doing service as granaries or stables, upon many Sauk County farms."[97] Other farmers of the period lacked their own hop house and would use their neighbors' hop houses.[98]

Such buildings checkered much of southern Wisconsin, but today only one remains in a recognizable fashion and publicly marked, although I know of at least one still standing unmarked on private property. The sole remaining hop house in Waukesha County is the Beaumont hop house, built around 1875—well after the initial boom.[99]

The Waukesha County Historical Society put up a marker for the unusual building in 1974. Others likely persist here and there as converted barns, but the 1860s were a long time ago and the barns of Wisconsin tend to have a limited lifespan, battered by blizzards and hailstorms and everything in between. My Wisconsin-born husband was constantly warned about playing in the slowly collapsing barns of his childhood, with a curt "Kids, don't play in the barn!" from his concerned grandmother left in charge of a football team's worth of cousins for weeks each summer. But in their heyday, these hop houses, like the barns of my husband's dairy farming relatives, would have gleamed in the August sun, a sign of success and possibility, new and clean and in good repair.

A few hop houses may still haunt the former hop farms, their timbers adapted to new uses, or even repurposed far beyond the farm, in the trend to use old barnwood as interior decor and furniture. An 1875 map recorded sixteen hop houses in Waukesha County alone, although some authors suggest that would have been an undercount.[100] Many hop houses were built of wood; others used wattle and daub or stone (figure 7.3). They differed quite a bit from the iconic and conical oast houses of England's hop-growing regions, often much more solid structures built to last, and built from the wealth of successful phases of the industry. Wisconsin's hop houses also seem to have disappeared much more thoroughly than the hop houses of New York as well.[101]

Like many of his neighbors, Silas Seymour built a wooden hop house (figure 7.4) in the early 1860s as his hop harvests grew, in order to dry his crop and to avoid having to take the hops to a neighbor's hop house. Based on his ledgers, I believe that Silas built the hop house in 1862. Years later, Silas's granddaughter Ruth Seymour Burmester would write of Silas's son Merton standing "in the sunshine in the old hop house door," long after the hop house had become little more than a storage shed.[102] Decades later, the now useless bedsteads once slept on by the crew of hop pickers were still stowed in the hop house: "What they were being saved for, Mama [Blanche Seymour] wondered, but Papa [Merton Seymour] would not let them

FIGURE 7.3. Original photo caption: "Stone Hop House, built by Dr. Taylor on section 27, Northeast corner of the Town of Greenfield." Photo by Harry Elsworth Cole, Sauk County, Wisconsin, ca. 1908. Wisconsin Historical Society, W012P7Z.

be destroyed. Now and again the children got one down for their playhouse, laid boards across them, put their dolls on them."[103] The family used the hop house to stash old furniture and toys, abandoned butter-making gear, and other items: "The butter churn, too, at length, was carried up the stairs in the hop house . . . and put in the little-used east end. Here stood Mary Ann's old spinning wheel, the yarn reel, the long skimming-pan rack, the massive old clothes wringer, the grain cradles and flails used by Silas, the broken ox yoke. And, dry and rocking unevenly on its worn pine rockers, cluttered with gunny sacks and mice-gnawed corn cobs and shriveled butternuts, the old Connecticut cradle, Abigail Bates' cradle, which had been Merton's baby bed," and Ella's baby bed as well.[104]

Later on, Merton piled up old machinery around the hop house to protect it from the pigs. But the hop house eventually returned to

FIGURE 7.4. The Hop House, at Silas Seymour's farm, date unknown (possibly mid-1900s). Ruth Seymour Burmester, *A Barn on the Place* (1996), 1-37.

the earth whence it came. When Burmester went to see the property on a birthday drive later in her life, she found "a couple of piles of black dirt . . . near the old woodpile site, and near the back door. They scooped out the place where they dug a 'grave' for the old hop house and wrecked buildings."[105] That old hop house is emblematic of the whole process I am analyzing. A building once at the top of its game became a moldering shed where the successive generations stored the obsolete gear of their parents and grandparents. The trappings of fecundity and hard physical work: a cradle, a spinning wheel, threshing tools, and a butter churn all lost their relevance until eventually the new owners dismantled the hop house and buried it in the earth.[106] The slow changes in buildings and inhabitants become visible in the overlay of documents, maps, and Google Earth that I used to trace this story through time. The surface of the land changes, alternately covered in hops or wheat and housing a succession of buildings that rise and fall. Above all this, in the bur oaks and the Norway spruce and the butternut trees, the winds sweep up the hills and down the valleys, and in the earth where old buildings decompose, substrata rest and shift, the worms and grubs and mycorrhizae go about their business, and old hop roots slumber on the edges of the new fields of today's crops. The Seymour hop house and its compatriots are a metaphor of sorts, the fading traces of a once dominant industry—some burned to the ground, some buried long ago, others hiding in plain sight as parts of barns or other outbuildings.

8

DEATH AND REBIRTH IN THE WISCONSIN COUNTRYSIDE

In the summer of 1876, Ella Seymour gathered twenty-six varieties of flowers from her family's garden to mark her twenty-fourth birthday. In reflecting on the occasion, she wrote ominously, "this summer my health is poor, and life is not all pleasure." In the same document, she recounted the heartbreaking death of her beloved sister Ida: "A sister came to be my playmate in childhood and my companion in youth. For twenty-one years she was my better half, shielding me from many hard knocks along our pathway of life," including protecting her from some of the cruelty of strangers' reactions to Ella's curved spine. "Last April [27, 1876] she journeyed to that home beyond the River. . . . Words can never tell how much she is missed."[1] The only explanation I have found of Ida's cause of death is unsurprisingly cryptic: "Ida was to begin her first term of teaching, got her feet wet, took cold, died of brain fever."[2] As Ella and Ida's grandniece Ruth Burmester wrote, imagining Ella's reaction, "Lovely young Ida, lifeless, cold. Oh no, it is a horrible nightmare! She waked in the night to cry, a nightmare. . . . The older girl felt bad to see her mother suffer, she knowing lonesomeness, too, but when four years later, her gentle spirit sought release from her . . . body, said to her, 'Dear mother, you must not grieve for me as you have for Ida.'"[3] There were oval pictures of Ella and Ida on the "south wall of the living room" in walnut frames: "Between them a motto, done in cross-stitch . . . it was the handiwork of Ella, made after Ida's

FIGURE 8.1. Original photo caption: "Hop Pickers posing by stands of harvested hops." Unknown photographer, Caledonia, Racine County, Wisconsin, ca. 1895. Wisconsin Historical Society, W012AQ7.

death. MANY A CLOUD HATH A SILVER LINING."[4] Ella herself soon followed Ida, passing on to join her sister on November 25, 1880, at the age of twenty-eight.

Ella and Ida and thousands of women like them made it possible for barrel after barrel of beer to be brewed. The brewers and their customers created a demand for Ella's labor and directly altered the prairies and swamps of Wisconsin, as replacements for wheat crops or on newly broken land and in the felling of saplings for millions of hop poles. Ella's story is singular, yet it reverberates across countless households of hop growers (figure 8.1). Elements of her story repeat dozens, hundreds, even thousands of times. Cycles of harvest, chores, illness, childbirth, and death. Ella was one point in a global system as the growing taste for beer in general and lager in particular transformed river valleys and villages. Ella and her role in the global industry call on us to more closely examine the landscapes we inhabit, to look for the people whose stories may dwell beneath the surface, haunt the corners of libraries and archives, or remain in the private memories of descendants.

The two most prevalent remnants of Wisconsin's hop industry rest beneath the surface of the earth, one alive and one dead. Every subject of this book is dead, and many of their bodies lie under the earth in Sauk County, Wisconsin. I sought out the graves of the hop farmers and their kin, moldering in that same earth. I was usually the lone visitor at each cemetery I saw, pacing through headstones on incomparably gorgeous summer days, or stomping through a deep March snow. The sun beat upon my shoulders as I towered above a small flat stone, its edges hidden beneath the thick cemetery grass, a single word carved into the granite: *Ella*. Nearby, an obelisk lists the Seymour family names, and just beyond it is an identical flat stone, reading *Ida*. The graves of hop farmers cluster together, reminiscent of the proximity of the records of their harvest in the handwritten pages of the US Census Bureau's decennial Census of Agriculture housed in the Wisconsin Historical Society Archives, and their farms stood shoulder to shoulder. There is physical proximity in the cemetery, although the burials (and at times the farms) are further subdivided by religion—a Lutheran cemetery full of German names, a Quaker cemetery that was the final resting place of a hop farmer who was also a vocal abolitionist, known for decrying not only slavery but also any Northerner who supported it.[5] As I stood in the Greenwood Cemetery in Reedsburg, in Sauk County, bones and cloth and wood decomposed quietly beneath my feet.

But not far from the lush green cemeteries, tangles of hop roots send out shoots every spring, decade after decade. Nearby the descendants and distant relatives of the hops those farmers planted a century and a half ago wind up the trees on the edges of the fields of corn and soybeans. Just as I looked for the headstones, I went in search of the hop roots coiling in the earth. The tendrils of these stories still curl through archives, databases, and local historical societies just as the hop rhizomes still lurk in the soil. The time I have spent in archives, cemeteries, and fields tells me that we are always in the middle of agricultural flux. We may not notice it. If we are lucky, our food (and drink) supply is stable, seemingly impervious to fluctuations in weather or pests or available arable land. One of the things that forgotten hop fields tell us, however, is that we cannot take the current arrangement of agricultural land uses for granted. These patterns have changed dramatically in the past, and they will change again in the future. The causes may vary: new regulations, new technologies that consume or conserve water and energy, changes in tastes or disposable income, wildfire, blight, and climate change, among others. These changes are not a part of some inevitable evolution but the result of a mix of struggles (over space and resources) and innovation, the pursuit of pleasure and the pursuit of profit. Even when longer eras of stability arrive, such as dairy in Wisconsin or hops in the Pacific Northwest, change may still be on the horizon.

One of the things I have learned from writing this book is that it does matter to leave messages for future generations. It matters to talk to the future, and in ways we'll never know. I gather up fragments of information from archives and landscapes because they are all I have to understand not only the past but also our place in the ongoing flow of time and change. What remnants are we leaving for the future? What will our descendants know of us in a century or two?

The things we consume leave marks on the earth and, sometimes, in the archive. Our sustenance comes from the earth, and so do our pleasures, like beer. The immense quantities of beer produced and consumed in the second half of the nineteenth century have left their mark across Milwaukee and other brewing capitals. Many of the old breweries still stand today, occupying whole city blocks and repurposed as condos, hotels, or offices. Former *tied houses* connected to the breweries—taverns with an obligation to sell that brewery's beer, sometimes owned by the brewery itself—still shape the cityscape with distinct architectural features, such as the ubiquitous Schlitz globe still seen above corner taverns today, despite the long ago demise of the tied house regime.[6] At a dentist appointment in the final days of writing this book, I looked out the seventh-floor window and saw at least three breweries, two dating back to the nineteenth century, the other one of the first brewpubs in town. The city still speaks of its beery past and looks toward the future. The rapid growth in nineteenth-century beer production affected both the urban landscapes of the Midwest's cities and the rural landscapes that produced the raw materials, including grain and hops. When a Milwaukee ironworker drank a lager at the bar in Puddlers Hall in the nineteenth century, or when I crack open a maibock on my porch on the first nice day of the year, we all are drinking a landscape.

Beer did indeed make Milwaukee famous, and at key moments in its development, brewers relied on the labor of women and girls for their hops. Women were central, as hop pickers and hostesses, to the successes of the breweries whose names we still know today. This book is, in part, a history of their success. The story of Wisconsin hops reveals the broader fact of consumers affecting landscapes and laborscapes. You, too, may walk among ghosts, beer-related or not, on any given day. Keep an eye out for them, search for them yourself, listen to the people who speak with and for the ghosts. You can use my methods and the methods of others to study the ghosts elsewhere. Several families, including Ella's, have left an outsize archival presence that allows me to take a deeper look at these questions. This is a fluke. Most of the people shaping this space and this plant left no such remnants. Ella and her relatives have left us letters, ledgers and account books, a diary, scraps of embroidery, typed-up texts of speeches and recollections, and even a self-published book that all help fill in the detail of a hop-growing life. And while I may not have as rich a trove for the other hop growers as I do for Ella and her family, thanks to the Census of Agriculture I do know a few details about every single person listed as a hop farmer from 1850 to 1870, nearly four thousand hop-growing households.

Growing up in California, with schoolteacher parents who enjoyed a good road trip, I was deeply aware of the wildly varying topography between my coastal hometown and the destinations of various family excursions. On school holidays we would pile into the station wagon and drive a few hours to the dry, golden Sierra foothills where my great-great-aunt Annabelle lived, or the plentiful national parks full of towering granite and redwoods, or the sunny suburbs of Los Angeles, swimming in my uncle's Thousand Oaks pool high atop old volcanic land. We drove through the scorching Death Valley and along the precipice of Highway 1 perched above the thundering Pacific Ocean. When I moved to Wisconsin, the landscape appeared comparatively gentle and unchanging. I found a rolling landscape full of dairy farms and a hint of woods somewhere up north, and a chilly lake lapping at the shore near my new home. Driving out on the grid of streets laid out across the state, in search of antique barns and pumpkin patches, and later, after marrying a Wisconsinite, driving past the farms of in-laws and heading deep into the countryside for mammoth family reunions full of strangers, I still mostly saw a landscape far more uniform than the one I grew up in.

But working on this book I acquired an acre-by-acre view of the topography. I began to see it another way. I began to recognize the giant centuries-old bur oaks hidden in the roadside tangle of younger ash and maple. I could see the tamarack swamps, the oak savanna, the stands of birch that all spoke to variations in geological conditions and geopolitics. I noticed the footprint of the glaciers in the drumlins and eskers. I sought instruction from knowledgeable people to understand how what looks like a vacant lot is in fact a prairie remnant and how to peer beneath the overgrowth to see the ancient corn hills and furrows of centuries of cultivation and fire.[7] I learned to read, in a very rudimentary way, the landscape of dying ash trees and dense, aging ironwood. This process has necessarily brought a sobering humility in the face of how much I have yet to learn, and it parallels my experience in the archive. What was once an inscrutable set of documents came into focus as the stories of individuals and communities, yet around the edges I can see the vague outlines of all that I have yet to learn and understand. When I began this work, I had no idea whether I would ever be able to pinpoint the location of a single hopyard. Now I know the identities and locations of thousands of hop farmers, as well as the ways their lives intermingled with the people and places around them, even as so many mysteries remain. I now know so much more about this node in the expansive nineteenth-century network of brewers, hop dealers, and beer drinkers affecting the world far beyond the edge of their beer glass.

Even in a family like the Seymours, with such unique and thorough records that have persisted into the present, there are tremendous gaps that we will never fill. The same will be true of our own lives someday. I move my body through the spaces Ella inhabited. I walk the graveyard where she was laid to rest not long after her beloved sister Ida. I watch the birds arrive and leave with the change of seasons, feel the weather blowing in, almost always from the northwest, and think about the seasons of Ella. The world has changed since she walked the earth in her buttoned-up Victorian boots. The sunsets unfold in a changed hue, the summers are hotter and wetter, when they are not colder and drier. No prairie chickens cross my path. But the hop roots still push up through the cold earth each spring. The raspberries still ripen into jewels in the edges of the nearby forests. I see the glint of woodpeckers in the still-bare trees of April and hear the clatter of sandhill cranes returning from their winter grounds. Each year is different, with varying alterations of the whorls on the earth's surface and the heat maps of the oceans, but as I stood in the cemetery one September day, silver blue clouds slid down from the north, a bit too soon, and I could feel in the air how Ella could write of a frost descending after the last hops were picked.

Wisconsin's nineteenth-century hop pickers worked in the last hot days of the summer, or the first cool days of the fall. At least today, September can come on quickly in Wisconsin. This often-glorious month can see a sweltering day of humidity and cicadas turn into a series of nights with hours of thunder, lightning, and howling winds. There are also peaceful afternoons that wipe away all memory of recent heat waves and all premonitions of the coming winter. The colors are softer everywhere. The goldenrod unfurls in the verges and the remnants of prairie, the leaves on the locust trees grow just a hint of gold around them, luscious waves of them blowing in the stiff winds the storms leave behind. Temperatures can be so mild that we can still sit outside in the evening, when most of the work is done. Such weather must have proved ideal for dancing by lantern light after a day of hop picking. The valleys shake off the humidity of the summer, the rivers and creeks run high from mid-September rain that gives way to sun and a westerly breeze. The land is laced with meaning, memory, sustenance, mourning, and sometimes joy. The searing heat of August has passed, and I cannot yet imagine the bitter cold that lies ahead, the bare branches of the slumbering trees. For Ella, every day, stormy or sunny, was full of work, described in the cadences of the chores required for the proper functioning of the household. Women like Ella and her relatives engaged in the paid and unpaid work essential to the production of the hops required by the increasingly industrialized breweries responding to and fostering the thirsts of growing numbers of beer drinkers the world over.

There is a bigger lesson here about asking, in the broadest sense, where our food and drink come from. What ghosts haunt the fields, barns, docks, and depots? We can ask these questions of any landscape: What once grew here? Who tended, processed, and consumed the plants that grew on this land? How did the people who once lived here nourish themselves? Ultimately this is a story about more than just hops. It is also a story about changes in the cultivation of the land, changes in consumer tastes, changes in power relations and labor practices, energy and technology, and how we get to where we are today. Let us seek out more ghosts. Let us leaf through the documents and tread the narrow path through the tall grasses to understand who once was here and to ponder who will take our place when we are gone. Let us meditate on what we lose by omitting Ella's story from the accounts of the rise of the nineteenth-century beer industry—that is, by ignoring the many ghosts that haunt the spaces where we dwell.

ACKNOWLEDGMENTS

One of the lessons I try to convey to my students, in beer class and beyond, is the value of reaching out to experts and colleagues throughout the research and writing process as well as the usefulness of building a sustaining network of friends, family, and whoever else you need to get through the day. I live what I teach, at least in this respect, and over the course of writing this book I have benefited from the guidance, wisdom, and friendship of more people than I can possibly include here. Along the way, I have done my best to keep a running list of the helpful, supportive folks, but I also apologize to anyone I may have overlooked or neglected to jot down in a notebook on the path toward completing this book.

Work on this book was supported by a fellowship at the Institute for Research in the Humanities (IRH) at the University of Wisconsin–Madison in 2023, as well as an Advancing Research and Creativity Award and a Research Assistance Fund award from the University of Wisconsin–Milwaukee. My semester as a UW System Fellow at the IRH was one of the most productive and enjoyable semesters of my quarter-century career. The collegiality, the rich conversations every Monday, and the chance to spend so much time at the adjacent Wisconsin Historical Society absolutely transformed this book.

Thanks, too, to Doug Mitchell (RIP), Kyle Wagner, James Toftness, and especially Elizabeth Branch Dyson, executive editor at the University of Chicago Press, who took on this wide-ranging proposal in the wake of the loss of two other editors. Mollie McFee has been an invaluable part of bringing this book to a close, and so many thanks to Carrie Olivia Adams for taking it on as well. Many thanks are due to Elizabeth Ellingboe, the production editor, and especially to Lori Meek Schuldt, the copy editor, whose meticulous and generous read of the manuscript allowed me to correct missing references, murky prose, and ill-placed images. Many thanks to the anonymous peer reviewers, whose comments helped me understand what the manuscript needed at crucial moments. John Wyatt Greenlee of Surprised Eel Mapping also deserves many thanks for creating the two maps in the book—what better way to illustrate the connectedness of hop farmers, Great Lakes, and far-off cities.

This book rests on the expertise, kindness, and generosity of dozens of archivists, librarians, brewers, hop growers, writers, readers, thinkers, and friends. At the top of the list are the hardworking people at UW-Milwaukee's interlibrary loan office. This book would have been impossible to write without their assistance. I ordered so many books from interlibrary loan that at one point they created an entire shopping cart dedicated to my voluminous orders (achievement unlocked). They seamlessly processed these requests and gave me access to a vibrant world of primary and secondary sources, both as hard copies and as scans of far-off documents and chapters. I cannot thank them enough. In addition, the UW-Milwaukee Archives and the American Geographic Society Library have been valuable resources. With many thanks to Heidi Alonzo, Stephen Appel, Georgia Brown, Beth Kucera, Abigail Nye, Jovanka Ristic, Katie Stollenwerk, Stephanie Surach, Kristin Woodward, and so many other brilliant colleagues.

Archivists and librarians across the US assisted as well. Above all, the Wisconsin Historical Society has made this project possible. Thank you to Jenny Garth, Lee Grady, Lisa Marine, Gayle Martinson, Nancy Mulhern, Leah Penzkover, Jacqueline Pozza Reisner, and so many other knowledgeable, helpful people. Lee deserves particular thanks for introducing me to the Census of Agriculture, which forms the backbone of this book. Thanks are also due to Kevin Abing and his colleagues at the Milwaukee County Historical Society, Mark Cerise at the US Department of Agriculture, Jenna Eddy at the H. H. Bennett Studio and Museum, Daniel Scholzen at the Molson-Coors Archive, Carly Still at the Cloisters, Douglas Bicknese at the National Archives and Records Administration, Craig Braunschweig at the Reedsburg Historical Society, and librarians and archivists at the National Agricultural Statistics Service, the California State Library, the Bancref Library, and the Library of Congress.

An especially heartfelt thank you to the people who read the whole manuscript: Bettina Arnold, Theresa McCulla, Jenn Lena, and Kay Wells. Also to people who read substantial pieces: Doug Hoverson, Anne Pycha, Anne Bramley, and Marne Kaeske. It is also a pleasure to thank my writing group, The Cascadia Subduction Zone, a.k.a. Writing Kidz, a.k.a. Subduction. Since 2016, a combination of Anne Basting, Liam Callanan, Aims McGuinness, Rick Popp, Jason Puskar, and Anne Pycha has provided warm friendship and incisive critique, as well as thematic beverages (and cheese) for our fireside meetings and summertime barbecues. I have learned so much from all of you, and I hope my writing reflects a fraction of what you've taught me.

Many thanks to beer scholars, brewers, and other friends and colleagues. To be clear, some of these folks are on beer history speed dial, while others are people who may have once shared a project-altering conversation between panels at a conference! A wide range, including Ana Acena, Brian Alberts, Jasmine Alinder, Jim Altwies, Laura Avedisian, Michael Benter, Allison Jahn Bluvas, George Jahn Bluvas, Camden Burd, Bonnie Byrd, Thomas Calkins, Marcia Carmichael, Jerry Charter, Christy Clark-Pujara, Dan Dettmers, David DiValerio, Josh Driscoll, Caroline Gottschalk Druschke, Tiah Edmunson-Morton, Alison Efford, Christine Evans, Daniel Freas, Liz Garibay, Antonio Paniagua Guzmán, Josh Havill, Stan Hieronymus, Jennifer Johung, Alexander Kaesbohrer, Stephen Kantrowitz, Stephen Kercher, Debbie Kolberg, Peter Kopp, Liz Anna Kozik, Wayne Kroll, James Levy, Gary Luther, Anna Mansson-McGinty, Adrienne Martini, Laura Mortimore, Jennifer Nickens, Rob Novak, Erin O'Donnell, Maureen Ogle, Alison Orton, Laura Paine, Jeremie Ruby-Strauss, Travis Rupp, Beth

Schlemper, Silvia Secchi, Kam Shapiro, Julia Skinner, Dave Snyder, Mike Stein, Jocelyn Szczepaniak-Gillece, Vijaya Tamla Rai (with extra gratitude for his assistance with the census data), Renee Tantala, Bobby Tanzilo, Jerry Thomasen, Michael Uhrich, Richard Unger, David Wegner, Sarah Weidner, and Jana Weiss.

To the approximately seventy-five students who have taken my beer seminar over the past few years—thank you for your creativity, enthusiasm, and curiosity! This book is better thanks to all of you. So many colleagues at UW-Milwaukee, in the Sociology Department, the Urban Studies Programs, the History Department, and beyond, have been supportive of this work at its many stages. This research has also been presented in various forms at the Association for the Study of Food and Society annual conference, in a barn in rural Wisconsin, in a bar on the South Side of Milwaukee, and at the formidable American Geographic Society Library on my home campus.

I also need to thank the Urban Studies Program, the Honors College, and the SURF Program, all at the University of Wisconsin–Milwaukee, for providing a long line of very helpful research assistants, including Bernard Apeku, Savannah Rose Hagen, Pete Lund, Hamideh Moayyed, Alexis Nehmer, Kostyn Tyksinski, and Vivian Wagner.

Thanks to my mother, Sandra Jordan, who has assisted in some way on every book I've written. In this case, she accompanied me on several research trips, patiently entertained herself while I talked to an archivist or leafed through files, and developed a helpful taste for India pale ale. I'm lucky to have such a mother! Likewise Jim Jordan (my father, who saw the beginning days of this book before passing away in 2018), Clement Jordan, Clyde Jordan, Carrie Diaz, and Carl Jordan have been very supportive in this process. Texting my mom and brother with updates about my to-do list was very motivating!

The biggest thanks are due to Dan Kern, which is why I dedicated this book to him. Thank you for making this an even more enjoyable process, for listening to my complaints when I hit roadblocks, and for accompanying me on so many journeys to breweries, history farms, obscure corners of Wisconsin and New York and points in between. And thank you in particular for two gifts that bookend this project—

the apple grafting knife that was the first present you ever gave me, as I was finishing a book about apples and tomatoes; and, perhaps even more consequentially, a small tabletop loom that you bought for me after I idly mused out loud, "I might want a loom," which has turned me into a weaver and, perhaps, in whatever comes next, someone who writes about weavers as well.

NOTES

PROLOGUE

1. Paine, "The Hops Era." (Full source details for this and other shortened citations of published works appear in the bibliography.)

2. There were notable exceptions, which I will detail subsequently, including several Black hop pickers, one Black hop farmer and his family, and two very large hop farms that briefly employed several hundred presumably Ho-Chunk hop pickers. Pickers of hops varied by location and decade, and later in this prologue I include more detail on the range of hop picker experiences, from the hop fields of Kent to the centrality of Chinese men and Indigenous families on the West Coast of the United States.

3. Unger, *Beer in the Middle Ages*, 58. I adopt an expansive notion of ghosts drawn from my own lifelong curiosity about the presence of the past all around me. It is not that I expect to actually encounter a specter in a hopyard; rather, the ghost in this context has to do with the challenge of discerning these long-ago figures in landscapes and archives, and how the search for these spirits can teach me about the past, and to some extent the future. The ghosts in this book are not familial for me, but I also draw inspiration from Crystal Wilkinson's invocation of kitchen ghosts: "The concept of the kitchen ghosts came to me years ago when I realized that my ancestors are always with me and that the women are most present when I'm chopping or stirring or standing at the stove." Wilkinson, *Praisesong for the Kitchen Ghosts*, 2. See also Gordon, *Ghostly Matters*.

4. *Economic Study of the Hop Industry in Oregon*.

5. Carney, "Whiteness and Settler Colonial Logics"; Hieronymus, *For the Love of Hops*; Kopp, *Hoptopia*; Larsen, *Hop King*; Summerhill, *Harvest of Dissent*; Tomlan, *Tinged with Gold*.

6. On cider, see (among many, many others) Bussey, *Illustrated History of Apples*; Jordan, *Edible Memory*, 73–112; Watson, *Cider, Hard and Sweet*. On whis-

key, see, for example, Mitenbuler, *Bourbon Empire*; Lender and Martin, *Drinking in America*.

7. See Dighe, "A Taste for Temperance"; Pilcher, *Hopped Up*; Dredge, *Brief History of Lager*; Ogle, *Ambitious Brew*.

8. See, for example, "Hop Pickers After Their Pay," *Wisconsin State Journal*, Dec. 11, 1868.

9. Historic Structures, "Pabst Brewing Company, Milwaukee."

10. Ella Seymour Diary, box 1, Seymour Family of Dellona, Sauk County, Wisconsin, Papers, 1842–1986 (esp. 1842–1891), Call Number M93-113, Wisconsin Historical Society, hereafter cited as Seymour Papers. Thomas Summerhill (*Harvest of Dissent*) also had access to diaries of hop pickers in upstate New York, but this is the only one I am aware of in Wisconsin, although there are a handful of published reminiscences.

11. See, for example, Bennett, *Ale, Beer, and Brewsters in England*; Nyuur and Sobiesu, "Brewing and the Beer Industry in Africa"; Rogerson, "African Traditional Beer"; Wade, *Filthy Queens*.

12. See, for example, Burman and Fennetaux, *The Pocket*; Flores-Villalobos, *The Silver Women*; Fuentes, *Dispossessed Lives*; Hahamovitch, *Fruits of Their Labor*; Kessler-Harris, *Out to Work*; Miles, *All That She Carried*; W. Moran, *Belles of New England*; Sleeper-Smith, *Indigenous Prosperity and the American Conquest*; Ulrich, *A Midwife's Tale*. In the same period covered in this book, women went to work in munitions plants and many other settings during the Civil War, including the Washington Armory, where twenty-one women died in an explosion in June 1864 (Bellamy, "Fireworks, Hoopskirts—and Death"). Indeed hop picking and hop picker hosting are simply two examples of so much women's work that contributed to larger-scale industries in this era.

13. On New York as the most significant hop-growing region in the nineteenth century, see Summerhill, *Harvest of Dissent*; Tomlan, *Tinged with Gold*; Osterud, *Bonds of Community*.

14. See, for example, Bauer, "Sudsy Sovereignty"; Bauer, *We Were All Like Migrant Workers Here*; Chan, *This Bittersweet Soil*; C. Daniel, *Bitter Harvest*; Kopp, *Hoptopia*; Raibmon, *Authentic Indians*; Vaught, *Cultivating California*.

15. Xan, *Wisconsin, My Home*, 149–50.

16. Hop Yard Account Book, Seymour Papers.

17. Bohn, "Hop Culture in Early Sauk County."

18. Bohn, "Hop Culture in Early Sauk County," 392.

19. Hops are by no means the only commodity crop to circulate on such a global scale in the nineteenth century. Jim Clifford captures the global scope of consumerism in his work on soap in the nineteenth century. The growing demand for a "pure" modern soap led to vast quantities of animal carcasses boiling in vats around the globe and the transformation of landscapes beneath the hooves and manure of the cattle and sheep destined to become soap. Importantly, the arrangement of animals and landscapes varied, as did the trade significance

of various locations—Russia, Australia, North America, among others (Clifford, "London's Soap Industry"). Along with animal industries, booms and busts of particular plants have wide-ranging and often global implications. See, for example, Pawley, *Nature of the Future*; MacFadyen, *Flax Americana*; Pluymers, *No Wood, No Kingdom*. In his pathbreaking work on the flax industry in Canada, Joshua MacFadyen identifies the central agents shaping the rise of flax—a plant not native to the Canadian plains, but which came to cover a very large amount of acreage in the nineteenth century (MacFadyen, *Flax Americana*). Also see Majumdar, "Recalcitrant Lifeworlds"; McDonell, *Quinoa Bust*.

20. If someone claims to know the precise date of the first use of hops in brewing, they are either joking or overly confident. There are tantalizing finds, such as the hops in the hold of a sunken ship on the coast of England, and medieval ledgers in Germany and France referencing hops being grown or delivered as a tribute to bishops, but there is no scholarly consensus as to the precise starting point of brewing with hops. Karl-Ernst Behre provides a fairly measured assessment of these early additives to beer; see Behre, "History of Beer Additives in Europe."

21. Amadou et al., "Millet-Based Traditional Processed Foods"; Pohl-Valero, "Scientific Lives of *Chicha*"; E. Rath, "It Gives the Rice a Kick."

22. Arnold, "'Drinking the Feast,'"; Behre, "History of Beer Additives in Europe"; Unger, *Beer in the Middle Ages*.

23. Acitelli, *The Audacity of Hops*; Hieronymus, *For the Love of Hops*.

24. Hoverson, *Drink That Made Wisconsin Famous*, 25.

25. Carney, "Whiteness and Settler Colonial Logics."

26. See, for example, Cornelius, *History in Indigenous Voices*; Kantrowitz, *Citizens of a Stolen Land*; Lonetree, "A Heritage of Resilience"; Lonetree, "Visualizing Native Survivance"; as well as the discussion in chapter 1.

27. Thompson, *Rise and Decline of the Wheat Growing Industry in Wisconsin*, 15. For more on wheat and other crops, see Zabinski, *Amber Waves*; Zappia, "Frontiers of Grain"; Ron, "When Hay Was King," where the focus is obviously hay, with comparative statistics for wheat.

28. Waisanen and Bliss, "Changes in Population and Agricultural Land," 84–13. For the explanation of "improved land," see United States Census Bureau, "1870 Census Instructions to Assistant Marshals."

29. Waisanen and Bliss, "Changes in Population and Agricultural Land," 84–13; see also Opie, *The Law of the Land*.

30. See, for example, Summerhill, *Harvest of Dissent*, 157; Thompson, *Rise and Decline of the Wheat Growing Industry in Wisconsin*.

31. Wisconsin Historical Society, "Dairy Farming in Wisconsin."

32. McQuillan, *Prevailing Over Time*; Wood, *Making Ontario*.

33. On tulips, see Goldgar, *Tulipmania*; Pollan, *The Botany of Desire*. On coffee, and the dangers of blights, see McCook, *Coffee Is Not Forever*. On rubber and iron ore, see Bunker and Ciccantell, *Globalization and the Race for Resources*, which describes how patterns of consumption in distant places affected the Amazon and

how the wealth of the rubber- and iron-using places impoverished the source of these raw materials. As with hops, the botanical qualities of the rubber tree largely dictated the terrain and the labor practices that made it profitable. Similarly, British planters turned the rainforest of Sri Lanka (called Ceylon at that time) into plantations of coffee, cinchona, and tea (Webb, *Tropical Pioneers*). These are all plants that originated elsewhere but that thrived in Sri Lanka and linked the island's ecological and economic fates to the tastes of consumers in distant lands. Like hops, these crops experienced varying degrees of boom and bust related to both consumer demand and blights. Coffee experienced a fungal blight around the same time the hop louse was invading Wisconsin hop fields. As in Wisconsin, growers turned to a range of crops to profit from the starkly changed landscape of Sri Lanka, with varying degrees of success and at times cataclysmic failure (Webb, *Tropical Pioneers*, 116, 128). By the end of the nineteenth century, tea had overtaken both cinchona and coffee (Webb, *Tropical Pioneers*, 135). In Wisconsin it was dairy that saved the day for decades to come, thanks in large part to the establishment of an agricultural extension system based out of the University of Wisconsin–Madison. For more on earlier systems of expertise and reform to combat agricultural crisis, see (among many others) Ron, *Grassroots Leviathan*.

34. Phillips, "Wisconsin's Black Farming Tradition." See also Clark-Pujara, "Race-Based Slavery"; Simms, *Settlin'*.

35. Olson, *The Depletion Myth*; Peace et al., "Maitland's Moment"; Pluymers, *No Wood, No Kingdom*.

36. Havill went on to add that "sport mutations likely gave rise to 'Early Cluster,' which is a variant that matures slightly earlier, whereas varieties like 'California Cluster' arose through clonal selection within the larger pool of 'Cluster' being grown in that region." Josh Havill, email messages to author, July 24, 2025, and December 8, 2025. Many thanks to Stan Hieronymus for suggesting that I reach out to Havill, and many thanks to Havill for his insights.

37. Although it focuses on the period after this book, see Slez, *Making of the Populist Movement*, for a rich discussion of the social, spatial, and political implications of railroads in the US.

38. See Reiherzer, *Winnebago County Beer*, as well as examples such as a mural depicting the area's hop history in City of Reedsburg, "Reedsburg Hops Mural."

39. Many of the sources in this book are the kinds of local histories that are inclined to erase or obscure Indigenous histories, and I do my best to take heed of Jean M. O'Brien's work on what she calls "firsting and lasting." These local histories produced from around twenty to sixty years after the events they recount (at least in Wisconsin) "created a particular reality, but not one that adequately accounted for Indian lives, survival, or history" (O'Brien, *Firsting and Lasting*, xviii). For additional critical approaches to archival and historical sources, see, for example, Chaudhuri et al., *Contesting Archives*.

40. This database is available as an Excel file by sending an email to jajordan

@uwm.edu. Throughout this book I will cite it as Jordan, Hop Farmer Database, as it is a unique source created from several primary sources. I first collected the names, townships, and harvest amounts of anyone growing hops from the handwritten hard copies of the Census of Agriculture held at the Wisconsin Historical Society Archives for 1850, 1860, and 1870. I then cross-referenced these thousands of handwritten entries with the digital population census records of Ancestry.com and FindAGrave.com to identify the farmer's birthplace and spouse. I now know the names, birthdates, hop harvests, and townships of nearly every hop farmer and nearly every hop farmer's inferred spouse (as indicated on Ancestry.com's searchable version of the population census) or other adult woman in the household for the census years of 1850, 1860, and 1870—the time of the rise and fall of Wisconsin's hop industry. Note that the use of the term "inferred" with regard to spouses and offspring is an artifact of the Ancestry.com database, where their transcription lists the inferred spousal and parental relationships based on ages and surnames. It is not an indication of any doubt regarding the veracity of a marriage, and it was only in 1880 that the census began instructing its enumerators to inquire about the relationships of all household members to the head of household (Szucs and Wright, "Census Records," 176). For the corresponding aggregate statistics—that is, the counts at the county and state level, which contain no individual farmer information—see "Agricultural Schedules: 1850 to 1900," in Walker, *Statistics*, 280–83. For more on the census, see M. Anderson, *The American Census*; Gauthier, *Measuring America*. I will also note that many of the names on Ancestry.com are incorrect. The optical character recognition was so bad in some cases that I corrected people's names on Ancestry.com as I worked through the database. My database also includes alternate spellings because in Ancestry.com, in some cases, a given person's name is not searchable with the correct spelling. At times I had to scroll through the neighbors of a known nearby hop farmer to find a badly transcribed name in the scanned, handwritten pages of the population census. Put another way, if anyone wants to replicate my work, not only will they need to search the name on Ancestry.com, but at times they will also need to scroll through the neighbors, comparing the agricultural census pages to the scanned Ancestry pages, to find a badly transcribed name.

41. Szucs and Wright, "Census Records."

42. See, for example, Bohn, "Hop Culture in Early Sauk County"; F. Canfield, *The Hop Pickers*. The Canfield book is a novel, but the author herself did pick hops near Baraboo in the 1860s, staying with the family of T. T. English.

43. In this case, a plat map is a map showing boundaries of counties, townships, farms, and other properties, drawn as part of the US General Land Office's Public Lands Survey.

44. See, for example, Reiherzer, *Winnebago County Beer*, as well as Corralitos Brewery's brewing with the McGrath hop found near the old McGrath farm in the Pajaro Valley in California (Hodges, "The McGrath Hop") as just two examples.

45. “Skunks are active and numerous; they enter hen coops and chickens disappear, but the animal is considered a benefit in the hop yard in digging worms out of the hills” (Dodge, “Notes on Growing Crops,” 195).

46. In doing so, I join the ongoing investigations into local and global patterns of cultural consumption of a range of goods. On alcoholic beverages, see (among many others) Bowen, *Divided Spirits*; Elzinga et al., “Craft Beer in the United States”; Jacobson, *Intoxicating Pleasures*; Maguire, “Taste for the Particular”; Mitenbuler, *Bourbon Empire*; Pilcher, “Imperial Hops”; Pilcher, *Hopped Up*; Pozner et al., “Watered Down”; Thurnell-Read, “Craft, Tangibility, and Affect”; Thurnell-Read, *Drinking Dilemmas*. On other goods, see, for example, Clifford, *West Ham and the River Lea*; DeSoucey, *Contested Tastes*; L. Miller, *Building Nature's Market*; Ocejo, *Masters of Craft*; Percival and Percival, *Reinventing the Wheel*; Wherry, *Culture of Markets*; and my own work on heirloom tomatoes, forgotten turnips, and the effects of remembering and forgetting on edible memories and landscapes, Jordan, *Edible Memory*.

47. Tsing, *Mushroom at the End of the World*.

48. In 1846, Waukesha County split from Milwaukee County, so technically it was still Milwaukee County when the Weavers arrived. On the first brewery in Wisconsin, see Apps, *Breweries of Wisconsin*, 14.

49. Martin Perkins suggests that most hop farmers in the area were English: “Many of the Sussex area growers in the Town of Lisbon shared an English nativity: names such as Swallow, Beaumont, and Smith joined the Weavers in local production.” Martin C. Perkins, “The History of Agriculture in Waukesha County (1834–1983),” in Langill and Loerke, *From Farmland to Freeways*, 187. Census data show that the early Waukesha hop farmers all came from England or New York, or both.

50. DeNorma, “Humulus Genetic Resources.” That said, people do brew with them, and there is at least one commercially grown *neomexicanus* available, the Zappa hop (named after musician Frank Zappa) from CLS Farms in the Yakima Valley.

51. Havill, email.

52. Beer historian Doug Hoverson has measured fourteen inches of growth on his own Cascade hop plants at the peak of the growing season in Minnesota. Doug Hoverson, email message to author, August 12, 2025.

53. Sleeper-Smith, *Indigenous Prosperity and the American Conquest*, 157.

54. Collot, *Journey in North America*.

55. Jefferson, *Message from the President* [. . .] *Communicating Discoveries Made*, 125.

56. Thwaites, *Bradbury's Travels*, 67–68.

57. Tomlan, *Tinged with Gold*, 23.

58. Ficker, “Christian Traugott Ficker's Advice to Emigrants,” 342.

59. Summerhill, *Harvest of Dissent*, 95.

60. Bohn, “Hop Culture in Early Sauk County,” 389.

61. Cole, *Standard History of Sauk County*, 98.

62. "Hop Culture," *Milwaukee Daily Sentinel*, Nov. 13, 1867.

63. F. Canfield, *The Hop Pickers*, 52.

64. Summerhill, *Harvest of Dissent*, 95.

65. "Emmet Wells' Weekly Hop Circular," *Wisconsin State Register*, Sept. 5, 1868. I use the spelling *Emmet* for Wells's first name throughout this book for consistency, but the newspapers of the time spelled his name as either *Emmet* or *Emmett*.

66. W. B. M., "A New Hop Kiln," *Wisconsin State Register*, Mar. 14, 1868.

67. Local beer researcher Gary Luther shared with me his assessment that, "varieties were wild, Grape, Humphrey Seedling, Canada, Cluster (rhizomes probably brought from New York)." Gary Luther, email message to author, February 21, 2017.

68. D. Smith, "Varietal Improvement in Hops," 1221.

69. Bissell, "Hop Culture in New York," 1675.

70. Rentmeester and Rentmeester, *De Vlamingen in Wisconsin / The Flemish in Wisconsin*, 32, 78.

CHAPTER ONE

1. Reilly, "Hop Growing History."

2. Blatz Brewing Company Records, 1862–1944, UWM Manuscript Collection 132, various volumes, University of Wisconsin–Milwaukee Archives (hereafter cited as Blatz Records); Pabst Brewing Company Records, 1873–1940, UWM Manuscript Collection 161, various volumes, University of Wisconsin–Milwaukee Archives (hereafter cited as Pabst Records, which also include the records from before 1889, when the name changed from Best to Pabst).

3. Bullard, *The Hop Farmer's Year*; Byrd, "Intertwined"; Tomlan, *Tinged with Gold*; Summerhill, *Harvest of Dissent*.

4. 1850 Census of Agriculture, as analyzed in Jordan, Hop Farmer Database.

5. Reilly, "Weaver Family."

6. Perkins, "History of Agriculture in Waukesha County," in Langill and Loerke, *From Farmland to Freeways*, 186; Tomlan, *Tinged with Gold*, 23; Reilly, "James Weaver and Hops."

7. Nearby Otsego County was the leading hop producer in 1840, clocking in at more than 168,000 pounds. *Compendium of the Enumeration of the Inhabitants*, 120.

8. Summerhill, "Farming on Shares," 151.

9. *Economic Study of the Hop Industry*.

10. Steiner, *Steiner's Guide to American Hops*, 43. There is even a historical plaque on the site of an early New York hop yard: "In 1808 James D. Coolidge Planted the First Hops Field in Madison County." See Historical Marker Database, "First Hop Yard."

11. A number of varieties of hops were grown in New York during the peak years: "English Cluster, Grape, Canada Red, Palmer Seedling and Humphrey Seedling." D. Smith, "Varietal Improvement in Hops," 1221.

12. DigiTreaties, "Cession 187."

13. Reilly, "David Bonham's Life."

14. The 1850, 1860, and 1870 population censuses did not record spouses (instead, as noted in the prologue, Ancestry.com infers which household members might be spouses, as well as which of the children in a household might be offspring of the head of household), but even in later census rolls, when the census taker recorded the spouse, people often lied about marital status. I have a prime example of such deception in my own family. In the mid-1860s, my great-great-great-grandfather ran off with the family's maid, who was my great-great-great-grandmother. He abandoned his wife and many children in Illinois and started a new family with his young servant, fleeing to the West Coast and lying to an 1880 census taker (and everyone else) about their marital status as they went on to have four children. In our family, this ruse lasted until the twenty-first century, when I happened to find a letter written by the abandoned eldest son on FindaGrave .com. A very intentional act of deceit hid a family scandal for more than a century, and I think it is safe to assume the census contains many such secrets.

15. "EASTERN HOPS for sale by the bale or less quantity, just rec'd at CUNNINGHAM's Drug Store," *Daily Sentinel and Gazette* (Milwaukee), Oct. 21, 1846, 1; another shopkeeper, L. Blossom, placed frequent ads offering to buy and sell hops (among other commodities): "HOPS, HOPS-Growth of 1846, of the best quality, for sale by the bale at the Eagle Brewery," *Daily Sentinel and Gazette*, Nov. 18, 1846; *Daily Sentinel and Gazette*, Feb. 10, 1847, 4, and "CASH. . . . and the highest price paid for Staves and Heading Barley and Hops, at the Eagle Brewery, by L. Blossom," *Daily Sentinel and Gazette*, Mar. 3, 1847, 4. I also want to note that the Newspapers.com database from which many of the historical references originate has imperfect scanning and character recognition. In other words, as on Ancestry .com, a search for a given phrase or word does not necessarily yield all instances of that term. There may be instances were a search for a headline or term listed here may not yield a result, whereas reading the digitized page will clearly show it.

16. "Ten Bales Eastern Hops First Sort," *Milwaukee Sentinel*, Sept. 20, 1848, 2.

17. "28 Bales Fresh Hops From 'Oneida' County, N.Y.," *Milwaukee Sentinel*, Apr. 9, 1850, 3.

18. "Wells and Hill have for sale at their Warehouse, on consignment, 20 tons saleratus" [and many other commodities], *Milwaukee Sentinel*, Dec. 30, 1851, 4; and "Hops—Just received, and for sale," Jan. 13, 1853, 3.

19. Derby, "History of the Port of Milwaukee," 4; see also Pawley, *Nature of the Future*.

20. Derby, "History of the Port of Milwaukee," 9.

21. Derby, "History of the Port of Milwaukee," 41.

22. Derby, "History of the Port of Milwaukee," 18.

23. For more on the scale of ecological change resulting from white settlement, see Liz Anna Kozik's truly innovative dissertation (Kozik, "Re-Peopling the Prairie"). In addition, see Blackhawk, *The Rediscovery of America*; Cronon, *Changes in the Land*; Cronon, *Nature's Metropolis*; Macfarlane, *Lives of Lake Ontario*; Secchi,

"Compounded Extraction"; Wood, *Making Ontario*. The Indigenous use of fire shaped the land that became Wisconsin: "Fire regimes changed in a multitude of ways during European settlement and development. Increased wildfire activity occurred, particularly along railways . . . while decreased fire activity occurred with EuroAmerican settlements." Guyette et al., "350 Years of Fire-Climate-Human Interactions," 2; See also McClain et al., "Patterns of Anthropogenic Fire"; Secchi, "Compounded Extraction."

24. Bernstein, *Wedding of the Waters*, 329.

25. Weaver, *Memories of Early Days*, 8.

26. Maritime History of the Great Lakes, "Table Showing the Tonnage of Steam Boats."

27. "How Many Shipwrecks Are in Lake Michigan?," *Milwaukee Journal-Sentinel*, Feb. 8, 2023.

28. Weaver, *Memories of Early Days*, 7, 10.

29. Weaver, *Memories of Early Days*, 10–11. This was not the only sighting of Great Lakes pirates, who ran illegal timber from Northern forests to Midwestern cities, as well as alcohol and guns. See Pure Michigan, "Michigan Pirates of the Great Lakes"; Varhola, *Shipwrecks and Lost Treasures*.

30. Stevens, *Making of Pioneer Wisconsin*, 23–24.

31. Stevens, *Making of Pioneer Wisconsin*, 41.

32. Haraszthy, "Documents."

33. Haraszthy, "Documents," 183.

34. "Marine," *Milwaukee Daily Sentinel*, Oct. 4, 1854.

35. Derby, "History of the Port of Milwaukee," 9–10.

36. Derby, "History of the Port of Milwaukee," 14.

37. Sussex-Lisbon Area Historical Society, "David Topping." By the time the 1850 census taker knocked on her door, Melinda had a total of nine children.

38. *1856–57 Milwaukee City Directory*, 465; *Erving, Burdick & Co.'s Milwaukee City Directory* for *1857–58*, 332. A comprehensive collection of these directories is held at the Milwaukee County Historical Society in downtown Milwaukee.

39. *Portrait and Biographical Record of Waukesha County*, 199.

40. Menomonee Valley Partners, "An Urban Escape." Manomin is also spelled *manoomin*, and there are strong arguments for capitalization, as found in a recent volume edited by Brittany Luby and colleagues: "Readers will also see variations in the spelling of 'Manomin' / 'Manoomin' / 'Mnoomin.' Given that Anishinaabewmowin developed in relation to the land, regional variations in pronunciation and spelling are both natural and expected" (Luby et al., *Manomin*, xii). Although many people continue to refer to this plant as "wild" rice, it is a plant that very often exists in connection to people, including long-standing practices of knocking seed heads into the water during harvesting to encourage future growth.

41. For the three-day estimate, see Keller, "Connecting the Dots on the Weavers."

42. Weaver, *Memories of Early Days*, 19.

43. Weaver, *Memories of Early Days*, 22.

44. Langill and Loerke, *From Farmland to Freeways*, 79.

45. Weaver, *Memories of Early Days*, 27.

46. 1860 Census of Agriculture, Schedule for Waukesha County, Wisconsin.

47. Weaver, *Memories of Early Days*, 44. For more on women in agricultural labor, see, for example, Egge, "Gender and Agriculture"; Jensen, "Butter Making"; Riney-Kehrberg, "Women in Agriculture"; Sachs, *Gendered Fields*.

48. Sasso and Joyce, "Ethnohistory and Archaeology," 177.

49. "In 1825, US officials called the region's Native nations together at the Mississippi River trading town of Prairie du Chien to establish geographical lines distinguishing the territory of the region's Ho-Chunk, Potawatomi, Menominee, Sauk, Meskwaki, and Ojibwe peoples. A Ho-Chunk leader protested in vain that hard territorial boundaries did not describe the nature of nationhood in the region, that its lakes and rivers were used in common by many peoples. But the Treaty of Prairie du Chien (1825) drew those lines nonetheless, stating (for the moment) which territories belonged to which native nations." Kantrowitz, *Citizens*, 23.

50. Lonetree, "Visualizing Native Survivance," 17, 18.

51. Loew, *Indian Nations of Wisconsin*, 3; also see Lurie, *Wisconsin Indians*.

52. Ho-Chunk Nation, "About Ho-Chunk Nation." Ned Blackhawk's *The Rediscovery of America* and Paulette Steeves's *The Indigenous Paleolithic of the Western Hemisphere* give vital context to this history. For more on the violence of this era, see Bowes, *Land Too Good for Indians*; Saunt, *Unworthy Republic*.

53. Lonetree, "Visualizing Native Survivance," 15.

54. Hilton, *Lake Michigan Passenger Steamers*, 54.

55. MIGenWeb, "Ships and Shipping News."

56. Maritime History of the Great Lakes, "Julia Palmer (Steamboat), storm damage."

57. Michigan Underwater Preserves, "Whitefish Point Underwater Preserve."

58. *Portrait and Biographical Record of Waukesha County*, 200.

59. Reilly, "James Weaver and Hops."

60. Reilly, "Weaver Family"; Reilly, "James Weaver and Hops."

61. Jordan, Hop Farmer Database. See also Gauthier, *Measuring America*.

62. Sussex-Lisbon Area Historical Museum, "James Weaver Letter to Cousin Richard Hardeman, December 13, 1839."

63. The children's birthdates, and the number of months from the previous child: March 1821, October 1822 (20), October 1824 (24), February 1826 (17), August 1827 (19), August 1829 (24), December 1831 (17), March 1833 (16), November 1834 (21), July 1836 (21), November 1837 (17), July 1839 (21), May 1841 (23), July 1842 (14), September 1843 (14), November 1845 (14). Reilly, "Hop Growing History"; see also Ancestry.com (subscription required to access, also available at many university and public libraries).

64. Sussex-Lisbon Area Historical Museum, "James Weaver Letter to Cousin Richard Hardeman, December 13, 1839."

65. Son William became a hop dealer and grew hops on Section 26 of the plat map. He married Mary Hewitt and had at least four children. His brother A. S. Weaver was fifteen years younger but also became a hop dealer and hop grower; he married Sarah Howard in 1866, after his return from fighting for the Union Army in the American Civil War. Western Historical Company, *History of Waukesha County*, 982–83.

66. *Atlas of Waukesha Co.*

67. Western Historical Company, *History of Waukesha County*, 744. See also Reilly, "First Town of Lisbon Settler."

68. Laubach, *Living a Land Ethic*, 19.

69. See, for example, H. Johnson, *Order Upon the Land*; Hatheway, *Surveying in Wisconsin in 1837*; Kassulke, "See Wisconsin Through the Eyes of 19th Century Surveyors"; Rück, "Continuity of Settler Colonial Narratives"; Schulte and Mladenoff, "Original US Public Land Survey Records."

70. Reedsburg is Township 12N, Range 4E, for example, and the notebook pages reveal succinct references to the trees: "W[hite] oak . . . B[urr or Black] oak . . . Land rolling . . . W and B oak thick undergrowth." Board of Commissioners of Public Lands, "Wisconsin Public Land Survey Records." Botanist John T. Curtis explained the process: "In the actual operation of surveying, each line was measured on the ground. At every half-mile interval on the lines in each direction, a corner point was established. These points were described by giving their bearings, in direction and distance, to two or four blazed trees nearest the corner. The species of each tree was listed as was its diameter. In this way settlers could fine [find] the exact spot with relative ease and locate their claim." Curtis, *Vegetation of Wisconsin*, 63–64.

71. Curtis, *Vegetation of Wisconsin*, 60.

72. Kassulke, "See Wisconsin Through the Eyes of 19th Century Surveyors."

73. David J. Mladenoff, "Interpreting the Maps," in Kassulke, *See Wisconsin Through the Eyes of 19th Century Surveyors*, 7.

74. "Shortly after the United States Government signed treaties with the indigenous peoples of Wisconsin, the General Land Office (GLO) conducted surveys of the treaty areas. These surveys mapped the state and laid out the Public Land Survey System grid of towns, sections, quarter sections, and quarter-quarter sections." Wisconsin Original Land Patents Database, "Wisconsin's Original Land Patent Data."

75. Lange, *Postglacial Vegetational History*, 8. Curtis reported that several vegetation maps were created in the nineteenth century: one by J. W. Hoyt in 1860, which was "remarkably accurate considering the nature of the information available to him," one by Joseph Knapp in 1871, which was "very generalized," and the first map in great detail by T. C. Chamberlin "based on land surveyors' data for

prairies, marshes, and swamps, and upon observations of members of the Geological Survey. . . . Its accuracy is extremely variable, apparently depending upon the botanical knowledge and interests of geologists who examine different regions of the state. . . . Another serious defect of the map is the failure to differentiate oak savanna from oak forest in the south" (Curtis, *Vegetation of Wisconsin*, 59).

76. Bergland and Hayes, *Studying Wisconsin*, 153, 154.

77. Pilar and Shreck, "Waukesha County."

78. E. Daniel, "Wisconsin's Oak Savannas."

79. Haraszthy, "Documents," 188.

80. Lange, *Postglacial Vegetational History*, 15; Marlin Johnson, "Natural Features and Land Use," in Langill and Loerke, *From Farmland to Freeways*, 27.

81. Hatheway, *Surveying in Wisconsin in 1837*, 396.

82. Lange, *Postglacial Vegetational History*, 17.

83. Western Historical Company, *History of Waukesha County*, 324, 327. The quoted passage silently omits the parenthetical scientific names for the species that were included in the original.

84. Western Historical Company, *History of Waukesha County*, 327.

85. Western Historical Company, *History of Waukesha County*, 328.

86. Over the last 250 years, "a network of amateurs, tradesmen, and bureaucrats introduced thousands of plant species from other continents, selected and hybridized varieties so that they would thrive in American settings . . . [and] sought to exclude or exterminate undesirable plants and plant pests. These activities fundamentally altered not only the vegetation, but also the economic activities, social relations, and common experiences of Americans." Pauly, *Fruits and Plains*, 1. See Burd, *Roots of Flower City*.

87. Coates, *American Perceptions of Immigrant and Invasive Species*; Pauly, *Fruits and Plains*.

88. Apps, *Breweries of Wisconsin*; Benter, *Roll Out the Barrels*; Hoverson, *Drink that Made Wisconsin Famous*; Kroll, *Wisconsin's Frontier Farm Breweries*.

89. Hoverson, *Drink That Made Wisconsin Famous*, 41.

90. Hoverson, *Drink that Made Wisconsin Famous*, 39.

91. *Directory of the City of Milwaukee for the Years 1847–48*, 54, 49.

92. Summerhill, *Harvest of Dissent*, 95.

93. Reilly, "Hop Growing History."

CHAPTER TWO

1. I assume this was the second edition of Lapham's book, reportedly "greatly improved" from the first edition. Lapham, *Wisconsin: Its Geography and Topography*.

2. Lapham, *Wisconsin: Its Geography and Topography*.

3. The Homestead Act was not passed until 1862, so Silas Seymour acquired his land under an earlier arrangements of land patents, as the US government sold

off the land it had claimed as its own when Wisconsin became a US territory. He is entered in the plat book on June 16, 1849, and his patent was signed on July 5, 1850, by President Zachary Taylor. For an image of Silas's land patent, see Bureau of Land Management, "General Land Office Records." For more on the patent system, see Family Search, "Wisconsin Land and Property." The same year that Silas filed his claim, Wakąjazi (Yellow Thunder) traveled to Mineral Point to file a claim of his own on forty acres a few miles west of Silas. Yellow Thunder "was a key leader of the disaffected bands of Ho-Chunk members who walked back to their ancestral homelands every time they were removed. In 1849 he purchased forty acres of land north of Baraboo which made him a legal landowner. His '40' became a haven for other Ho-Chunk people." Sauk County Historical Society, "Yellow Thunder—Wakąjazi."

4. "Neil had driven out past the Cemetery way north of town and by way of the Old Spence Fish Farm, so we came down Highway H from the north so we could see better, get a good view. I had him stop at the NW corner of the Six Acre field to see if S.J.'s old 'marker stone' was there yet. It wasn't. The road has been widened so much there, as well as all along down through past the meadow, that it probably was moved when road work was done." Burmester, *A Barn on the Place*, vi. This was a lightly fictionalized book written by Ella's niece, her brother Merton's daughter ("While almost all of the stories are true, not everything occurred in the exact order in which it is told"; Burmester, *A Barn on the Place*, n.p.). The only copy that I am aware of resides in the library stacks at the Wisconsin Historical Society.

5. "Documents: Silas J. Seymour Letters III," 461.

6. H. Smith, *History of the City of Buffalo*, 105.

7. Curtis, *Vegetation of Wisconsin*, 465. Those population counts excluded most of the Indigenous population because of certain distinctions made by the US Census Bureau. For example, for the 1860 census, "Indians *not taxed* are not to be enumerated. The families of Indians who have renounced tribal rule, and who under state or territory laws exercise the rights of citizens, are to be enumerated" (J. Collins, "Native Americans in the Census, 1860–1890"). See Kantrowitz, *Citizens of a Stolen Land*, for an in-depth discussion of Ho-Chunk citizenship. In Waukesha County in the same period, and with the same caveats, the enumerated population went from 2,256 people in 1840 to 19,258 people just ten years later (M. Johnson, "Natural Features and Land Use," in Langill and Loerke, *From Farmland to Freeways*, 34).

8. "The white pioneers in Sauk County could be divided into 2 groups: 'Yankees'—people mostly of English background, but also of Irish, Scottish or Welsh origins, who came mainly from the eastern states; and immigrants from continental Europe, who came mainly from Germany and Switzerland." Yankees settled in Prairie du Sac and German and Swiss in Sauk City. "Swiss . . . and Germans pioneered in the Honey Creek region; Bavarians clustered in the Plain area; Yankees, linked closely with the settlement in Prairie du Sac, moved onto the

Sauk Prairie, and with Scotch Irish and Welsh, onto the Cassell Prairie; Yankees also moved into Troy Township, and in Winfield and Dellona Townships . . . Welsh moved into the Spring Green area; and Norwegians and Danes . . . pioneered in Big Hollow." Lange, *A County Called Sauk*, 28.

9. Lange, *Postglacial Vegetational History*, 21.

10. Reilly, "Hop Growing History."

11. "Another possibility was the sugar beet. The wartime scarcity of cane sugar had prompted Wisconsinites to experiment with beets as well as sorghum. Not till 1868, however, did the state's first sugar refinery appear, near Fond du Lac. This was the work of two German immigrants, one of them the former foreman of a refinery in Germany." Current et al., *History of Wisconsin: Civil War Era*, 461.

12. "Documents: Silas J. Seymour Letters II," 334.

13. "Documents: Silas J. Seymour Letters III," 460.

14. "Seymour Letters," 196.

15. "Seymour Letters," 195.

16. "Seymour Letters," 196.

17. Burmester, *A Barn on the Place*, 16-12.

18. In 1863, a congressman reported about one thousand Ho-Chunk people living in Sauk and neighboring counties, still moving from one place to the next (Onsager, "Removal of the Winnebago," 117). In 1867, reports describe that "they lived a nomadic life [in Sauk and neighboring counties], supporting themselves by hunting, trapping, fishing, and picking and selling berries. They raised considerable corn and potatoes in Juneau County and also made a business of raising riding ponies for sale" (Onsager, "Removal of the Winnebago," 118–19). See also Tetzloff, "Diminishing Winnebago Estate"; Tetzloff, "To Do Some Good Among the Indians."

19. "Documents: Silas J. Seymour Letters II," 330.

20. "Documents: Silas J. Seymour Letters II," 331.

21. "Documents: Silas J. Seymour Letters II," 336.

22. "Documents: Silas J. Seymour Letters II," 331.

23. "Documents: Silas J. Seymour Letters II," 331.

24. "Documents: Silas J. Seymour Letters II," 332.

25. "Seymour Letters," 198.

26. "Documents: Silas J. Seymour Letters II," 332.

27. Nevol, "Deadly Summers."

28. "Seymour Letters," 193.

29. Ruth Seymour Burmester to Lorna Lutes Sylvester, 13 December 1972, in Baker, "Conine Family Letters, 1852–1863," 129.

30. Baker, "Conine Family Letters, 1849–1851," 358. The letter was dated May 25, 1851.

31. Baker, "Conine Family Letters, 1849–1851," 356.

32. Burmester, *A Barn on the Place*, 7-6.

33. Mary Ann Conine Seymour, "'Reminiscences of Forty Years Ago,' A Speech given on the fortieth anniversary of her wedding to Silas J. Seymour," in Baker, "Conine Family Letters, 1849–1851," 359.

34. Baker, "Conine Family Letters, 1849–1851," 359.

35. Baker, "Conine Family Letters, 1849–1851," 333.

36. Burmester, *A Barn on the Place*, 7-6.

37. Burmester, *A Barn on the Place*, 19-1.

38. Baker, "Conine Family Letters, 1849–1851," 361.

39. "Documents: Silas J. Seymour Letters III," 469–70n.

40. Baker, "Conine Family Letters, 1849–1851," 360.

41. Burmester, *A Barn on the Place*, 1-17.

42. Burmester, *A Barn on the Place*, 1-17.

43. Burmester, *A Barn on the Place*, 7-6.

44. Baker, "Conine Family Letters, 1852–1863," 165.

45. Burmester, *A Barn on the Place*, 7-6.

46. Burmester, *A Barn on the Place*, 16-6.

47. Based on my analysis of all recorded hop growers in the 1860 Census of Agriculture schedules held at the Wisconsin Historical Society. Jordan, Hop Farmer Database.

48. Lange, *Postglacial Vegetational History*, 11.

49. Curtis, *Vegetation of Wisconsin*, 46.

50. Lange, *Postglacial Vegetational History*, 11.

51. Seymour Papers.

52. Lange, *Postglacial Vegetational History*, 14.

53. Densmore, "Understanding and Using Early Nineteenth Century Account Books."

54. *Economic Study of the Hop Industry*, 18.

55. 1860 Census of Agriculture Schedule for Sauk County, Wisconsin, Wisconsin Historical Society Archives.

56. Silas lost a brother in the war but did not fight himself.

PART TWO

The title of this section is a nod to the eminent Lost Lagers, two beer historians who have done so much to link the history of beer with its contemporary expression. Particular thanks to Mike Stein (half of Lost Lagers) for always being ready to answer my obscure beer history queries.

CHAPTER THREE

1. "Hops and Hop Culture," *Wisconsin State Journal*, Mar. 9, 1868.

2. It is possible this is a wild hop. Jesse Cottington also tried to adapt wild hops for brewing, given the number of wild hops that grew nearby. Handwritten mss., Writers' Program Wisconsin: Writings and Research Notes, 1935–1942, Wis Mss

MM Box 15, Wisconsin Historical Society (hereafter cited as Writers' Program Wisconsin). I have explored the possibility of testing this hop's genetics, but one of the leading experts believes it would not be fruitful.

3. On Saaz, see L. Alberts, "Žatec, Cradle of Saaz Hops."

4. "Another account of early hops growing involves a Hungarian who settled in what is now Sauk County in the early 1840s. Count Agostin Haraszthy is said to have founded the village of Sauk City (for a brief time named for him) and planted the first hopyard in the area in 1842. The count, after a few years, moved on to California, but he left behind the seeds of the hop craze." Paine, "The Hops Era," 25. I'm not convinced, and neither is Dan Dettmers, who wrote to me via email on January 25, 2017, "I presume as part of this project you are looking into the life of Agoston Haraszth? Many claim he was the 'father of hops' in Wisconsin but I've seen no evidence to this beyond modern historians pointing at each other. The late Jim Packard and I discussed this many times as he was a big fan of the Count. We agreed its [*sic*] logical he probably planted hops in Sauk, we couldn't find proof."

5. Donohoe, "Agostin Haraszthy," 153.

6. For My Cousins, "Sauk County, Wisconsin."

7. W. Canfield, *Map of Sauk County, Wisconsin.*

8. Dictionary of Wisconsin Biography Rejected Entries, 1950s, Wis Mss SY, Box 1, Folder 2, Wisconsin Historical Society.

9. Wisconsin: County Court (Sauk County); Probate Place: Sauk, Wisconsin; Notes: Probate Cases, Reel 35, Box 83, Cont—Box 87, Cont., Wisconsin Historical Society.

10. Krug, *History of Reedsburg*, 111.

11. One source lists Agnes having been sixteen when the family emigrated, but that is impossible given her birth date in 1834. *Biographical Review*, 217.

12. Writers' Program Wisconsin; New York Heritage Digital Collections, "History of Waterville Collection." The Foothill Hops Farm Brewery in Munnsville, New York, has an extensive display of the hop history of the region.

13. Krug, *History of Reedsburg*, 111; see also Writers' Program Wisconsin.

14. Krug, *History of Reedsburg*, 20.

15. Writers' Program Wisconsin.

16. French, *American Sketchbook*, 126.

17. See, for example, *Reedsburg Remembers*, 74.

18. Some records say that the hop kiln was 12 by 12 feet, others that it was 24 by 12 feet.

19. Krug, *History of Reedsburg*, 111.

20. Western Historical Company, *History of Sauk County*, 619.

21. Western Historical Company, *History of Sauk County*, 619.

22. Krug, *History of Reedsburg*, 112.

23. Western Historical Company, *History of Sauk County*, 619.

24. Steiner, *Steiner's Guide to American Hops*, 45.

25. *Reedsburg Remembers*, 78.

26. Apps, *Breweries of Wisconsin*, 185. Doug Hoverson's more recent and encyclopedic account says that the brewery was founded by a John M. Hettinger, who built it in 1849. Hettinger's "first work was the building of a shanty, to protect his wife and children from the storms; then he built a brewery, and painted it red; and although he insisted upon calling it the Fort Winnebago Brewery, the people disregarded his wishes, and persistently styled it the Old Red Brewery." Hoverson lists another brewery in Portage that may have been Cottington's customer, City Brewery, where Charles Haertel "began brewing at the northeast corner of Cook and Clark streets in 1852." While he initially brewed around twelve barrels a week, a few years later production reached two thousand barrels a year, "making it one of the largest in the state outside Milwaukee" and a very large consumer of hops. Hoverson, *Drink That Made Wisconsin Famous*, 587–88.

27. Hoverson, *Drink That Made Wisconsin Famous*, 473.

28. Schuette, *Loganville, Our Heritage*, 29.

29. J. Moran and Hopkins, *Wisconsin's Weather and Climate*, 2.

30. Jordan, Hop Farmer Database.

31. DeLeers, "Object History: Plank Roads"; "Plank Road Meeting," *Milwaukee Daily Sentinel*, Feb. 3, 1849.

32. Derby, "History of the Port of Milwaukee," 132.

33. Without the railroad, this entire story would have quite literally taken a different path. See Cronon, *Nature's Metropolis*. Notably, neither hops nor beer appear in William Cronon's legendary volume on the rise of Chicago.

34. Cole, *A Standard History of Sauk County*, 9.

35. 1850 Census of Agriculture Schedule for Wisconsin, vol. 37–38, Waukesha County, Wisconsin Historical Society.

36. Perkins, "History of Agriculture in Waukesha County," in Langill and Loerke, *From Farmland to Freeways*, 186.

37. Tomlan, *Tinged with Gold*, 23.

38. Based on my analysis of the agricultural census and the population census. Jordan, Hop Farmer Database, and 1850 US Census Schedule for Wisconsin, Wisconsin Historical Society.

39. 1850 Census of Agriculture Schedule for Wisconsin, vol. 37–38, Waukesha County, Wisconsin Historical Society. In 1850, James Weaver had 150 improved acres, 43 unimproved acres, $4,000 cash value of farm, $150 value of implements, 9 horses, 7 "milch cows," 4 working oxen, 3 other cattle, 14 sheep, 10 swine, $564 value of stock, 500 bushels of wheat, 500 bushels of oats, 100 pounds of wool, 50 pounds of "Irish potatoes," 75 bushels of barley, 250 pounds of butter, and 20 tons of hay.

40. Stan Hieronymus, email to author, December 8, 2022. Other sources confirm this figure; for example: "The average 31-gallon barrel of brew takes" 1½ pounds of hops (McIntyre, "Let's Recall the . . . Heyday in Hops," 4). The lone possible home brewer was John Quiggle of Merrimack, but even his 8-pound hop harvest was a lot for a home brewer, and there were breweries nearby where he

might have offloaded a few pounds, perhaps? These included Leinenkugel's, Sauk City Brewery, and Stinglhammer's in nearby Sauk City. Of the 1860 farmers, the most prolific was John Kyle in Loganville at 6,000 pounds, but Harvey Canfield, A. B. Case, SVR Ableman, and Benjamin Colton all grew 1,000 or more pounds. As listed in the 1860 Census of Agriculture (Jordan, Hop Farmer Database), the hop farmers of Sauk County that year were Harvey Canfield (Baraboo), AB Case (Excelsior), SVR Ableman (Excelsior), John Quiggle (Merrimack), B Colton (New Buffalo), Benjamin James (Spring Green), Adam Fey (Troy), Daniel Corson (Washington), and John Kyle (Troy). They hailed from the states of Connecticut, New York, Ohio, and Pennsylvania, and the countries of England, Prussia, and Wales. Ten of them were married, and their wives hailed from (unsurprisingly) Connecticut, New York, Ohio, Pennsylvania, England, and Wales. I also suspect that some were bearers of knowledge about hops—many of the wives of hop farmers were originally from New York, and that seems a possible conduit for knowledge about how to grow this sometimes finicky plant. The hands of these women—almost all white settlers—shape ecologies and commodities. If you were to simply read through the agricultural census schedules, you'd have little sense of these expansive effects.

41. Jordan, Hop Farmer Database.

42. Unger, *Beer in the Middle Ages*.

43. Xan, *Wisconsin, My Home*, 102.

44. Ragatz and Ragatz, "Memoirs of a Sauk Swiss," 217.

45. Krynski and Little, "Hannah's Letters," 190.

46. Based on my analysis of the handwritten, individual-level agricultural census records held as hard copies at the Wisconsin Historical Society Archives (Jordan, Hop Farmer Database; see the finding aid at https://digital.library.wisc.edu/1711.dl/wiarchives.uw-whs-ser01675) combined with the digitized population census available on Ancestry.com, these 1860 farmers and their wives came from the states of Massachusetts, New Hampshire, New York, Ohio, and Vermont, and from the countries of Canada, England, Germany, Ireland, Scotland, and Wales. By 1870, there were 68 hop farmers in Waukesha County—a modest sum compared with the 1,121 hop farmers in Sauk County. By this time, there were 11 German hop farmers in Waukesha County, but 42 people from England growing hops there (Jordan, Hop Farmer Database).

47. That same year, California—which would soon become a reigning hop state—grew a mere 80 pounds of hops. See Kennedy, *Agriculture of the United States in 1860*, xcv.

48. "Productions of Agriculture: Table IV.—State of Wisconsin," in Walker, *Statistics*, 283.

49. Advertisement, *Evergreen City Times*, Mar. 24, 1854, 4.

50. *Wisconsin and Iowa Farmer, and Northwestern Cultivator* 7, no. 2 (1855): 55.

51. J. Moran and Hopkins, *Wisconsin's Weather and Climate*, 115–16.

52. "Commercial," *Milwaukee Daily Sentinel*, Jan. 26, 1852.

53. *Transactions of the Wisconsin State Agricultural Society*, vol. 3, 59–60.

54. About 180–200 pounds per bale seems to have been the general standard, but it could vary depending on how many leaves and stems ended up in the hops, whether they had seeds, and how well the hops had been dried and pressed. "American Hops," *Milwaukee Daily Sentinel*, Nov. 15, 1854.

55. For more on Silas Allen, see Reiherzer, *Winnebago County Beer*, and the virtual exhibit in Wisconsin Oral History Project, "The Lands We Share."

56. See, for example, Bauer, "Sudsy Sovereignty"; Bauer, *We Were All Like Migrant Workers Here*; Chan, *This Bittersweet Soil*; C. Daniel, *Bitter Harvest*; Kopp, *Hoptopia*; Raibmon, *Authentic Indians*; Vaught, *Cultivating California*.

57. Bauer, "Sudsy Sovereignty"; Bauer, *We Were All Like Migrant Workers Here*.

58. Cordle, *Out of the Hay*; O'Neill, *Pull No More Bines*; Galbraith, "Health Supervision of Hop and Fruit Pickers"; Sutherland and Walton, *Hop Pickers' Hovels*; Kent Archive, "Hops in Kent"; Carr and Hanbury, "Utilizing Discomfort to Better Support Gypsy, Romany and Traveller Young People's Experiences."

59. British Hop Association, "Kent and the South East."

60. Orwell, *Diaries*.

61. H. Parker, *The Hop Industry*, 73.

62. H. Parker, *The Hop Industry*, 166. See also the websites for the German Hops Museum (https://www.hopfenmuseum.de/en/) as well as the phenomenal HopfenBierGut in Spalt (https://hopfenbiergut.de/en-gb/startseite).

63. See also Komori, "Canadian 'War of the Two Sugars,'" on the racialization of sugar beet labor in Canada.

64. See Tiya Miles's powerful account of the work (and life and love) of enslaved women and their descendants (Miles, *All That She Carried*) as well as Seth Rockman's discussion of the work of enslaved weavers and seamstresses (Rockman, *Plantation Goods*) and Marisa Fuentes's study of enslaved women, violence, and the archive (Fuentes, *Dispossessed Lives*).

65. C. Collins, "Cholera and Typhoid Fever in Kent"; Street, *Beasts of the Field*, 284.

66. Bohn, "Hop Culture in Early Sauk County," 392.

67. *Transactions of the Wisconsin State Agricultural Society*, vol. 3, 59–60.

68. Summerhill, *Harvest of Dissent*, 108.

69. Summerhill, *Harvest of Dissent*, 47.

70. See W. Moran, *Belles of New England*, and Eisler, *Lowell Offering*, for example.

71. See Ulrich, *A Midwife's Tale*, on weaving; Jensen, "Butter Making," on how the production of butter by women was economically significant and understudied; R. Miller, *Entangled Lives*. Also see Coulthard, *The Barn*, for a discussion of the risks involved for women working as domestic servants or other laborers in unfamiliar households. Even the Thomas Hardy novel *Tess of the D'Urbervilles* clearly shows women engaged in a range of agricultural work (some posing a range of risks), including fieldwork and milkmaids.

72. Summerhill, *Harvest of Dissent*, 249n69.

73. Summerhill, *Harvest of Dissent*, 160.

74. Western Historical Company, *History of Sauk County*, 429.

75. W. Canfield, *Map of Sauk County, Wisconsin.*

76. *Baraboo News Republic*, May 19, 1859, 3.

77. *Baraboo Republic*, Sept. 1, 1859, 1. In 1851, a farmer named S. Antisdale in Beloit had won a prize for hops at the state fair. See *Wisconsin and Iowa Farmer, and Northwestern Cultivator* 3, no. 11 (1851): 210.

78. *Wisconsin and Iowa Farmer, and Northwestern Cultivator* 5, no. 11 (1853): 250.

79. Western Historical Company, *History of Jefferson County*, 644.

80. Hibbard, "History of Agriculture," 149.

81. For more on Scandinavian immigration in this era, see Rasmussen, *Civil War Settlers.*

82. Jordan, Hop Farmer Database.

83. Reiherzer, *Winnebago County Beer*, 39.

84. *Wisconsin State Journal*, Aug. 21,1866, 2.

85. *Bi-monthly Report of the Agricultural Department* (1864), 30.

86. Kennedy, *Agriculture of the United States in 1860*, xcv, xcvi.

87. The archives at the University of Wisconsin–Milwaukee hold extensive papers related to Pabst/Best and Blatz for the period in question. Unfortunately, the brewery records that survive for Schiltz at the Milwaukee Public Library do not reach back to the nineteenth century.

88. See, for example, *1856–57 Milwaukee City Directory*; *Erving, Burdick & Co.'s Milwaukee City Directory for 1857–58*; Hoverson, *Drink That Made Wisconsin Famous*, 40.

89. Hoverson, *Drink That Made Wisconsin Famous*, 521.

90. Hoverson, *Drink That Made Wisconsin Famous*, 517.

91. *1860–1861 Directory of the City of Milwaukee.*

92. *Edwards' Annual Directory.*

93. Tolan, "Historical Perspective on Milwaukee's Brewing Renaissance." Some folks (including a guide for a tour I once took of one of Milwaukee's biggest breweries) claim that the Chicago Fire also significantly aided the growth in the fame of Milwaukee's beer industry, but Hoverson (*Drink That Made Wisconsin Famous*) is skeptical, in part because Milwaukee beer was already being shipped to Chicago in significant amounts before the fire.

94. "Annual Statement of the Trade and Commerce of Milwaukee, for the Year 1860," *Milwaukee Daily Sentinel*, Jan. 1, 1861. Hoverson, *Drink That Made Wisconsin Famous*, 45. See also Wisconsin Historical Society, "Brewing and Prohibition."

95. In 1853, port records held on microfilm at the Wisconsin Historical Society Archives in Madison list a shipment of one ton of hops into the port. State Historical Society of Wisconsin, Division of Archives and Manuscripts P68-2018. United States—Department of Treasury RG 36: Records of the Bureau of Cus-

toms Selected records of the Milwaukee, Wisconsin, Collector. Micro 105 Reel 1 1851–1900, 153.

96. *Das Tägliche Banner*, Mar. 15, 1852.

97. "Brewers seemingly have always found a way to obtain grain and hops, though sometimes at considerable trouble and not in the desired quantities. The general trend has been for the geographical expansion of brewing to predate that of barley and hop production. At the time when New York State was the center of production for barley and hops, breweries were already established in Wisconsin . . . At certain times and places, it was true that local farmers were induced to grow barley and hops in order to supply local brewery demands, but the long-term trend has been that barley and hop production has shown adjustment to purely ecological factors entirely independent of the brewing industry." Baldwin, "Historical Geography of the Brewing Industry," 33–34. Right around the boom, Wisconsin's supply of hops exceeded the demand of in-state breweries, but brewers still had a preference for a range of hops and continued to buy from other states and countries alongside their Wisconsin purchases.

98. Jordan, Hop Farmer Database, 1850 and 1860.

99. Blatz Records, including vols. 47, 48, 51; Pabst Records, vols. 28–30.

100. Hoverson, *Drink That Made Wisconsin Famous*, 21.

101. Drawing on examples from 1836 through 1844, one thousand pounds of "pressed hops" were for sale by S. D. Cowles & Co (*Weekly Wisconsin*, Sept. 8, 1836, 3); Bassett's drugstore advertised hops for sale in a Green Bay paper (*Wisconsin Democrat*, Nov. 11, 1837, 3); W. B. Slocum had one hundred pounds of hops for sale, alongside timothy and clover seed (*Southport Telegraph*, May 30, 1843, 3); Jared Lake had hops for sale in South Port (*South Port American*, Dec. 2, 1843), 3; and S. D. Cowles offered a single bale of hops for sale, "just received," along with dried peaches, Ohio butter, and cheese (*Racine Advocate*, Apr. 23, 1844, 3).

102. *Directory of the City of Milwaukee for the Years 1847–48*, 23; *Directory of the City of Milwaukee for the Years 1848–1849*, 227.

103. "American Hops," *Milwaukee Daily Sentinel*, Nov. 15, 1854.

104. "Hops in Sauk County," *Daily Free Democrat*, Nov. 20, 1855, 2.

105. Hoverson, *Drink That Made Wisconsin Famous*, 29.

106. Dredge, *Brief History of Lager*; Hoverson, *Drink That Made Wisconsin Famous*, 37.

107. Andrew Robichaud ("Frozen Over") has especially interesting takes on ice, including the ways that ice disrupts time, slowing rot (of meat, beer, or even corpses) and shifting the seasons of brewing, slaughter, and harvest. Jeffrey Pilcher (*Hopped Up*, 82) notes that at first the brewers of lager used caves dug into hillsides to achieve the low temperatures required for bottom fermentation, along with the plentiful Midwestern ice, but by the 1860s, they were building ice houses that were easier to manage. But natural ice was the main cooling mechanism for lager until refrigeration became viable and scalable for brewing in the 1880s. See also *One Hundred Years of Brewing*, 74, on seasonality.

108. Hoverson, *Drink That Made Wisconsin Famous*, 37; see also Dredge, *Brief History of Lager*. Pilcher (*Hopped Up*, 74) pinpoints the rise of Pilsener to October 5, 1842.

109. Pilcher, *Hopped Up*, 82, 99.

110. Efford, *German Immigrants*, 40.

111. Walzer, "Beer Gardens and Beer Halls."

112. Walzer, "Beer Gardens and Beer Halls."

113. B. Alberts, "Beer to Stay," 149. See also Ogle, *Ambitious Brew*.

114. B. Alberts, "Beer to Stay," 188. Alberts provides a nuanced discussion of the shifting battle lines between lager and temperance in the nineteenth century.

115. Historic Structures, "Pabst Brewing Company."

116. Historic Structures, "Pabst Brewing Company."

CHAPTER FOUR

1. Hopyard Account book and 1859 ledger, Seymour Papers.

2. "Will It Pay?," *Wisconsin State Register*, May 12, 1866.

3. In her descriptions of these two sisters in her ancestral family, Ruth Burmester noted, "Ellen Augusta 'Ella' 1852–1880 (had deformed back), Ida Jane 1855–1876." Burmester, *A Barn on the Place*, 1-19.

4. Seymour Family file, box 1, Ella Seymour, Seymour Papers. This essay was not in her diary but a separate document, one that seemed to be meant for others to read.

5. Burmester, *A Barn on the Place*, 19-1.

6. Cole, *Standard History of Sauk County*, 95.

7. Schlitz Audubon Nature Center, "Climate and the Tension Zone in Wisconsin."

8. Lange, *A County Called Sauk*, 3.

9. *Reedsburg Remembers*, 1.

10. *Reedsburg Remembers*, 1.

11. Wisconsin Historical Society, "Beer in Wisconsin." In 1860, the city brewed 36,000 barrels of beer; by 1873, production had risen to 260,120 barrels (Merk, *Economic History of Wisconsin*, 154). Exports in this period fluctuated wildly. In 1864, the US exported 3.6 million pounds of hops—one year later, only a tenth as much, 349,987 pounds. Between 1865 and 1875, imports of hops varied from a low of 21,568 in 1869 to a high of 5.6 million pounds in 1872. In 1862–63, Blatz was buying thousands of pounds of hops from several dealers, including Eddy & Wilber and Hinds & Allen (Blatz Records, vol. 47, cf. 7, 42, 83). In the 1860 census, Wisconsin grew 130,000 pounds of hops. Jefferson County led the way with 46,000 pounds, while Sauk County grew 19,300 pounds and Waukesha County 18,000 pounds.

12. Wisconsin Historical Society, "Letters by Relatives of Laura Ingalls Wilder."

13. Wisconsin Historical Society, "Letters by Relatives of Laura Ingalls Wilder." See also Janik, "Ma and Pa Ingalls Married."

14. The figure of $82.50 is my best guess at the number. The handwriting is hard

to read, and she crossed out the original number she wrote. Twenty pickers is also a lot for such a small harvest, unless at least some of those pickers were extended family and not paid separately.

15. The 1860 census breakdown included people from the following places. New York: 15 men, 13 women; England: 4 men, 4 women; Vermont: 3 men, 2 women; Connecticut and Germany: 2 men, 2 women; Ireland: 2 men, 1 woman; Ohio: 2 women; New Jersey: 1 man, 1 woman; Rhode Island: 1 man; Scotland: 1 man; New Hampshire: 1 woman; Pennsylvania, 1 woman. Jordan, Hop Farmer Database.

16. W. Anderson, *Laura's Album*, 13.

17. Perkins, "History of Agriculture in Waukesha County," in Langill and Loerke, *From Farmland to Freeways*, 186.

18. Lange, *A County Called Sauk*, 69.

19. Mandel, *Settlers of Dane County*, 14.

20. *Transactions of the Wisconsin State Agricultural Society*, vol. 7, 36.

21. Paine, "The Hops Era."

22. Mueller, *Only in Sumpter*, 24. County fairs continued to offer prizes for hops and other goods. In 1863, someone named AB Case won a dollar for his bale of hops at the Annual County Fair and Cattle Show (*Baraboo News Republic*, Oct. 14, 1863). Again in 1864, a one-dollar premium was offered for the best bale of hops (*Baraboo News Republic*, Mar. 30, 1864).

23. Blatz Records, vol. 47, 12, 200; vol. 48, 4.

24. "The hop crop of this country increased from 6,000 bales in 1839 to 80,000 in 1862. Owing to unfavorable seasons, the crops of 1863 and 1864 were but 65,000 and 45,000 respectively. The cultivation of the hop has been mainly confined to the high central lands of New York. In 1859 the crop of that state was more than 90 per cent of that of the entire Union; Vermont, which ranks next as a hop grower, producing but one sixteenth part as many." *Milwaukee Daily Sentinel*, Jan. 20, 1865.

25. Fred Miller Notebook ca. 1877–1888, MP20141201-116, Molson-Coors Archive, Milwaukee, Wisconsin.

26. Blatz Records, vol. 48, including pages 7, 10, 17, 23, 70, 76–78, 85–86.

27. Blatz Records, vol. 47, 200.

28. Hoverson, *Drink That Made Wisconsin Famous*, 512.

29. Hoverson, *Drink That Made Wisconsin Famous*, 43.

30. For example, Hoverson, *Drink That Made Wisconsin Famous*, 512.

31. See, for example, Blatz Records, vols. 35, 51, 272.

32. "How Lager Beer is Made," *Milwaukee Daily Sentinel*, Jan. 1, 1866.

33. Tomlan, *Tinged with Gold*, 48.

34. Scot, *Perfite Platforme*; Rudd and Rudd, *Cultivation of Hops*.

35. See, for example, Tomlan, *Tinged with Gold*; Summerhill, *Harvest of Dissent*.

36. "Hops—The Rise and Reign of Lager Beer," *Milwaukee Daily Sentinel*, Jan. 30, 1865.

37. *Documents of the Assembly of the State of New York*, 913.

38. *Waukesha Plain-Dealer*, Sept. 19, 1865.

39. Byrd, "Intertwined," 16.

40. *Sparta Eagle*, Jul. 17, 1867.

41. *Wisconsin State Journal*, May 19, 1876.

42. Hittim A. Gain, letter to the editor, *Milwaukee Daily Sentinel*, Feb. 26, 1866.

43. *Baraboo Republic*, Oct. 3, 1866, 1.

44. *Baraboo Republic*, Oct. 3, 1866, 1.

45. In 1865, Best, predecessor to Pabst, produced 10,908 barrels of beer. By 1873, it was brewing more than 100,000 barrels, a nearly tenfold increase in just eight years (Merk, *Economic History of Wisconsin*, 154). By 1884, Best was brewing over 385,000 barrels (Buck, *Pioneer History of Milwaukee*, 346). The hopping rate was approximately 2 pounds of hops per barrel, as Pabst consumed 800,314 pounds of hops that year (Buck, *Pioneer History of Milwaukee*, 348). While we can assume some change in hopping rate and recipe between 1865 and 1884, extrapolating that figure can at least give us some sense of the relationship between Wisconsin hop production and Wisconsin hop consumption. In the 1866 figures (which are presumably for 1865's harvest), Wisconsin produced 829,377 pounds of hops. In the entire US in 1864, 13 million pounds of hops were grown; 3,657,181 barrels of beer (31 gallons to the barrel) were brewed.

46. Winnebago County grew 67,000 pounds in 1865 ("Wisconsin Items," *Milwaukee Daily Sentinel*, Dec. 28, 1865). Between 1860 and 1865, hop production in Winnebago County increased from almost 17,000 pounds to 67,000 pounds—a huge shift in the agriculture of the county (Noyes, "Chapter XXIV Farm, Factory Pace Quickens," 240).

47. Langson, *Seventh Annual Statement*, 28.

48. "Wisconsin: Her Early History," *Milwaukee Daily Sentinel*, Aug. 1, 1865.

49. *Janesville Gazette*, Jul. 8, 1867.

50. Western Historical Company, *History of Sauk County*, 204.

51. *Baraboo Republic*, Aug. 29, 1866, 3.

52. Horatio Hodge, "Notes of a Tourist," *Milwaukee Daily Sentinel*, Sept. 29, 1866.

53. Hodge, "Notes of a Tourist."

54. *Milwaukee Daily Sentinel*, Sept. 1, 1866, 1. Doug Hoverson was kind enough to share his newspaper files with me, a very useful source to augment the various newspaper databases.

55. "Hop Culture in Wisconsin," *Wisconsin State Journal*, Aug. 14, 1866.

56. Dell Pilot, "Crops," *Milwaukee Daily Sentinel*, Oct. 13, 1866.

57. "Grapes in Sauk County: The Hop Crop of 1866," *Milwaukee Daily Sentinel*, Apr. 24, 1866.

58. "Items," *Milwaukee Daily Sentinel*, Jun. 2, 1866.

59. Dell Pilot, "From Sauk County," *Milwaukee Daily Sentinel*, Aug. 22, 1866. For more on pests, including the "hop worm," see "The Her Cnor [Hop Crop]," *Milwaukee Daily Sentinel*, Jul. 1, 1867. Note the terrible work of the optical character reader (OCR), which interprets an article titled "The Hop Crop" as "The Her Cnor."

60. "From Columbia County," *Milwaukee Daily Sentinel*, Dec. 6, 1866.

61. "Hauptkerle sind doch unsere Temperenzler," *Der Westbote*, Jun. 28, 1866.

62. Hittim A. Gain, letter to the editor, *Milwaukee Daily Sentinel*, Feb. 26, 1866.

63. For example, "Mrs. Hanna Dix of Hilbert . . . arrived with a group of girls from Germany when she was twenty-two [ca. 1869] and for a time earned her living by picking hops" ("The Society and the State," 509).

64. F. Canfield, *The Hop Pickers*, 66, 140.

65. Jensen, *Calling This Place Home*, 9.

66. Thoreau quoted in Meine and Keeley, *The Driftless Reader*, 48.

67. "Wisconsin Items," *Milwaukee Daily Sentinel*, Aug. 27, 1866.

68. "Wisconsin Items," *Wisconsin State Journal*, Oct. 19, 1866.

69. "Hops," *Waukesha Freeman*, reprinted in *Wisconsin State Register*, Feb. 24, 1866.

70. "Wisconsin Items," *Milwaukee Daily Sentinel*, Sept. 10, 1866.

71. Merk, *Economic History of Wisconsin*, 39.

72. Merk, *Economic History of Wisconsin*, 39.

73. Paine, "The Hops Era," 28.

CHAPTER FIVE

1. Trimpey, *Becky: My First Love*, 13.

2. In Silas Seymour's yard in 1867, my calculations suggest that each worker picked approximately 32 pounds of hops each day, but those would have been wet rather than dried hops. "In a yard of eight acres, 50 hands, of whom 40 are misses or women, are employed during the picking season; boys are too boisterous generally, and not counted profitable hands." "Hops and Their Culture," *Milwaukee Daily Sentinel*, Mar. 26, 1866.

3. Lampard, *Rise of the Dairy Industry*.

4. The estimated range of poles per acre from Paine, "The Hops Era," 26; Lapham et al, *Report on the Disastrous Effects*, 93.

5. "Increase of Hop Culture in Wisconsin," *Milwaukee Daily Sentinel*, Jun. 29, 1867.

6. Fuller, Warren & Co., "City Items," *Milwaukee Daily Sentinel*, May 8, 1867.

7. "The Hop Crop of Sauk County," *Wisconsin State Register*, Aug. 17, 1867.

8. "State News," *Milwaukee Daily Sentinel*, Aug. 6, 1867.

9. "The Eastern Hop Crop," *Milwaukee Daily Sentinel*, Aug. 9, 1867.

10. Steiner, *Steiner's Guide to American Hops*, 46.

11. Current et al., *History of Wisconsin: Civil War Era*, 459. Writers of the day often used the word blight to describe hops injured by fungus and/or insects.

12. Women are a noticeable absence in a book like William Cronon's *Nature's Metropolis*. Women rarely appear, yet it is simply told as "history" rather than what it is—a story of the work of men, often reliant on the unmentioned work of women. I have had people incorrectly describe my research being on "women in

the hop industry." It is an analysis of the hop industry, and women turn out to be integral to that industry—they may be making "women's history," but they are also making "history," and including them helps us take a step toward telling a more accurate story.

13. This phrase recently appeared in a Miller ad campaign, purportedly honoring the first professional woman brewer in North America (A. Parker, "No Women, No Beer.") One example of the work returning women to their rightful place in the histories of great industries and economies is Joan Flores-Villalobos's study on the centrality of Black Caribbean women's labor to the creation of the Panama Canal and the ways their earnings gave them some amount of power and ability to resist some of the violence and exploitation of the system in place (Flores-Villalobos, *The Silver Women*). And no canal gets built without work that is often coded as "women's work": laundry and cooking, for starters.

14. F. Canfield, *The Hop Pickers*, 42.

15. S. Rath, *Pioneer Photographer*, 31.

16. F. Canfield, *The Hop Pickers*, 25.

17. Leroy Gates, "Simple and Practical Method of Hop Growing," *Prairie Farmer*, Dec. 14, 1867, 372.

18. "Hops," *Milwaukee Daily Sentinel*, Sept. 10, 1867.

19. Gates, "Simple and Practical Method."

20. Krug, *History of Reedsburg*, 113.

21. Bohn, "Hop Culture," 389–90.

22. However, an important addendum might be the case of the so-called Orphan Trains, a project of the Children's Aid Society in New York that sent tens of thousands of children to midwestern farms between the 1850s and 1890. See Gilfoyle, "Revising the Newsboy," 1171. While "Orphan Train" may be the more well-known term today, professor of social work Karen Staller argues that the term promotes an inaccurate myth around a larger system of child welfare programs and "placing-out" systems (Staller, *New York's Newsboys*, 50).

23. See, for example, F. Canfield, *The Hop Pickers*, 20, along with other sources cited here.

24. "Hops," *Milwaukee Daily Sentinel*, Sept. 10, 1867. Lager required fewer hops than ales in general, and "after the Civil War, with the increasing production of lager, the hopping ratio had already fallen to about 1.8 pounds per barrel." Steiner, *Steiner's Guide to American Hops*, 46.

25. Bohn, "Hop Culture"; Trimpey, *Becky: My First Love*.

26. Pickles, "From the Lemonweir Valley," *Milwaukee Daily Sentinel*, Sept. 19, 1867. I assume that "Pickles" is a pen name, as many of the reporters in these papers write with comical or pun-laden aliases.

27. Street, *Beasts of the Field*, 342, 388.

28. *Vernon County Censor*, Sept. 12, 1866, 2.

29. See for example, *Baraboo Republic*, Aug. 15, 1866, 3; *Wisconsin State Journal*, Aug. 21, 1866, 2.

30. Paine, "The Hops Era."
31. F. Canfield, *The Hop Pickers*, 132.
32. Schuette, *Loganville, Our Heritage*, 67; Lange, *A County Called Sauk*, 67.
33. "State News," *Milwaukee Daily Sentinel*, Sept. 7, 1867.
34. "State News," *Milwaukee Daily Sentinel*, Sept. 21, 1867.
35. Steiner, *Steiner's Guide to American Hops*, 55.
36. They spent the first few months in Wisconsin sleeping outdoors. Not long after they had finally built a small house, Mary Ann, already in ill health, died (Durbin, "Two Wisconsin River Stories," 180). Gates remarried the following spring to another Dells resident, Elizabeth A. Finnegan, and eventually scandal erupted when she left him with their young son and moved in with another man: "She began living elsewhere with a man named Horton. . . . In August of 1866 'old man Gates,' as he was commonly known, sold most of his landholdings to his family. His reasons for doing so are a matter of conjecture, but subsequent events suggest that either he was starting to close out his affairs in anticipation of retiring and leaving the area or that he needed money to expand a hop-growing operation" (Durbin, "Two Wisconsin River Stories," 181).
37. Durbin, "Two Wisconsin River Stories," 182.
38. McIntyre, "Let's Recall the . . . Heyday in Hops."
39. Burmester, *A Barn on the Place*, 18-9.
40. "Gone Hop Picking," *Wisconsin State Register*, Sept. 7, 1867.
41. *Baraboo Republic*, Oct. 3, 1866.
42. "Hop Pickers," *Wisconsin State Register*, Sept. 11, 1869.
43. *Watertown News*, Aug. 26, 1868, 3.
44. *Wisconsin State Journal*, Sept. 1, 1868, 4.
45. "Hop Pickers," *Wisconsin State Register*, Sept. 11, 1869.
46. John Rooney, "Hop Culture in Days Long Past," *Baraboo News*, Oct. 26, 1911.
47. Family Search, "Wisconsin Military Records."
48. Rosholt, *Our County, Our Story*, 184.
49. Steiner, *Steiner's Guide to American Hops*, 56.
50. McIntyre, "Let's Recall the . . . Heyday in Hops," 52.
51. Pickles, "From the Lemonweir Valley."
52. Summerhill, *Harvest of Dissent*, 109.
53. Cole, *Standard History of Sauk County*, 96.
54. "In 1867, John Rooney went into business with his stepfather. They sold their crop for 56 cents a pound that year and made $1,100 over expenses." Schuette, *Loganville, Our Heritage*, 30.
55. Rooney quotations in Cole, *Standard History of Sauk County*, 97.
56. Cole, *Standard History of Sauk County*, 97.
57. 1870 Population Schedule for Freedom Township, Sauk County, Wisconsin, enumerated on August 12, 1870, p. 7, on Ancestry.com.
58. Gates, "Simple and Practical Method."
59. Bohn, "Hop Culture in Early Sauk County," 390.

60. "Dorothy Canfield Fisher's Mother Once with a Merry Hop-Picking Party at Baraboo," *Madison Democrat*, Aug. 23, 1919.

61. Kilsdonk, "Review of Culture and Agriculture," 126.

62. On attempts to develop mechanized picking, see, for example, *Semi-Weekly Wisconsin*, Sept. 2, 1868, 2.

63. Merk, *Economic History of Wisconsin*, 41.

64. *Baraboo Republic*, Aug. 15, 1866, 3.

65. Willie Hopper, "All About Hops," *Wisconsin State Register*, Sept. 14, 1867.

66. Mueller, *Only in Sumpter*, 25.

67. Summerhill, *Harvest of Dissent*.

68. With thanks to Adrienne Martini for this insight.

69. *Waukesha Plain-Dealer*, Waukesha, Wisconsin, Sept. 29, 1868, 3.

70. F. Canfield, *The Hop Pickers*, 121, 123.

71. "Development of Farming in Sauk County," Writers' Program Wisconsin. James Altwies was one of the first to point out to me that there were thousands and thousands of "hop maidens" who traveled to Wisconsin for the harvest (from very far away, on packed train cars). Some people claim that because of the phytoestrogens in the hops, which he says is part of why women did the picking instead of men, the women all started menstruating a week after they started picking. I have found no evidence to support this claim, which also doesn't mean it's not true. His colleague looked for a spike in birth rates after the hop harvest and didn't find one, but that also seems almost impossible to gauge, given the geographic range of the pickers, the poor quality of birth statistics at the time, and the other tremendous noise that would be in that data.

72. Bohn, "Hop Culture in Early Sauk County," 393.

73. From an interview conducted at an unknown date in the twentieth century with Mrs. Harry Allen, John Allen, and Anastasia Furman, all of Allenville, by Robert Gard and Elaine Reetz, as recounted in Gard and Reetz, *Trail of the Serpent*, 143.

74. Xan, *Wisconsin, My Home*, 149–50.

75. "The Hoppenfest," *Wisconsin State Register*, Sept. 26, 1868.

76. "The Hoppenfest."

77. Archer, "Wisconsin Man Inventor," 237.

78. Bohn, "Hop Culture in Early Sauk County," 392.

79. Gard and Reetz, *Trail of the Serpent*, 143.

80. Krueger, "Motherhood on the Wisconsin Frontier," 64.

81. Steiner, *Steiner's Guide to American Hops*, 55.

82. "Simple and Practical Method of Hop-Growing," *Farmer's Magazine*, Jan. 1868, 209. Nineteenth-century author Peter Lund Simmons explained the use of sulfur thus: "Brimstone [sulfur] is burnt on the stove for the purpose of bleaching . . . when the hop is bright and free from disease, and a light green colour is desired, only two or three pounds are used to a kiln of about twenty boxes. . . . The brimstone is placed in a little dish on the stove, a small quantity at a time, and this is repeated until the moisture is expelled from the hop" (Simmonds, *Hops*, 102–3).

83. Krueger, *Wisconsin Stories*, 10.

84. Krueger, *Wisconsin Stories*, 12.

85. Krueger, *Wisconsin Stories*, 14.

86. Jensen, "Calling this Place Home," 15.

87. Current et al. *History of Wisconsin: Civil War Era*, 531.

88. Burmester, *A Barn on the Place*, 20-4.

89. Sutherland and Walton, *Hop Pickers' Hovels*, 6.

90. H. Parker, *The Hop Industry*, 74.

91. Rolvenden History Group, *Hopping in Rolvenden*.

92. Galbraith, "Health Supervision of Hop and Fruit Pickers," 459.

93. Street, "'We Are Not Slaves,'" 218.

94. *Waukesha Plain-Dealer*, Sept. 29, 1868, 3.

95. McIntyre, "Let's Recall the . . . Heyday in Hops," 52.

96. See, for example, Rothman, "Sex and Self-Control"; Dayton, "Taking the Trade"; Sunne, "Abortion in Iowa."

97. See, for example, Cordle, *Out of the Hay and into the Hops*; O'Neill, *Pull No More Bines*.

98. A. H. B., "Letter from Mauston," *Milwaukee Daily Sentinel*, Sept. 2, 1868.

99. A. H. B., "Letter from Mauston."

100. A. H. B., "Letter from Mauston."

101. On the conditions in Kent, England, see, for example, O'Neill, *Pull No More Bines*.

102. A. H. B., "Letter from Mauston."

103. "Hop Picking." *Wisconsin State Register*, Sept. 21, 1867.

104. Krug, *History of Reedsburg*, 111.

105. "As more hopyards were planted, a few analysts warned of the inevitable result of the trend. In a May 13, 1867, article, the *Milwaukee Sentinel* condemned the crazed farmers of the state and those reporters who published 'estimates of costs of raising hops so erroneous that they are calculated to seriously mislead the uninformed.' They further warned that the current crop was 'nearly equal to the home market and the next one [was] sure to overstock it'" (Paine, "The Hops Era," 29).

106. "Hops and Hop Culture. Future Prospects of the Crop. Choice and Preparation of the Ground. The Mode of Cultivation. Picking, Curing and Packing, a Full Account of all the Processes." Furnished for the *Wisconsin State Journal* by W. S. Grubb, Baraboo, Sauk County, Wisconsin, March 9, 1868.

107. John Rooney, "Hop Culture in Days Long Past," *Baraboo News*, Oct. 26, 1911. Some of the dealers of the 1860s included Dixon and Son, Hansen & Co of Kilbourn City, and Ramsey, Mackey and Young of Reedsburg.

108. Rooney quoted in "Night Riders," *Madison Capitol Times*, Feb. 14, 1921.

109. *Reedsburg Remembers*, 82.

110. Lange, *A County Called Sauk*.

111. "State Items," *Milwaukee Daily Sentinel*, Feb. 2, 1867.

112. Current et al., *History of Wisconsin: Civil War Era*, 549.

113. Rumney, "Hops Cultivation in Wisconsin," 53.

114. Bohn, "Hop Culture in Early Sauk County," 394.

115. Merk, *Economic History of Wisconsin*, 41.

116. Eisley and Tishler, "Honey Creek Swiss Settlement," 9.

117. *Wisconsin State Journal*, Jan. 13, 1874.

118. Bohn, "Hop Culture in Early Sauk County," 393.

119. Paine, "The Hops Era."

120. "Marine Intelligence," *Milwaukee Daily Sentinel*, Oct. 7, 1867.

121. Great Lakes Vessel History, "Detroit (Wooden)."

122. "Marine Intelligence," *Milwaukee Daily Sentinel*, Oct. 18, 1867.

123. Great Lakes Vessel History, "Detroit (Wooden)."

124. *Gazetteer and Directory*, 30.

125. *Gazetteer and Directory*, 168.

126. Smithsonian National Museum of American History Behring Center, "On the Water."

127. Smithsonian, "On the Water."

128. Smithsonian, "On the Water."

129. Derby, "History of the Port of Milwaukee," 256.

130. "State Items," *Milwaukee Daily Sentinel*, Sept. 21, 1867.

131. "State Items." Lill might be referring to the Lill & Diversey Brewery, which was the successor to the first commercial brewery in Chicago, Haas & Sulzer. This was an ale brewery, despite the German founders. Mosher, "Chicago."

132. "Multiple News Items," *Wisconsin State Register*, Oct. 5, 1867.

133. Burmester, *A Barn on the Place*, 1-18.

134. For more on the importance of forests for trade and power, see, for example, Clifford and Castonguay, "British Ghost Acres"; Pluymers, *No Wood, No Kingdom*.

135. *Annual Report of the State Board of Agriculture*, 89.

136. S. Rath, *Pioneer Photographer*, 28.

137. See, for example, Peace et al., "Maitland's Moment"; Olson, *The Depletion Myth*.

138. Burrows, "Cultivation of Underwood," 612.

139. See, for example, Cordle, *Out of the Hay and into the Hops*.

140. "State News," *Milwaukee Daily Sentinel*, Jan. 5, 1869.

141. Western Historical Company, *History of Sauk County*, 367.

142. Mueller, *Only in Sumpter*, 24.

143. "The Culture of Hops," *Milwaukee Daily Sentinel*, Nov. 13, 1867.

144. Dell Pilot, "From Sauk County," *Milwaukee Daily Sentinel*, Aug. 22, 1866.

145. Dell Pilot, "Crops," *Milwaukee Daily Sentinel*, Oct. 13, 1866.

146. Gates, "Simple and Practical Method."

147. "Hop Culture," *Practical Farmer and Rural Advertiser of the Middle States*, Jan. 1868, 6.

148. "Hop Poles," *Milwaukee Daily Sentinel*, Sept. 26, 1866.

149. Dell Pilot, "Letter from Kilbourn City," *Milwaukee Daily Sentinel*, Feb. 6, 1867.

150. "Mauston," *Milwaukee Daily Sentinel*, Feb. 20, 1867.

151. Dell Pilot, "Quantity, Durability, Prices, &c., of Different Kinds of Hop Poles," *Milwaukee Daily Sentinel*, Mar. 6, 1867.

152. "Simple and Practical Method of Hop-Growing," *Farmer's Magazine*, Jan. 1868, 209.

153. Pilot, "Quantity, Durability, Prices, &c."

154. "Marine Intelligence," *Milwaukee Daily Sentinel*, Sept. 5, 1867.

155. "State News," *Milwaukee Daily Sentinel*, Nov. 20, 1867.

156. Cole, *Standard History of Sauk County*, 95.

CHAPTER SIX

1. The chapter title quotation comes from Western Historical Company, *History of Sauk County Wisconsin*, 655.

2. *Wisconsin State Journal*, Jan. 15, 1868, 2.

3. "State News," *Milwaukee Daily Sentinel*, Jan. 23, 1868.

4. "State News," *Milwaukee Daily Sentinel*, Dec. 23, 1867. The changing attitude of settlers toward wetlands deserves further inquiry, some of which appears in Adam King's paper "Lead, Land, and Cranberries: The Ho-Chunk Experience in the 19th Century." King argues that competition over cranberry bogs and other berrying terrain contributed to the 1873 attempt to kidnap Ho-Chunk residents of Wisconsin and force them to move to Nebraska. He quotes a June 23, 1873, letter written by a white advocate of Ho-Chunk sovereignty: "The primary cause of the desire for their removal is found in the following facts: Northern Wisconsin has a large area of what is known as cranberry marshes . . . a permanent source of living and income for the Indians. Within the past 2 or 3 years the attention of the whites has been drawn to these marshes as a source of wealth" (28). King points to newspaper coverage of an 1871 purchase by a white-owned company, including land "used by the Ho-Chunk as a summer home and a means of survival and income" (30). Many thanks to Jackie Pozza Reisner, curator of American Indian Collections at the Wisconsin Historical Society, for sharing this resource with me.

5. "State News," *Milwaukee Daily Sentinel*, Jan. 20, 1868.

6. A. H. B., "Letter from Mauston," *Milwaukee Daily Sentinel*, Mar. 12, 1868.

7. Emmet Wells ("Dealer in Hops exclusively and only on Commission. No. 59 Pearl Street. Consignments respectfully solicited") was not a disinterested observer of the hop market—he had a very vested interest in it, as he was a hop dealer himself, with offices, at various times in the 1860s, at 43 Front Street and 59 Pearl Street in Lower Manhattan. "Emmet Wells' Weekly Circular," *Baraboo Republic*, Feb. 5, 1868. The Pearl St. address is visible here, for example: "The Hop Market: Emmet Wells' Weekly Hop Circular," *Wisconsin State Journal*, Dec. 1, 1868, 1.

8. "Emmet Wells' Weekly Hop Circular," *Baraboo Republic*, Feb. 5, 1868, 3.

9. Northern Brewer, "Cluster Hops Pellets"; Northern Brewer, "Hallertau Hops Pellets."

10. "Emmet Wells' Weekly Hop Circular," *Wisconsin State Register*, Feb. 15, 1868.

11. "Emmet Wells' Weekly Hop Circular," *Wisconsin State Register*, Apr. 4, 1868.

12. "Emmet Wells' Weekly Hop Circular," *Wisconsin State Register*, May 9, 1868.

13. "Emmet Wells' Weekly Hop Circular," *Wisconsin State Register*, June 20, 1868, emphasis added.

14. Ure Porter, "Hops," *Wisconsin State Register*, May 2, 1868.

15. "The Hop Crop of Sauk County," *Wisconsin State Register*, Aug. 17, 1867.

16. "Emmet Wells' Weekly Hop Circular," *Wisconsin State Register*, June 20, 1868, 3.

17. *Wisconsin State Register*, Jun. 17, 1868.

18. "Multiple News Items," *Wisconsin State Register*, Jul. 4, 1868.

19. "State News," *Milwaukee Daily Sentinel*, Jun. 29, 1868.

20. "Emmet Wells' Weekly Hop Circular," *Wisconsin State Register*, Jul. 4, 1868.

21. "Emmet Wells' Weekly Hop Circular," *Wisconsin State Register*, Jul. 11, 1868.

22. *Baraboo Republic* quoted in "Hops," *Wisconsin State Register*, Jul. 18, 1868.

23. "Kilbourn and Baraboo Items," *Wisconsin State Register*, Jul. 25, 1868.

24. "Emmet Wells' Weekly Hop Circular," *Wisconsin State Register*, Jul. 25, 1868.

25. "Emmet Wells' Weekly Hop Circular," *Wisconsin State Register*, Jul. 25, 1868.

26. "Emmet Wells' Weekly Hop Circular," *Wisconsin State Register*, Jul. 25, 1868.

27. "Ure Porter on Hops," *Wisconsin State Register*, Aug. 8, 1868.

28. "Emmet Wells' Weekly Hop Circular," *Wisconsin State Register*, Aug. 8, 1868.

29. "Hop Picking, &c.," *Wisconsin State Register*, Aug. 29, 1868.

30. "Hop Picking, &c."

31. "Hop Picking, &c."

32. Merk, *Economic History of Wisconsin*, 1916.

33. Pickles, "From the Lemonweir Valley"

34. D. C. W., "Letter from Portage," *Milwaukee Daily Sentinel*, Sept. 1, 1868.

35. Reilly, "Hop Growing History."

36. *Wisconsin State Register*, May 2, 1868.

37. *Watertown News*, Aug. 5,1868.

38. *Baraboo Republic*, Sept. 2, 1868.

39. *Semi-Weekly Wisconsin*, May 13, 1868.

40. *Wisconsin State Journal*, Jul. 10, 1868, 1.

41. *Watertown News*, Jul. 22, 1868.

42. D. C. W., "Letter from Portage."

43. A. H. B., "Letter from Mauston," *Milwaukee Daily Sentinel*, Sept. 2, 1868.

44. A. H. B., "Letter from Mauston."

45. *Wisconsin State Journal*, Sept. 1, 1868, 4.

46. McMynn, *Nineteenth Annual Report of the Superintendent*, 130.

47. "Multiple News Items," *Milwaukee Daily Sentinel*, Aug. 29, 1868.

48. S. Rath, *Pioneer Photographer*, 31.

49. *Baraboo Republic*, Sept. 2, 1868, 2. I assume the bakery was located in Baraboo.

50. *Wisconsin Mirror*, Sept. 2, 1868.

51. S. Rath, *Pioneer Photographer*, 31.

52. "State Items," *Milwaukee Daily Sentinel*, Sept. 2, 1868.

53. *Biographical History of La Crosse*, 252.

54. Kantrowitz, *Citizens of a Stolen Land*, 92. Also see the following: "The Sparta *Democrat* says 'Mr. H. Greve has engaged the services of about 200 Indians for hop picking." *Baraboo Republic*, Sept. 16, 1868, 3. I continue to seek details of the Ho-Chunk experience of hop picking, a reminder that a finished book can still contain threads that reach into the future.

55. Steve Kantrowitz suggested I look through the Charles E. Brown papers at the Wisconsin Historical Society, which I did, to no avail.

56. One group of Ho-Chunk residents had hired a lawyer to help defend them from removal in the early 1870s. "H.W. Lee, Esq., was employed as attorney by the Indians, and on conferring with Mr. Delano, Secretary of the Interior, he was informed by Ed. R. Smith, Indian Commissioner, that there was no authority for the forcible removal of the Indians, 'that the act simply appropriated money to defray the expense of removal, but did not provide that they should be removed.' On the receipt of this information, [they] at once left the camp and went about their usual work, cutting wood, harvesting, picking hops and berries, and whatever they could get to do. The special agent, being without Indians to transport, secured the assistance of United States troops from Fort Snelling, who, with the assistance of the civil authorities, . . . succeeded in transporting between 700 and 800 of them to Nebraska, where 240 died, and the rest found their way back to Wisconsin in the Spring of 1874. . . . Many of them are now actual settlers in Portage, Marathon, and Jackson counties." Western Historical Company, *History of Northern Wisconsin*, 728.

57. Bauer, "Sudsy Sovereignty"; Carney, "Whiteness and Settler Colonial Logics"; Kopp, *Hoptopia*.

58. *Wisconsin State Journal*, Sept. 3, 1868, 2.

59. *Wisconsin State Journal*, Sept. 3, 1868, 2.

60. Correspondence of the Sentinel, "From the West," *Milwaukee Daily Sentinel*, Sept. 4, 1868.

61. A. H. B., "Letter from Mauston."

62. "It requires two or three years to get a yard into bearing, and if started when hops are at the highest, it will come into bearing just when they are the lowest, and vice versa." "Hop Culture," *Milwaukee Daily Sentinel*, Oct. 28, 1869.

63. Writers' Program Wisconsin.

64. "Emmet Wells' Weekly Hop Circular," *Wisconsin State Register*, Jul. 25, 1868.

65. Krug, *History of Reedsburg*, 114.

66. Krug, *History of Reedsburg*, 114.

67. Just ahead of the lynch mob, Sheriff Lewis raced his buggy alongside a canal and scooped up the accused man, who was fleeing the mob on foot. The buggy foundered on the way back to the jail, so Lewis and the accused man ran as fast as they could so the sheriff could get him to the comparative safety of a jail cell. When the mob caught up with them at the jail, Lewis clobbered the ringleader of the mob over the head with a pair of shackles. The mob dispersed, and the accused man was later acquitted at court in Madison. "Murder at Portage City," *Milwaukee Daily Sentinel*, Aug. 18, 1857. See also *History of Columbia County*, 493–94.

68. "The first new hops we have noticed in market were 14 bales which came to-day, Friday, from the yard of E.F. Lewis. They are in prime order and neatly baled. They are stored in Wentworth's warehouse." "Multiple News Items," *Wisconsin State Register*, Sept. 5, 1868.

69. "Hop Picking," *Wisconsin State Register*, Sept. 5, 1868.

70. "Thus far no buyer has entered the field here. A dispatch from Mauston says that 40 cents a pound has been offered there, but we are inclined to doubt it. Our home dealers are generally of the belief that no extensive purchases will be made until hops are baled." *Semi-Weekly Wisconsin*, Sept. 2,1868, 2.

71. *Der Wanderer*, Sept. 12, 1868.

72. Langson, *Eleventh Annual Statement*, 41.

73. *Vernon County Censor*, Sept. 2, 1868, reprinting an article from *Wisconsin Mirror*, 2.

74. *Wisconsin State Journal*, Sept. 16, 1868.

75. "The Hop Crop and Prices—The Latest," *Wisconsin State Journal*, Sept. 19, 1868, 2.

76. Writers' Program Wisconsin. "In 1867, the price of hops was from 40 to 55 cents per pound, while in 1869 it was from 10 to 15 cents, some of poor quality selling as low as 3 cents." Butterfield, *History of Dane County, Wisconsin*, 156.

77. Hibbard, "History of Agriculture," 152.

78. "HOPS: The Sauk County Crop Blighted," *Wisconsin State Journal*, Sept. 16, 1868. Jerry Apps (*Breweries of Wisconsin*, 29) incorrectly dates the crash as happening in 1867. It most decidedly happened in 1868, not 1867.

79. "Troubles Between Hop-Growers and Pickers," *Milwaukee Daily Sentinel*, Sept. 26, 1868.

80. "Troubles Between Hop-Growers and Pickers."

81. *Vernon County Censor*, Sept. 12, 1866, 2.

82. *Wisconsin State Journal*, Sept. 16, 1868.

83. *Wisconsin State Journal*, Dec. 11, 1868.

84. *Wisconsin State Journal*, Dec. 11, 1868.

85. Western Historical Company, *History of Sauk County*, 618.

86. Cole, *Standard History of Sauk County*, 526.

87. Merk, *Economic History of Wisconsin*, 42.

88. United States Census Schedules for Wisconsin, 1870, ser. 1677, vol. 7, Sauk

County, Wisconsin Historical Society Library and Archives, Madison, and Jordan, Hop Farmer Database.

89. "Agricultural Schedules: 1850 to 1900," in Walker, *Statistics*, 281.

90. "Oconomowoc—Hops in this vicinity look well, and if they get through the next two weeks all right, there will be a good yield. In and around Hartland, the hop yards do not look thrifty, and the yield must necessarily be very light." *Waukesha Plain-Dealer*, Aug. 11, 1868, 3.

91. I have seen only one claim to suggest that the hop crash was related to the temperance movement, and I have found no evidence to support it: "The eventual demise of hop cultivation in Wisconsin was caused by pressure from religious groups opposed to the consumption of malted beverages and growing competition from new hop-growing regions in California and the Pacific Northwest and revitalized hop growing in New York." J. Moran and Hopkins, *Wisconsin's Weather and Climate*, 28.

92. From William S. Grubb, Hop Commission Dealer, Baraboo, Sauk Co., Wis. "Hops," *Wisconsin State Journal*, Sept. 16, 1868.

93. Cole, *Standard History of Sauk County*, 1918.

94. E. F. Lewis, "Proportionate Hop Cultivation," *Wisconsin State Register*, June 12, 1869.

95. "Lewis' Hop Yard, &c.," *Wisconsin State Register*, Aug. 22, 1868.

96. *Watertown Democrat*, Sept. 6, 1866, 3.

97. "Emmet Wells' Weekly Hop Circular," *Wisconsin State Register*, Jun. 13, 1868.

98. "Emmet Wells' Weekly Hop Circular," *Wisconsin State Register*, Jul. 25, 1868.

99. "Emmet Wells' Weekly Hop Circular," *Wisconsin State Register*, Jul. 25, 1868.

100. "City Matters," *Milwaukee Daily Sentinel*, Jun. 9, 1869.

101. Western Historical Company, *History of Milwaukee*, 1458–59.

102. Buck, *Pioneer History of Milwaukee*, 348. Note that this is from the 1886 version of this book, not the 1876 version.

103. Western Historical Company, *History of Milwaukee*, 1462.

104. Buck, *Pioneer History of Milwaukee*, 348.

105. Barton, *Industrial History of Milwaukee*, 126–27.

106. Paine, "The Hops Era."

107. "Marine Intelligence," *Milwaukee Daily Sentinel*, Oct. 20, 1868.

108. "Marine Intelligence," *Milwaukee Daily Sentinel*, Nov. 5, 1868; "Marine Intelligence," *Milwaukee Daily Sentinel*, Nov. 7, 1868; "Marine Intelligence," *Milwaukee Daily Sentinel*, Nov. 28, 1868. The *Alpena* later sank in the "Big Blow" of 1880, and all aboard perished in one of the biggest storms to hit Lake Michigan (MSRA, "Alpena"). The *City of Fremont* (renamed the *Adiramled* in 1908) also later foundered and sank—in June 1912, in Lake Ontario (Great Lakes Shipwreck Files, "Adiramled"), but all aboard survived because they were able to get into "one of the lifeboats 10 minutes before the steamer went to the bottom of the lake" (Shipwrecks of Upstate NY, "Lake Ontario Ship Wrecks: S.S. Adiramled").

109. "Emmet Wells' Weekly Hop Circular," *Wisconsin State Register*, Oct. 31,

1868. This policy adopted by brewers affected the hop growers: "The resolution adopted unanimously by the last National Convention of Brewers, to buy hops only as they needed them for use, has had, and will have, more to do with the present prices than any 'rings,' or all the meetings at hop centers of all the growers in Wisconsin." Shanghai Chandler, "Hops, and Something Else About 'Em," *Wisconsin State Register*, Oct. 31, 1868. The steamers *Manitowoc* and *Alpena* continued to bring hops around Lake Michigan, including seventy bales to Chicago on the *Alpena*. "Marine Intelligence," *Milwaukee Daily Sentinel*, Oct. 16, 1868; "Marine Intelligence," *Milwaukee Daily Sentinel*, Sept. 24, 1868.

110. "The Hop Market: Emmet Wells' Weekly Hop Circular," *Wisconsin State Journal*, Dec. 11, 1868.

111. "State News," *Milwaukee Daily Sentinel*, Nov. 12, 1868.

112. "Hop Market—A New Move," *Wisconsin State Register*, Dec. 5, 1868.

113. Muza Hawkins, "Village of Ironton," in *Reedsburg Remembers*, 87. Even in the 1850s, English brewers were using US hops: Whitbread brewed ales with various combinations of American, English, and Belgian, according to their brewing logs from 1850 to 1858. Pattinson, *London! Brewing Capital*, 393.

114. "Multiple News Items," *Wisconsin State Register*, Dec. 5, 1868.

115. Like Kopp's findings in Oregon, hop growing in Wisconsin was always a translocal affair: "Oregon farmers depended on the importation of rootstock, knowledge, technology, and goods not only from Europe and the eastern United States but also from Asia, Latin America, and Australasia. They also relied upon a seasonal labor supply of people from all of these areas as a supplement to local Euro-American and indigenous communities to harvest their crops. In turn, Oregon hop farmers reciprocated in exchanges of plants and ideas with growers and scientists around the world, and, of course, sent their cured hops into the global marketplace." Kopp, *Hoptopia*, 4.

116. "Emmet Wells' Weekly Hop Circular," *Wisconsin State Journal*, Nov. 25, 1868.

117. *Wisconsin State Journal*, Nov. 25, 1868.

118. McIntyre, "Let's Recall the . . . Heyday in Hops," 5.

119. "It is not more than fifteen years ago that the culture of hops was first attempted in this state, and 'choice' Wisconsin hops are now known all over the world." "The Hop Crop of Wisconsin," *Semi Weekly Wisconsin*, Sept. 16, 1868.

120. *Wisconsin State Journal*, Sept. 16, 1868, 2.

121. *Bi-monthly Report of the Agricultural Department*, 409.

122. Kopp, *Hoptopia*.

123. Reilly, "James Weaver and Hops."

124. "Exports of hops from New York from Sept. 1st 1868 to Sept. 1st, 1869: To Liverpool and London 71,030 bales, Cuba 228 bales, China 398, Australia 437, Brazil 306, New Granada 263, Mexico 289, British West Indies 31, Venezuela 20, Chili 18, Central America 10, Peru 4, Miscellaneous 7, British North American Colonies 153, Total Exports 73, 224. Exports from other American ports: From Boston 2213

bales, Baltimore 115 bales, Philadelphia 401 bales, Portland 1634 bales . . . Grand total 77,687." "Emmet Wells' Weekly Hop Circular," *Semi-Weekly Wisconsin*, Sept. 18, 1869.

CHAPTER SEVEN

1. "Emmet Wells' Weekly Hop Circular: New York," *Semi-Weekly Wisconsin*, Sept. 18, 1869.

2. Wikipedia, "RMS *Scotia*," last modified July 26, 2025, 15:55 (UTC), https://en.wikipedia.org/wiki/RMS_Scotia.

3. USDA, "Productions of Agriculture: Table IV.—State of Wisconsin," in Walker, *Statistics*, 283. Note that the totals can vary slightly by source, owing to a combination of errors by compilers in later interpretations of handwriting, as well as omissions of particular pages or townships. When I tallied the totals in each handwritten section of the agricultural census for Wisconsin in 1870, I found a few instances where my calculations strayed from the official numbers in this document, but in most cases my calculations were correct and the compilers were incorrect. See specific notes in Jordan, Hop Farmer Database.

4. "Hop Culture," *Milwaukee Daily Sentinel*, Oct. 28, 1869.

5. "Monetary and Commercial," *Milwaukee Daily Sentinel*, Feb. 18, 1869.

6. "The Hop Market: Emmet Wells' Weekly Hop Circular," *Wisconsin State Journal*, Jan. 19, 1869.

7. "Monetary and Commercial," *Milwaukee Daily Sentinel*, May 13, 1869.

8. "Monetary and Commercial," *Milwaukee Daily Sentinel*, Feb. 18, 1869.

9. "State News," *Milwaukee Daily Sentinel*, Feb. 22, 1869.

10. "Regulating Industry and Values," *Milwaukee Daily Sentinel*, Apr. 24, 1869.

11. "Multiple News Items," *Wisconsin State Register*, Jul. 3, 1869.

12. "The Hop Crop," *Wisconsin State Register*, Sept. 11, 1869; "The Hop Crop," *Milwaukee Daily Sentinel*, Sept. 30, 1869.

13. A.h.b., "Letter from Mauston," *Milwaukee Daily Sentinel*, Sept. 11, 1869.

14. Jordan, Hop Farmer Database.

15. Fowler's wife, Elisabeth, was also listed as "Indian" in the census (Ancestry.com). In addition, at least one man, Moses Paquette, was listed as white in the census but had Indigenous grandparents (Waggoner, *"Neither White Men Nor Indians,"* 5).

16. The census taker listed Martha Jackson as "Mulatto," a category that was included in the census collections of 1850–90, 1910, and 1920. The 1870 definition was "quadroons, octoroons and all persons having any perceptible trace of African blood." K. Parker et al., "Chapter 1: Race and Multiracial Americans in the US Census."

17. Cox, *Bone and Sinew of the Land*, xv.

18. Cox, *Bone and Sinew of the Land*, 190.

19. Cox, *Bone and Sinew of the Land*, 193.

20. Clark-Pujara, "Race-Based Slavery," 41.
21. Jordan, Hop Farmer Database.
22. Clark-Pujara, "Race-Based Slavery."
23. Jordan, Hop Farmer Database.
24. Western Historical Company, *History of Sauk County*, 751.
25. French, *American Sketchbook*, 126.
26. *Transactions of the Oneida Historical Society at Utica*, 149.
27. Myrick, *The Hop*, 41.
28. Usher, *Wisconsin: Its Story*, 1311.
29. *Weekly Wisconsin*, Nov. 24, 1869.
30. *Monthly Reports of the Dept. of Agriculture* (1870), 338.
31. McIntyre, "Let's Recall the . . . Heyday in Hops," 52.
32. *Wisconsin State Journal*, Sept. 16, 1868.
33. *Wisconsin State Journal*, Oct. 11, 1870.
34. *Wisconsin State Journal*, Sept. 9, 1871.
35. *Wisconsin State Journal*, Sept. 9, 1871.
36. Mueller, *Only in Sumpter*, 27.
37. *Reedsburg Free Press*, Jan. 3, 1873.
38. *Portrait and Biographical Record of Excelsior County*, 200.
39. *Portrait and Biographical Record of Excelsior County*, 200.
40. Keller, "Roberta Jean Brown Duckett."
41. Butterfield, *History of Dane County*, 204–5.
42. "The News," *Milwaukee Daily Sentinel*, Aug. 27, 1870.
43. *Wisconsin State Journal*, Sept. 7, 1872.
44. *Wisconsin State Journal*, Sept. 7, 1872.
45. [Frank Moore], "The Winnebago Indians," *Wisconsin State Register*, Jan. 18, 1873, 2.
46. Moore quoted in Onsager, "Removal of the Winnebago," 205.
47. Kantrowitz, *Citizens of a Stolen Land*, 11. In the same year that Ella began keeping her diary, the Washington correspondent for the *Milwaukee Sentinel* followed the debates taking place in Congress about the violent expulsion of Ho-Chunk and other Indigenous residents. The reporter, Frank Moore, asked why Ho-Chunk residents would leave "the abundant huckleberry ridges, cranberry marshes, muskrat house and catfish sloughs of Wisconsin for the 'rich soil' of the far-away South" (*Milwaukee Sentinel*, 1873, 1). Moore mentioned Yellow Thunder (Wakąjazi) owning forty acres not far from the Dells and Blue Wing (Ahuchoga) owning forty acres in Monroe County. Lawrence Onsager references a letter written by Hunt about meeting with Winneshiek, who said he and other Ho Chunk "would not leave the graves of their ancestors in Wisconsin until they are compelled to do so by force" (Onsager, "Removal of the Winnebago," 203). In the winter of 1873–74, the federal government made yet another attempt at violent removal (Onsager, "Removal of the Winnebago," 220). Ella's well-recorded domesticity, the

vivid sense of home she conveys in her writing, is adjacent to this ongoing, violent refusal to allow Ho-Chunk people to be at home in the same space.

48. DeKaury, *Narrative of Spoon Decorah*, 13.

49. Onsager, "Removal of the Winnebago," 119, 124. According to Frank Moore, "They earn by hunting fur, catching fish, picking hops, picking huckleberries and picking cranberries, more than enough each year to give them a comfortable livelihood" (quoted in Onsager, "Removal of the Winnebago," 143). The Ho-Chunk communities in this area continued to pick hops, as well as cranberries, into the 1870s (Onsager, "Removal of the Winnebago," 205).

50. Onsager, "Removal of the Winnebago," 216, citing the *Juneau County Argus*, Dec. 25, 1873: "At six p.m., seventy-three [Ho-Chunk people] were placed on the westbound train for Sparta. They arrived there at three-thirty a.m. on the 21st and Lt. Stafford delivered the captives to Captain Thomas. The captive [Ho-Chunk] were lodged over Sunday, under guard, in H. Greve's hop house, near the railroad depot." A report was written in September 1869, in New Lisbon, by D. A. Griffith, "special Indian agent." The report lists gathering and selling blueberries and cranberries, the cultivation of corn and potatoes on a small scale, and that Ho-Chunk residents of the area "also assist at harvesting and picking hops. They are well off in ponies, and in winter engage in hunting and trapping." Griffith, "No. 147: United States Special Agency for Stray Bands," 447.

51. King, "Lead, Land, and Cranberries," 28.

52. Summerhill, *Harvest of Dissent*, 162.

53. Summerhill, *Harvest of Dissent*, 163.

54. Summerhill, *Harvest of Dissent*, 161. For more on migrant labor, see in particular Hahamovitch, *Fruits of Their Labor*; Hahamovitch, *No Man's Land*; Suits, "Hoboes, Wheat, and Climate Precarity."

55. Population census schedule for California, 1870Sacramento County, on Ancestry.com. See, for example, Center Township, Sacramento County, p. 8, where thirty-eight Chinese men are enumerated, all with the occupation of hop picker.

56. Bauer, *We Were All Like Migrant Workers Here*; Bauer, "Sudsy Sovereignty"; Carney, "Whiteness and Settler Colonial Logics"; Chan, *This Bittersweet Soil*; Kopp, *Hoptopia*; Vaught, *Cultivating California*.

57. This is not the daughter in law of Hiram and Deborah Pelton, but rather seems to have been married to Jason Pelton, son of J. and Sarah Pelton.

58. Even as late as 1873, Ella's mother was still using her spinning wheel. Her mother-in-law was a weaver, and I found a brief mention of a loom at the Silas Seymour place, and several references to knitting, including knitting stockings.

59. See, for example, Blatz Journal, October 1873, Blatz Records, vol. 51, 323.

60. *Transactions of the Wisconsin State Agricultural Society*, vol. 12, 25.

61. *Transactions of the Wisconsin State Agricultural Society: W. W. Field Secretary's Annual Report*, 25.

62. Sussex-Lisbon Area Historical Museum, "William Weaver Letter to Cousin John Hardeman."

63. *Wisconsin State Journal*, Jan. 13, 1874.

64. Brown, *The Small Book.*

65. *Monthly Reports of the Dept. of Agriculture* (1874), 362.

66. Illinois, Michigan, Alabama, and many other states all tried their hand. On Illinois, for example, see *Monthly Reports of the Dept. of Agriculture* (1872), 345.

67. *Monthly Reports of the Dept. of Agriculture for the Year 1875*, 495.

68. Hoverson, *Drink That Made Wisconsin Famous*, 517.

69. Hoverson, *Drink That Made Wisconsin Famous*, 508.

70. This brewery was first known as Empire, then as Best and Company, finally acquiring the name of Pabst in 1889 (Pabst Mansion Milwaukee, "Pabst Brewing Company"). The figure of 100,000 pounds of hops for 100,000 barrels is definitely approximate. Brewers' recipes varied, including balancing old hops with new hops to avoid too strong a hop flavor. These recipes were using somewhere between 1 and 2 pounds of hops per brewer's barrel, or per thirty-one gallons. I sought the guidance of Stan Hieronymus on this question, and his estimate was 1–2 pounds per barrel.

71. Barton, *Industrial History of Milwaukee*, 126.

72. Hoverson, *Drink That Made Wisconsin Famous.*

73. Chris Foran, "Milwaukee's Oldest Bars: Taverns that Have Passed the 100-Year Mark," *Milwaukee Journal-Sentinel*, Oct. 9, 2023. Puddlers Hall is still going strong. In reading this article I was struck by how many of the oldest bars in town are places my husband and I went when we were courting, not out of any intentional pursuit of the oldest taverns but just because these places are still part of the fabric of life in Milwaukee.

74. Such purchases can be found year after year in the Blatz ledgers, daybooks, journals, and other papers held at the University of Wisconsin–Milwaukee Archives. See, for example, Blatz Records, vols. 11, 35, 47, 48, 51, 78, 79, 272, and 286.

75. On hops being damaged by seawater, see Milwaukee Brewery General Journal, Aug. 24, 1874–Mar. 17, 1875, Blatz Records, vol. 79, 119.

76. Blatz Records, vol. 35, 13, 17.

77. On Miller's contract, see Frederick Millers Notebooks, Molson-Coors Archive, Milwaukee. On the Blatz purchases, see, for example, Blatz Records, vol. 47, Milwaukee Brewery Cash Book Dec. 1, 1862–Dec. 27, 1864, 12, 200.

78. *Annual Report of the Commissioner of Agriculture: For the Year 1878 (1879)*, 278.

79. *Annual Report of the Commissioner*, 278.

80. Paine, "The Hops Era," 29. See also Rumney, "Hops Cultivation in Wisconsin."

81. US Department of Agriculture, "Table I.—Summary for the Tenth Census, 1880."

82. "Hop Harvest on at Pabst Farm," *Evening Wisconsin*, Sept. 15, 1908.

83. Barton, *Industrial History of Milwaukee*, 126–27.

84. Pabst Records, vols. 28–30.

85. Pattinson, "When American Hops Moved West."

86. Butterfield, *History of Dane County*, 206.

87. In 1872, Wisconsin had 292 breweries. In 1876, Milwaukee brewed 321,611 "barrels of lager beer"; by comparison, "in 1865 it furnished 65,666 barrels of beer, and in 1870 108,845 barrels. . . . A large quantity of the beer made was shipped to eastern and southern cities. . . . The fame of Milwaukee lager beer is widely extended" (Butterfield, *History of Dane County*, 205).

88. Blatz Records, vol. 51, 385.

89. Gurda, *Milwaukee: City Built on Water*, 52.

90. Gurda, *Milwaukee: City Built on Water*, 52–53.

91. Draeger and Speltz, *Bottoms Up*, 10.

92. Hoverson, *Drink That Made Wisconsin Famous*, 1.

93. Lange, *A County Called Sauk*, 67; see also Western Historical Company, *History of Sauk County*, 158.

94. In Wisconsin, dairying became the fix for a long time. Both hops and dairying later benefited greatly from federal and state interventions, with university extensions and other systems of very intentionally supporting these industries. Wisconsin's Extension wasn't founded until 1891, although the university itself was founded in 1848. Apps, *Breweries of Wisconsin*; Ogle, *Ambitious Brew*.

95. See for example, Marshall, "Michigan Hops"; New York State Brewers Association, "Farm Brewery"; Wisconsin Hop Exchange, "Quality First, Local Always."

96. Joseph Spaulding, whose hop house is pictured in figure 7.2, was born in Maine in 1820, married to a woman named Judith who was born in Ohio in 1821. They harvested 1,200 pounds of hops in 1869. Jordan, Hop Farmer Database. See also Wisconsin Historical Society, "Property Record [. . .] Joseph Spaulding Hop House."

97. Cole, *Standard History of Sauk County*, 95.

98. Perkins, "History of Agriculture in Waukesha County," in Langill and Loerke, *From Farmland to Freeways*, 187.

99. Historical Marker Database, "Beaumont Hop House."

100. Calkins and Laatsch, "Hop Houses of Waukesha County," 186.

101. Kevin Kain, "Caught on the Hop—Wayward Lane Brewing and the History of New York's Hop Houses," *Pellicle*, Aug. 23, 2021; LaDuke, "Hop Houses in Otsego County."

102. Burmester, *A Barn on the Place*, 1-2.

103. Burmester, *A Barn on the Place*, 19-1.

104. Burmester, *A Barn on the Place*, 10-23.

105. "Bobby (Neil's son) . . . had said that the hop house was down. Only he didn't know it was the old hop house, he just said it was the building on the north side of the yard." Burmester, *A Barn on the Place*, vi.

106. The hop house was definitely still standing as late as 1941, when Silas's

granddaughter Ruth and her husband built a new barn. Burmester, *A Barn on the Place*, vi.

CHAPTER EIGHT

1. Seymour Papers.

2. Burmester, *A Barn on the Place*, 1-18.

3. Burmester, *A Barn on the Place*, 7-7.

4. A piece of Ella's needlework, stitched for the US centennial in 1876, resides in an archive in Madison, but the mourning cross-stitch may still reside in a relative's home or may have vanished.

5. Charles Kelley, for example, was a passionate abolitionist and "promoter of the Underground Railroad" who grew 1,200 pounds of hops in Baraboo in 1869. *Reedsburg Remembers*, 110.

6. Tanzilo, "Urban Spelunking: Schlitz Tied Houses." See also Ronnenberg, *Material Culture of Breweries*; Appel, "Building Milwaukee's Breweries."

7. Gartner, "Raised Field Landscapes"; Kozik, "Re-Peopling the Prairie."

BIBLIOGRAPHY

ARCHIVES

Note: Archival sources that have been published or are available online are listed in the "Published Sources" section that follows this list of repositories for papers and other documents.

Molson-Coors Archive, Milwaukee
Fred Miller Notebooks ca. 1877–1888, MP20141201-116.
University of Wisconsin–Milwaukee Archives
Blatz Brewing Company Records, 1862–1944, UWM Manuscript Collection 132.
Pabst Brewing Company Records, 1873–1940, UWM Manuscript Collection 161.
Wisconsin Historical Society, Division of Library, Archives, and Museum Collections, Madison
Dictionary of Wisconsin Biography Rejected Entries, 1950s, Box 1, Folder 2, Call Number Wis Mss SY.
Seymour Family of Dellona, Sauk County, Wisconsin, Papers, 1842–1986 (esp. 1842–1891), Call Number M93-113.
United States Census Schedules for Wisconsin, 1850–1870, Series 1675, 1676, 1677.
Writers' Program. Wisconsin: Writings and Research Notes, 1935–1942, Call Number Wis Mss MM Box 15.

PUBLISHED SOURCES

Acitelli, Tom. *The Audacity of Hops: The History of America's Craft Beer Revolution*. Chicago Review Press, 2013.
Alberts, Brian. "Beer to Stay: Brewed Culture, Ethnicity, and the Market Revolution." PhD diss., Purdue University, 2018.

Alberts, Leen. "Žatec, Cradle of Saaz Hops and Landmark of Commercial Hop Cultivation." *Brewery History*, no. 181 (Winter 2019): 43–50.

Amadou, I., O. S. Gbadamosi, and Guo-Wei Le. "Millet-Based Traditional Processed Foods and Beverages—A Review." *Cereal Foods World* 56, no. 3 (2011): 115–121.

Anderson, Margo. *The American Census: A Social History*. Yale University Press, 1988.

Anderson, William, comp. *Laura's Album: A Remembrance Scrapbook of Laura Ingalls Wilder*. HarperCollins, 1998.

Annual Report of the Commissioner of Agriculture: For the Year 1878 (1879). US Government Printing Office, 1879.

Annual Report of the State Board of Agriculture. Vol. 3. Missouri State Board of Agriculture, 1868.

Appel, Susan K. "Building Milwaukee's Breweries: Pre-Prohibition Brewery Architecture in the Cream City." *Wisconsin Magazine of History* 78, no. 3 (1995): 163–99.

Apps, Jerry. *Breweries of Wisconsin*. University of Wisconsin Press, 1992.

Archer, Myfanwy Morgan. "Wisconsin Man Inventor of Folding Film Roll Kodak Features." *Wisconsin Magazine of History* 16, no. 3 (1933): 235–43.

Arnold, Bettina. "'Drinking the Feast': Alcohol and the Legitimation of Power in Celtic Europe." *Cambridge Archaeological Journal* 9, no. 1 (2009): 71–93.

Atlas of Waukesha Co. Wisconsin, Drawn from Actual Surveys and the County Records to Which is Added a Railroad & Sectional Map of the State of Wisconsin. Harrison and Warner, 1873.

Baker, Donald E., ed. "The Conine Family Letters, 1849–1851: Employed in Honest Business and Doing the Best We Can." From materials contributed by Ruth Seymour Burmester. *Indiana Magazine of History* 69, no. 4 (1973): 320–65.

Baker, Donald E., ed. "The Conine Family Letters, 1852–1863: 'Just Think How We Are Scattered.'" From materials contributed by Ruth Seymour Burmester. *Indiana Magazine of History* 70, no. 2 (1974): 122–78.

Baldwin, William Owen. "Historical Geography of the Brewing Industry: Focus on Wisconsin." PhD diss., University of Illinois, 1966.

Barton, Elmer E. *Industrial History of Milwaukee, the Commercial, Manufacturing and Railway Metropolis of the North-west: Its Great Natural Resources and Advantageous Location as a Shipping Point, with a Review of Its General Business Interests, Including History of Milwaukee Chamber of Commerce, Statistical and Descriptive, to which is Added a Series of Sketches of the Prominent Places and People of the Cream City, the Rise and Progress of Firms, Institutions, and Corporations*. Published by the author, 1886.

Bauer, William J. "Sudsy Sovereignty: Indigenous Workers and the Hops Industry of the Pacific Slope." *Labor: Studies in Working-Class History of the Americas* 12, no. 1–2 (2015): 71–86.

Bauer, William J. *We Were All Like Migrant Workers Here: Work, Community, and*

Memory on California's Round Valley Reservation, 1850–1941. University of North Carolina Press, 2009.

Behre, Karl-Ernst. "The History of Beer Additives in Europe—A Review." *Vegetation History and Archaeobotany* 8 (1999): 35–48.

Bellamy, Jay. "Fireworks, Hoopskirts—and Death: Explosion at a Union Ammunition Plant Proved Fatal for 21 Women." *Prologue Magazine* 44, no. 1 (Spring 2012). https://www.archives.gov/publications/prologue/2012/spring/arsenal.

Bennett, Judith M. *Ale, Beer, and Brewsters in England: Women's Work in a Changing World, 1300–1600*. Oxford University Press, 1999.

Benter, Michael D. *Roll Out the Barrels: Brewers of Eastern Dodge County, Wisconsin, 1850–1961*. Benterprises, 2013.

Bergland, Martha, and Paul G. Hayes. *Studying Wisconsin: The Life of Increase Lapham*. Wisconsin Historical Society Press, 2014.

Bernstein, Peter L. *Wedding of the Waters: The Erie Canal and the Making of a Great Nation*. W. W. Norton, 2010.

Bi-monthly Report of the Agricultural Department. US Government Printing Office, 1864.

Bi-monthly Report of the Agricultural Department. US Government Printing Office, 1868.

Biographical History of La Crosse, Trempealeau and Buffalo Counties. Lewis Publishing Company, Chicago, 1892.

Biographical Review: The Leading Citizens of Livingston and Wyoming Counties, New York. Biographical Review, 1895.

Bissell, Emery Gilbert. "Hop Culture in New York." *American Journal of Pharmacy*, November 1877, 538–43.

Blackhawk, Ned. *The Rediscovery of America: Native Peoples and the Unmaking of US History*. Yale University Press, 2023.

Board of Commissioners of Public Lands. "Wisconsin Public Land Survey Records: Original Field Notes and Plat Maps; Township 12 North, Range 4 East." UW-Madison Libraries. Accessed November 29, 2025. https://digicoll.library.wisc.edu/cgi-bin/SurveyNotes/SurveyNotes-idx?type=article&byte=2560319&twp=T012NR004E.

Bohn, Belle Cushman. "Hop Culture in Early Sauk County." *Wisconsin Magazine of History* 18, no. 4 (1935): 389–94.

Bowen, Sarah. *Divided Spirits: Tequila, Mezcal, and the Politics of Production*. University of California Press, 2015.

Bowes, John P. *Land Too Good for Indians: Northern Indian Removal*. University of Oklahoma Press, 2016.

British Hop Association. "Kent and the South East." Accessed August 5, 2025. https://www.britishhops.org.uk/hops/history/kent-south-east/.

Brown, Sue, ed. *The Small Book, Or The Journals of David Wilson Small*. Anundsen, 1995. https://www.familysearch.org/library/books/idviewer/233746.

Buck, James Smith. *Pioneer History of Milwaukee: 1854–1860*. Milwaukee News, 1886.

Bullard, Albert C. *The Hop Farmer's Year: The Seasons, Tools & Methods of Hop Growers in New York State's Golden Age of Hops*. Square Circle Press, 2015.

Bunker, Stephen G., and Paul S. Ciccantell. *Globalization and the Race for Resources*. Johns Hopkins University Press, 2005.

Burd, Camden. *The Roots of Flower City: Horticulture, Empire, and the Remaking of Rochester, New York*. Cornell University Press, 2024.

Bureau of Land Management. "General Land Office Records." Accession No. MW-1008-018. Accessed August 6, 2025. https://glorecords.blm.gov/details/patent/default.aspx?accession=1008-018&docClass=MW&sid=rd3p12wo.cf0#patentDetailsTabIndex=1.

Burman, Barbara, and Ariane Fennetaux. *The Pocket: A Hidden History of Women's Lives*. Yale University Press, 2019.

Burmester, Ruth Seymour. *A Barn on the Place*. Published posthumously by the author's family, 1996.

Burrows, A. J. "Cultivation of Underwood." *Forestry: A Journal of Forest and Estate Management*. November 1882, 609–14.

Bussey, Dan. *The Illustrated History of Apples in the United States and Canada*. JAK KAW Press, 2016.

Butterfield, Consul Willshire. *History of Dane County, Wisconsin*. Western Historical Company, 1880.

Byrd, Bonnie L. "Intertwined: New York Hop Production During the Rise of the American Brewing Industry." Master's thesis, SUNY at Albany, 2014.

Calkins, Charles F., and William G. Laatsch. "The Hop Houses of Waukesha County, Wisconsin." *Pioneer America* 9, no. 2 (1977): 180–92.

Canfield, Flavia A. Camp. *The Hop Pickers: Girl Life in the Sixties*. Harcourt, Brace, 1922.

Canfield, Wm. C. *Map of Sauk County, Wisconsin*. Louis Lipman Practical Lithographer, 1859. Library of Congress. Accessed August 5, 2025. https://www.loc.gov/item/2012593174/.

Carney, Megan A. "Whiteness and Settler Colonial Logics in the Pacific Northwest Hops and Craft Beer Industries." *Food, Culture & Society* 26, no. 5 (2023): 1032–55.

Carr, Sally, and Ali Hanbury. "Utilizing Discomfort to Better Support Gypsy, Romany and Traveller Young People's Experiences of Education." In *Critical Pedagogies of Discomfort in Practice and Professional Education*, edited by Fiona Cullen, Mike Seal, and Michael Whelan. Bloomsbury, 2025.

Chan, Sucheng. *This Bittersweet Soil: The Chinese in California Agriculture, 1860–1910*. University of California Press, 1986.

Chaudhuri, Nupur, Sherry J. Katz, and Mary Elizabeth Perry, eds. *Contesting Archives: Finding Women in the Sources*. University of Illinois Press, 2010.

City of Reedsburg. "Reedsburg Hops Mural." Accessed August 12, 2025. https://www.reedsburgwi.gov/index.asp?SEC=DFD59405-6470-4E56-87AD-43AB9F73E21F&DE=3B4561E8-8CC5-464E-B58D-1088C994409E.

Clark-Pujara, Christy. "Race-Based Slavery and People of African Descent on the Midwestern Frontier," *Middle West Review* 10, no. 2 (2024): 57–43.

Clifford, Jim. "London's Soap Industry and the Development of Global Ghost Acres in the Nineteenth Century." *Environment and History* 27, no. 3 (2021): 471–97.

Clifford, Jim. *West Ham and the River Lea: A Social and Environmental History of London's Industrialized Marshland, 1839–1914*. University of British Columbia Press, 2017.

Clifford, Jim, and Stéphane Castonguay. "British Ghost Acres and Environmental Changes in the Laurentian Forest During the Nineteenth Century." *Journal of Historical Geography* 78 (2022): 126–38.

Coates, Peter. *American Perceptions of Immigrant and Invasive Species: Strangers on the Land*. University of California Press, 2006.

Cole, Harry Ellsworth, ed. *A Standard History of Sauk County, Wisconsin*. Lewis, 1918.

Collins, Christopher. "Cholera and Typhoid Fever in Kent." Kent Archaeological Society Paper No. 4 (2021). Kent Archaeological Society. Accessed August 13, 2025. https://www.kentarchaeology.org.uk/papers/cholera-and-typhoid-fever-in-kent.

Collins, James P. "Native Americans in the Census, 1860–1890." *Prologue Magazine* 38, no. 2 (Summer 2006). https://www.archives.gov/publications/prologue/2006/summer/indian-census.html.

Collot, Georges-Henri-Victor. *A Journey in North America, Containing a Survey of the Countries Watered by the Mississippi, Ohio, Missouri, and other Affluing Rivers*. Vol. 1. Paris, 1826. Printed for Arthus Bertrand. https://www.americanjourneys.org/aj-088a/.

Compendium of the Enumeration of the Inhabitants and Statistics of the United States. Special report prepared at the request of the Department of State. Thomas Allen, 1841. https://www.nass.usda.gov/AgCensus/archive/files/1840.pdf.

Cordle, Celia. *Out of the Hay and into the Hops: Hop Cultivation in Wealden Kent and Hop Marketing in Southwark, 1744–2000*. University of Hertfordshire Press, 2011.

Cornelius, Carol. *A History in Indigenous Voices: Menominee, Ho-Chunk, Oneida, Stockbridge, and Brothertown Interactions in the Removal Era*. Wisconsin Historical Society Press, 2023.

Coulthard, Sally. *The Barn: The Lives, Landscapes, and Lost Ways of an Old Yorkshire Farm*. Head of Zeus, 2021.

Cox, Anna-Lisa. *The Bone and Sinew of the Land: America's Forgotten Black Pioneers and the Struggle for Equality*. PublicAffairs, 2018.

Cronon, William. *Changes in the Land: Indians, Colonists, and the Ecology of New England*. Hill and Wang, 1983.

Cronon, William. *Nature's Metropolis: Chicago and the Great West*. Norton, 1992.

Current, Richard Nelson, Jack Holzhueter, and Paul Hass. *The History of Wisconsin: The Civil War Era, 1848–1873*. Wisconsin Historical Society, 2014.

Curtis, John T. *The Vegetation of Wisconsin: An Ordination of Plant Communities*. University of Wisconsin Press, 1959.

Daniel, Cletus E. *Bitter Harvest: A History of California Farmworkers, 1870–1941*. University of California Press, 1982.

Daniel, Eddee. "Wisconsin's Oak Savannas (And Why You Should Appreciate Them)." *Milwaukee Magazine*, May 24, 2017. https://www.milwaukeemag.com/oak-savannas-milwaukee-county/.

Dayton, Cornelia Hughes. "Taking the Trade: Abortion and Gender Relations in an Eighteenth-Century New England Village." *William and Mary Quarterly* 48, no. 1 (1991): 19–49.

DeKaury, Spoon. *Narrative of Spoon Decorah*. Collections of the State Historical Society of Wisconsin 13. State Historical Society of Wisconsin, 1895. http://www.wisconsinhistory.org/turningpoints/search.asp?id=34.

DeLeers, Michael. "Object History: Plank Roads." Wisconsin 101. September 2019. https://wi101.wisc.edu/object-history-plank-roads/.

DeNorma, Jeanine S. "Humulus Genetic Resources." National Clonal Germplasm Repository: Corvallis, OR, Agricultural Research Service, US Department of Agriculture. Modified September 3, 2020. https://www.ars.usda.gov/pacific-west-area/corvallis-or/national-clonal-germplasm-repository/docs/ncgr-corvallis-humulus-germplasm/#introduction.

Densmore, Christopher. "Understanding and Using Early Nineteenth Century Account Books." *Midwestern Archivist* 5, no. 1 (1980): 5–19.

Derby, William Edward. "A History of the Port of Milwaukee—1835–1910." PhD diss., University of Wisconsin–Milwaukee, 1963.

DeSoucey, Michaela. *Contested Tastes: Foie Gras and the Politics of Food*. Princeton University Press, 2016.

Dighe, Ranjit S. "A Taste for Temperance: How American Beer Got to Be So Bland." *Business History* 58, no. 5 (2016): 752–84.

DigiTreaties. "Cession 187." Accessed August 18, 2025. https://digitreaties.org/treaties/cession/187/.

Directory of the City of Milwaukee for the Years 1847–48. Wilson & King, 1847.

Directory of the City of Milwaukee for the Years 1848–49. Rufus King, 1848.

Documents of the Assembly of the State of New York: Ninetieth Session—1867. Vol. 17, no. 243. Printing House of C. Van Benthuysen & Sons, 1867. https://www.google.com/books/edition/Documents_of_the_Assembly_of_the_State_o/-mwbAQAAIAAJ?hl=en&gbpv=1.

"Documents: Silas J. Seymour Letters II." *Wisconsin Magazine of History* 32, no. 3 (1949): 328–38.

"Documents: Silas J. Seymour Letters III." *Wisconsin Magazine of History* 32, no. 4 (1949): 456–71.

Dodge, J. R., ed. "Notes on Growing Crops." *Monthly Reports of the Department of Agriculture for the Year 1869*. US Government Printing Office, 1869.

Donohoe, Joan Marie. "Agostin Haraszthy: A Study in Creativity." *California Historical Society Quarterly* 48, no. 2 (1969): 153–63.

Draeger, Jim, and Mark Speltz. *Bottoms Up: A Toast to Wisconsin's Historic Bars and Breweries*. Wisconsin Historical Society Press, 2012.

Dredge, Mark. *A Brief History of Lager: 500 Years of the World's Favourite Beer*. Kyle Books, 2019.

Durbin, Richard D. "Two Wisconsin River Stories." *Wisconsin Magazine of History* 77, no. 3 (1994): 163–95.

An Economic Study of the Hop Industry in Oregon. Station Bulletin 288. Agricultural Experiment Station, Oregon State Agricultural College, June 1931.

Edwards' Annual Directory to the Inhabitants, Institutions, Incorporated Companies, Manufacturing Establishments, Business, Business Firms, etc., etc., in the City of Milwaukee for 1867. Richard Edwards, 1867.

Efford, Alison Clark. *German Immigrants, Race, and Citizenship in the Civil War Era*. Cambridge University Press, 2013.

Egge, Sara. "Gender and Agriculture." In *A Companion to American Agricultural History*, edited by R. Douglas Hurt. John Wiley and Sons, 2022.

1856–57 Milwaukee City Directory. J. M. Van Slyck, 1856.

1860–1861 Directory of the City of Milwaukee. Milwaukee: Starr & Son, 1860.

Eisler, Benita, ed. *Lowell Offering: Writings by New England Mill Women 1840–1845*. Lippincott, 1977.

Eisley, Jane, and William H. Tishler. "The Honey Creek Swiss Settlement in Sauk County: An Expression of Cultural Norms in Rural Wisconsin." *Wisconsin Magazine of History* 73, no. 1 (1989): 2–20.

Elzinga, Kenneth G., Carol Horton Tremblay, and Victor J. Tremblay. "Craft Beer in the United States: History, Numbers, and Geography." *Journal of Wine Economics* 10, no. 3 (2015): 242–74.

Erving, Burdick & Co.'s Milwaukee City Directory for 1857–58. Steam Press of King, Jermain, 1857.

Family Search. "Wisconsin Land and Property." Last modified June 13, 2025, 09:52. https://www.familysearch.org/en/wiki/Wisconsin_Land_and_Property.

Family Search. "Wisconsin Military Records." Last modified March 18, 2025, 11:32. https://www.familysearch.org/en/wiki/Wisconsin_Military_Records#Civil_War_(1861_to_1865).

Ficker, Christian Traugott. "Christian Traugott Ficker's Advice to Emigrants (II)." *Wisconsin Magazine of History* 25, no. 3 (1942): 331–55.

Flores-Villalobos, Joan. *The Silver Women: How Black Women's Labor Made the Panama Canal*. University of Pennsylvania Press, 2023.

For My Cousins. "Sauk County, Wisconsin: Maps and Written History (as of 1878)." Updated February 20, 2012. http://www.formycousins.com/1878/1878atlas-Sauk.html.

French, Bella, ed. *The American Sketchbook: History of Reedsburg, Wis.* Vol. 2, no. 2. Sketch Book Company, 1875.

Fuentes, Marisa J. *Dispossessed Lives: Enslaved Women, Violence, and the Archive*. University of Pennsylvania Press, 2016.

Galbraith, S. Nicol. "The Health Supervision of Hop and Fruit Pickers in South West Kent." *Journal of State Medicine* 41, no. 8 (1933): 457–75.

Gard, Robert E., and Elaine Reetz. *The Trail of the Serpent: The Fox River Valley Lore and Legend*. Wisconsin House, 1973.

Gartner, William Gustav. "Raised Field Landscapes of Native North America." PhD diss., University of Wisconsin–Madison, 2003.

Gauthier, Jason G., ed. *Measuring America: The Decennial Censuses from 1790 to 2000*. US Department of Commerce, 2002.

Gazetteer and Directory of the Chicago, Milwaukee & St. Paul Railway and Branches, the Western Union and the Sabula, Ackley & Dakota Railroads: Embracing All Alphabetical Directories, with Sketches of All Towns Lying Along the Lines of the Above Railroads, Distance Tables and Other Information. Polk, Murphy, 1875.

Gilfoyle, Timothy J. "Revising the Newsboy." *Journal of Urban History* 49, no. 5 (2023): 1171–82.

Goldgar, Anne. *Tulipmania: Money, Honor, and Knowledge in the Dutch Golden Age*. University of Chicago Press, 2007.

Gordon, Avery. *Ghostly Matters: Haunting and the Sociological Imagination*. 2nd ed. University of Minnesota Press, 2008.

Great Lakes Shipwreck Files. "Adiramled." Accessed November 13, 2025. https://greatlakesrex.wordpress.com/alphabetical-shipwreck-list/a/.

Great Lakes Vessel History: The Vessel Histories of Sterling Berry. "Detroit (Wooden)." Accessed August 6, 2025. https://www.greatlakesvesselhistory.com/histories-by-name/d/detroit-wooden.

Griffith, D. A. "No. 147: United States Special Agency for Stray Bands, etc." In *Report of the Commissioner of Indian Affairs, Made to the Secretary of the Interior, For the Year 1869*. US Government Printing Office, 1870.

Gurda, John. *Milwaukee: A City Built on Water*. Wisconsin Historical Society Press, 2018.

Guyette, Richard P., Michael C. Stambaugh, Daniel C. Dey, Joseph M. Marschall, Jay Saunders, and John Lampereur. "350 Years of Fire-Climate-Human Interactions in a Great Lakes Sandy Outwash Plain." *Forests* 7, no. 189 (2016): 1–19.

Hahamovitch, Cindy. *The Fruits of Their Labor: Atlantic Coast Farmworkers and the Making of Migrant Poverty, 1870–1945*. University of North Carolina Press, 1997.

Hahamovitch, Cindy. *No Man's Land: Jamaican Guestworkers in America and the Global History of Deportable Labor*. Princeton University Press, 2011.

Haraszthy, Agoston. "Documents: Haraszthy's Wisconsin Experience." *Wisconsin Magazine of History* 23, no. 2 (1939): 182–206. Originally published in 1844.

Hatheway, Franklin. *Surveying in Wisconsin in 1837*. Edited by Reuben Gold Thwaites. Collections of the State Historical Society of Wisconsin, 1900.

Hibbard, Benjamin Horace. "The History of Agriculture in Dane County, Wisconsin." PhD diss., University of Wisconsin–Madison, 1902.

Hieronymus, Stan. *For the Love of Hops: The Practical Guide to Aroma, Bitterness, and the Culture of Hops*. Brewers Publications, 2012.

Hilton, George Woodman. *Lake Michigan Passenger Steamers*. Stanford University Press, 2002.

Historic Structures. "Pabst Brewing Company, Milwaukee, Wisconsin." Accessed August 6, 2025. https://www.historic-structures.com/wi/milwaukee/pabst_brewing.php.

Historical Marker Database. "Beaumont Hop House." Revised June 16, 2016. https://www.hmdb.org/m.asp?m=76446.

Historical Marker Database. "First Hop Yard." Revised August 13, 2020. https://www.hmdb.org/m.asp?m=154097.

History of Columbia County, Wisconsin. Western Historical Company, 1880.

Ho-Chunk Nation. "About Ho-Chunk Nation." Accessed October 29, 2025. https://ho-chunknation.com/about/.

Hodges, Elizabeth. "The McGrath Hop." *Edible Monterey Bay*, Summer 2016. https://www.ediblemontereybay.com/online-magazine/summer-2016/the-mcgrath-hop/.

Hoverson, Doug. *The Drink That Made Wisconsin Famous: Beer and Brewing in the Badger State*. University of Minnesota Press, 2019.

Jacobson, Lisa. *Intoxicating Pleasures: The Reinvention of Wine, Beer, and Whiskey After Prohibition*. University of California Press, 2024.

Janik, Erika. "Ma and Pa Ingalls Married This Week in 1860." Wisconsin Public Radio. February 1, 2016. https://www.wpr.org/ma-and-pa-ingalls-married-week-1860.

Jefferson, Thomas. *Message from the President of the United States, Communicating Discoveries Made in Exploring the Missouri, Red River, and Washita, by Captains Lewis and Clark, Doctor Sibley, and Mr. Dunbar; with a Statistical Account of the Countries Adjacent*. New York, 1806. Printed by Hopkins & Seymour. http://www.americanjourneys.org/aj-090/.

Jensen, Joan M. "Butter Making and Economic Development in Mid-Atlantic America from 1750 to 1850." *Signs*13, no. 4 (1988): 813–29.

Jensen, Joan M. *Calling This Place Home: Women on the Wisconsin Frontier, 1850–1925*. Minnesota Historical Society Press, 2006.

Johnson, Hildegard Binder. *Order Upon the Land: The US Rectangular Land Survey and the Upper Mississippi Country*. Oxford University Press, 1976.

Jordan, Jennifer A. *Edible Memory: The Lure of Heirloom Tomatoes and Other Forgotten Foods*. University of Chicago Press, 2015.

Kantrowitz, Stephen. *Citizens of a Stolen Land: A Ho-Chunk History of the Nineteenth-Century United States*. University of North Carolina Press, 2023.

Kassulke, Natasha. *See Wisconsin Through the Eyes of 19th Century Surveyors*. Board of Commissioners of Public Lands, Wisconsin. Publication number

PUB-CE-4018, 2009. Accessed November 28, 2025. https://bcpluat.wisconsin.gov/SharedDocuments/Land/DNR-OriginalLandSurveyArticle.pdf.

Keller, Fred. "Connecting the Dots on the Weavers." *NW/Sussex Sun*, November 10, 2016.

Keller, Fred. "Roberta Jean Brown Duckett." *Living Sussex Sun*, March 16, 2010 (publication of Sussex-Lisbon Area Historical Society).

Kennedy, Joseph Camp Griffith. *Agriculture of the United States in 1860; Compiled from the Original Returns of the Eighth Census*. US Government Printing Office, 1864. https://www.nass.usda.gov/AgCensus/archive/files/1860b-03.pdf.

Kent Archives. "Hops in Kent." Kent County Council. Accessed August 14, 2025. https://www.kentarchives.org.uk/hops-in-kent/.

Kessler-Harris, Alice. *Out to Work: A History of Wage-Earning Women in the United States*. Oxford University Press, 2003.

Kilsdonk, Betty. "Review of Culture and Agriculture by Tom McKay and Deborah Kmetz." *Public Historian* 8, no. 4 (1986): 125–27.

King, Adam. "Lead, Land, and Cranberries: The Ho-Chunk Experience in the 19th Century." BA thesis, University of Wisconsin–Eau Claire. UW Minds. Accessed December 2, 2025. https://minds.wisconsin.edu/bitstream/handle/1793/54470/KingSpring2011.pdf.

Komori, Jane. "The Canadian 'War of the Two Sugars': Homegrown Sugar Beets and the Racial Stratification of Labour." *Historical Materialism* 31, no. 3 (2023): 252–75.

Kopp, Peter Adam. *Hoptopia: A World of Agriculture and Beer in Oregon's Willamette Valley*. University of California Press, 2016.

Kozik, Liz Anna. "Re-Peopling the Prairie: History, Ecology, and How They Can Better Inform Prairie Science." PhD diss., University of Wisconsin–Madison, 2023.

Kroll, Wayne. *Wisconsin's Frontier Farm Breweries 1830's–1880's*. Published by the author, 2003.

Krueger, Lillian. "Motherhood on the Wisconsin Frontier." In *Wisconsin: From Native Matriarchies to the New Millennium*, edited by Genevieve McBride. Wisconsin Historical Society Press, 2014.

Krueger, Lillian. *Wisconsin Stories: Motherhood on the Wisconsin Frontier*. State Historical Society of Wisconsin, 1980. Reprinted from *Wisconsin Magazine of History*, 29 (December 1945): 157–83; (March 1946): 333–46.

Krug, Merton Edwin. *History of Reedsburg and the Upper Baraboo Valley*. Democrat Printing Company, 1929.

Krynski, Elizabeth, and Kimberly Little. "Hannah's Letters: The Story of a Wisconsin Pioneer Family, 1856–1864; Part I." *Wisconsin Magazine of History* 74, no. 3 (1991): 162–95.

LaDuke, John. "Hop Houses in Otsego County, New York." Master's thesis, Memorial University of Newfoundland, October 2015.

Lampard, Eric. E. *The Rise of the Dairy Industry in Wisconsin: A Study in Agricultural Change, 1820–1920*. State Historical Society of Wisconsin, 1963.

Lange, Kenneth I. *A County Called Sauk: A Human History of Sauk County, Wisconsin*. Sauk County Historical Society, 1976.

Lange, Kenneth I. *A Postglacial Vegetational History of Sauk County and Caledonia Township, Columbia County, South Central Wisconsin*. Technical Bulletin No. 168. Department of Natural Resources, Madison, WI, 1990.

Langill, Ellen D., and Jean Penn Loerke, eds. *From Farmland to Freeways: A History of Waukesha County, Wisconsin*. Waukesha County Historical Society, 1984.

Langson, William J. *Seventh Annual Statement of the Trade and Commerce of Milwaukee for the Year Ending December 31, 1864, Reported to the Milwaukee Chamber of Commerce*. Starr & Son, 1865.

Langson, William J. *Eleventh Annual Statement of the Trade and Commerce of Milwaukee for the Year Ending December 31, 1868, Reported to the Milwaukee Chamber of Commerce*. Jermain & Brightman, 1869.

Lapham, Increase Allen. *Wisconsin: Its Geography and Topography, History, Geology, and Mineralogy*. 2nd ed. I. A. Hopkins, 1846. https://archive.org/details/wisconsinitsgeog01laph/page/n5/mode/2up?view=theater.

Lapham, Increase Allen, Joseph Gillett Knapp, and H. Crocker. *Report on the Disastrous Effects of the Destruction of Forest Trees, Now Going on So Rapidly in the State of Wisconsin*. Commission to Ascertain Effects of the Destruction of Forest Trees, 1867.

Larsen, Dennis M. *Hop King: Ezra Meeker's Boom Years*. Washington State University Press, 2016.

Laubach, Stephen A. *Living a Land Ethic: A History of Cooperative Conservation on the Leopold Memorial Reserve*. University of Wisconsin Press, 2014.

Lender, Mark Edward, and James Kirby Martin. *Drinking in America: A History*. Revised and expanded ed. Free Press, 1987.

Loew, Patty. *Indian Nations of Wisconsin: Histories of Endurance and Renewal*. Wisconsin Historical Society Press, 2013.

Lonetree, Amy. "A Heritage of Resilience: Ho-Chunk Family Photographs in the Visual Archive." *Public Historian* 41, no. 1 (2019): 34–50.

Lonetree, Amy. "Visualizing Native Survivance: Encounters with My Ho-Chunk Ancestors in the Family Photographs of Charles Van Schaick." In *People of the Big Voice: Photographs of Ho-Chunk Families by Charles Van Schaick, 1879–1942*, edited by Tom Jones, Michael Schmudlach, Matthew Daniel Mason, Amy Lonetree, and George A. Greendeer. State Historical Society of Wisconsin, 2011.

Luby, Brittany, Margaret Lehman, Andrea Bradford, Samantha Mehltretter, and Jane Mariottie, eds. *Manomin: Caring for Ecosystems and Each Other*. With Niisaachewan Anishinaabe Nation. University of Manitoba Press, 2024.

Lurie, Nancy Oestreich. *Wisconsin Indians*. Wisconsin Historical Society Press, 2002.

MacFadyen, Joshua. *Flax Americana: A History of the Fibre and Oil That Covered a Continent*. McGill-Queen's University Press, 2018.

Macfarlane, Daniel. *The Lives of Lake Ontario: An Environmental History*. McGill-Queen's University Press, 2024.

Maguire, Jennifer Smith. "The Taste for the Particular: A Logic of Discernment in an Age of Omnivorousness." *Journal of Consumer Culture* 18, no. 1 (2016): 3–20.

Majumdar, Aparajita. "Recalcitrant Lifeworlds: Decolonizing the History of Human-Plant Relations." *Environmental Humanities* 16, no. 1 (2024): 79–99.

Mandel, David. *Settlers of Dane County: The Photographs of Andreas Larsen Dahl*. Dane County Cultural Affairs Commission, 1985.

Maritime History of the Great Lakes. "Julia Palmer (Steamboat), storm damage, 1 Nov 1847." Accessed November 29, 2025. https://images.maritimehistoryofthegreatlakes.ca/60983/data.

Maritime History of the Great Lakes. "Table showing the tonnage of Steam Boats on lake Erie, their Age, number of Berths, number of Hands employed, &c." Accessed August 6, 2025. https://www.maritimehistoryofthegreatlakes.ca/documents/ShipLists/BRA1835.htm. Article first published in *Bethel Magazine*, January 1836.

Marshall, Brenda. "Michigan Hops: The Women Behind the Bines." CraftBeer.com. November 14, 2025. https://www.craftbeer.com/full-pour/michigan-hops-the-women-behind-the-bines.

McClain, William E., Charles M. Ruffner, John E. Ebinger, and Greg Spyreas. "Patterns of Anthropogenic Fire Within the Midwestern Tallgrass Prairie 1673–1905: Evidence from Written Accounts." *Natural Areas Journal* 41, no. 4 (2021): 283–300.

McCook, Stuart. *Coffee Is Not Forever: A Global History of the Coffee Leaf Rust*. Ohio University Press, 2019.

McDonell, Emma. *Quinoa Bust: The Making and Unmaking of an Andean Miracle Crop*. University of California Press, 2025.

McIntyre, Elwood. "Let's Recall the . . . Heyday in Hops." *Better Crops with Plant Food*, February 1956.

McMynn, John G. *Nineteenth Annual Report of the Superintendent of Public Instruction of the State of Wisconsin, 1866*. Atwood & Rublee, 1867.

McQuillan, D. Aidan. *Prevailing Over Time: Ethnic Adjustment on the Kansas Prairies 1875–1925*. University of Nebraska Press, 1990.

Meine, Curt, and Keefe Keeley, eds. *The Driftless Reader*. University of Wisconsin Press, 2017.

Menomonee Valley Partners. "An Urban Escape, Nature and Trails [. . .] Find It All in the Menomonee River Valley." Accessed November 23, 2025. https://www.thevalleymke.org.

Merk, Frederick. *Economic History of Wisconsin During the Civil War Decade*. Wisconsin Historical Society, 1916.

Michigan Underwater Preserves. "Whitefish Point Underwater Preserve." Accessed November 29, 2025. https://www.michiganpreserves.org/whitefish-point-underwater-preserve/.

MIGenWeb. "Ships & Shipping News—Lake Superior." Michigan Genealogy on the Web, Part of The USGenWeb Project. Accessed August 6, 2025. https://www.migenweb.org/chippewa/history/shipping.htm.

Milero, Pilar, and Cody Shreck. "Waukesha County." *Encyclopedia of Milwaukee*. Accessed August 5, 2025. https://emke.uwm.edu/entry/waukesha-county/.

Miles, Tiya. *All That She Carried: The Journey of Ashley's Sack, a Black Family Keepsake*. Random House, 2022.

Miller, Laura J. *Building Nature's Market: The Business and Politics of Natural Foods*. University of Chicago Press, 2017.

Miller, Marla R. *Entangled Lives: Labor, Livelihood, and Landscapes of Change in Rural Massachusetts*. Johns Hopkins University Press, 2019.

Mitenbuler, Reid. *Bourbon Empire: The Past and Future of America's Whiskey*. Penguin, 2016.

Monthly Reports of the Dept. of Agriculture. US Government Printing Office, 1870.

Monthly Reports of the Dept. of Agriculture. US Government Printing Office, 1872.

Monthly Reports of the Dept. of Agriculture. US Government Printing Office, 1874.

Monthly Reports of the Dept. of Agriculture for the Year 1875. US Government Printing Office, 1876.

Moran, Joseph M., and Edward J. Hopkins. *Wisconsin's Weather and Climate*. University of Wisconsin Press, 2002.

Moran, William. *The Belles of New England: The Women of the Textile Mills and the Families Whose Wealth They Wove*. Thomas Dunn, 2002.

Mosher, Randy. "Chicago." In *Oxford Companion to Beer*, edited by Garrett Oliver. Oxford University Press, 2012. Accessed August 5, 2025, via Craft Beer & Brewing website. https://beerandbrewing.com/dictionary/KHCvNfQYqW.

Mueller, Erhart. *Only in Sumpter*. Worzalla, 1977.

Myrick, Herbert. *The Hop: Its Culture and Cure, Marketing and Manufacture*. Orange Judd, 1909.

Nevol, Nykole. *Deadly Summers: Infant and Child Deaths in 19th Century Rochester, New York*. SUNY Geneseo. Accessed August 6, 2025. https://knightscholar.geneseo.edu/cgi/viewcontent.cgi?article=1137&context=great-day-symposium.

New York Heritage Digital Collections. "History of Waterville Collection." Accessed August 5, 2025. https://nyheritage.org/collections/history-waterville-collection.

New York State Brewers Association. "Farm Brewery." Accessed December 11, 2025. https://newyorkcraftbeer.com/farm-brewery/.

Northern Brewer. "Cluster Hops Pellets 1 oz." Accessed August 6, 2025. https://www.northernbrewer.com/products/cluster-hop-pellets.

Northern Brewer. "Hallertau Hops Pellets 1 oz." Accessed August 6, 2025. https://www.northernbrewer.com/products/german-hallertau-hop-pellets.

Noyes, Edward. "Chapter XXIV Farm, Factory Pace Quickens." In *Prairies, Pines, and People: Winnebago County in a New Perspective*, edited by James I. Metz. Oshkosh Northwestern, 1976.

Nyuur, Richard B., and Pauline Sobiesu. "The History and Development of Brewing and the Beer Industry in Africa." In *Brewing, Beer and Pubs: A Global Perspective*, edited by Ignazio Cabras, David Higgins, and David Preece. Palgrave Macmillan, 2016.

O'Brien, Jean M. *Firsting and Lasting: Writing Indians Out of Existence in New England*. University of Minnesota Press, 2010.

Ocejo, Richard E. *Masters of Craft: Old Jobs in the New Urban Economy*. Princeton University Press, 2018.

Ogle, Maureen. *Ambitious Brew*. Blue Willow Books, 2019.

Olson, Sherry H. *The Depletion Myth: A History of Railroad Use of Timber*. Harvard University Press, 1971.

One Hundred Years of Brewing: A Complete History of the Progress Made in the Art, Science and Industry of Brewing in the World, Particularly During the Last Century. H. S. Rich, 1901.

O'Neill, Gilda. *Pull No More Bines: An Oral History of East London Women Hop Pickers*. Women's Press, 1990.

Onsager, Lawrence. "The Removal of the Winnebago Indians from Wisconsin to Nebraska in 1873–4." Master's thesis, Loma Linda University, 1985.

Opie, John. *The Law of the Land: Two Hundred Years of American Farmland Policy*. University of Nebraska Press, 1994.

Orwell, George. *Diaries*. Liveright, 2012.

Osterud, Nancy Grey. *Bonds of Community: The Lives of Farm Women in Nineteenth-Century New York*. Cornell University Press, 1991.

Pabst Mansion Milwaukee. "Pabst Brewing Company." Accessed November 30, 2025. https://www.pabstmansion.com/history/pabst-brewing-co/.

Paine, Laura. "The Hops Era: Wisconsin's Agricultural Gold Rush." *Wisconsin Academy Review*, June 1990, 23–29.

Parker, Alex. "No Women, No Beer: Miller Lite Celebrates America's Forgotten Women Brewers." *Beer & Beyond* (blog), Molson Coors Beverage Company, June 22, 2022. https://www.molsoncoorsblog.com/miller-lite-mary-lisle-brewster-alewives.

Parker, Kim, Julia Menasce Horowitz, Rich Morin, and Mark Hugo Lopez. "Chapter 1: Race and Multiracial Americans in the US Census." In *Multiracial in America: Proud, Diverse, and Growing in Numbers*. Pew Research Center. June 11, 2015. https://www.pewresearch.org/social-trends/2015/06/11/chapter-1-race-and-multiracial-americans-in-the-u-s-census/.

Parker, Hubert H. *The Hop Industry*. P. S. King & Son, 1934.

Pattinson, Ronald. *London! Brewing Capital*. Kilderkin, 2009.

Pattinson, Ronald. "When American Hops Moved West." *Shut Up About Barclay Perkins* (blog), February 5, 2018. https://barclayperkins.blogspot.com/2018/02/when-american-hops-moved-west.html.

Pauly, Philip J. *Fruits and Plains: The Horticultural Transformation of America*. Harvard University Press, 2007.

Pawley, Emily. *The Nature of the Future: Agriculture, Science, and Capitalism in the Antebellum North*. University of Chicago Press, 2020.

Peace, Thomas, Jim Clifford, and Judy Burns. "Maitland's Moment: Turning Nova Scotia's Forests into Ships for the Global Commodity Trade in the Mid-Nineteenth Century." In *Moving Natures: Mobility and the Environment in Canadian History*, edited by Ben Bradley, Jay Young, and Colin M. Coates. University of Calgary Press, 2016.

Percival, Bronwen, and Francis Percival. *Reinventing the Wheel: Milk, Microbes, and the Fight for Real Cheese*. University of California Press, 2017.

Phillips, Kynala. "Wisconsin's Black Farming Tradition." *Belt Magazine*, August 20, 2021.

Pilcher, Jeffrey M. *Hopped Up: How Travel, Trade, and Taste Made Beer a Global Commodity*. Oxford University Press, 2024.

Pilcher, Jeffrey M. "Imperial Hops: Beer in the Age of Empire," *Global Food History* 10, no. 1 (2024): 52–67.

Pluymers, Keith. *No Wood, No Kingdom: Political Ecology in the English Atlantic*. University of Pennsylvania Press, 2021.

Pohl-Valero, Stefan. "The Scientific Lives of *Chicha*: The Production of a Fermented Beverage and the Making of Expert Knowledge in Bogotá, 1889–1939." *Osiris* 35 (2020): 204–27.

Pollan, Michael. *The Botany of Desire: A Plant's-Eye View of the World*. Random House, 2001.

Portrait and Biographical Record of Waukesha County, Wisconsin: Containing Biographical Sketches of Old Settlers and Representative Citizens of the County, Together with Biographies and Portraits of All the Presidents. Excelsior, 1894.

Pozner, Jo-Ellen, Michaela DeSoucey, J. Cameron Verhaal, and Katarina Sikavica. "Watered Down: Market Growth, Authenticity, and Evaluation in Craft Beer." *Organization Studies* 43, no. 3 (2022): 321–45.

Pure Michigan: Official Travel & Tourism Website for Michigan. "Michigan Pirates of the Great Lakes." Accessed August 13, 2025. https://www.michigan.org/article/trip-idea/michigan-pirates-great-lakes.

Ragatz, Oswald, and Lowell Joseph Ragatz. "Memoirs of a Sauk Swiss." *Wisconsin Magazine of History* 19, no. 2 (1935): 182–227.

Raibmon, Paige. *Authentic Indians: Episodes of Encounter from the Late-Nineteenth-Century Northwest Coast*. Duke University Press, 2005.

Rasmussen, Anders Bo. *Civil War Settlers: Scandinavians, Citizenship, and American Empire, 1848–1870*. Cambridge University Press, 2022.

Rath, Eric C. "It Gives the Rice a Kick: Sweetness and Kōji in Early Modern Sake Brewing." *Gastronomica: The Journal of Food and Culture* 23, no. 4 (2023): 30–41.

Rath, Sara. *Pioneer Photographer: Wisconsin's H. H. Bennett*. Tamarack Press, 1979.

Reedsburg Remembers: 100th Anniversary. Historical Committee, Reedsburg Centennial July 3–5, 1948. Souvenir program and centennial history.

Reiherzer, Lee. *Winnebago County Beer: A Heady History*. American Palate, 2019.

Reilly, Michael R., comp. and ed. "David Bonham's Life." Sussex-Lisbon Area Historical Museum. Revised September 3, 2012. https://slah.us/david-bonhams-life/.

Reilly, Michael R. "First Town of Lisbon Settler—Thomas Spencer Redford or?" Sussex-Lisbon Area Historical Museum. Revised May 28, 2013. https://slah.us/first-town-of-lisbon-settler-thomas-spencer-redford-or/.

Reilly, Michael R., comp. and ed. "Hop Growing History in Lisbon, Waukesha County, and Wisconsin." Sussex-Lisbon Area Historical Museum. Revised July 2014. https://slah.us/hop-growing-history-in-lisbon-and-waukesha-county/.

Reilly, Michael R. "James Weaver and Hops." Sussex-Lisbon Area Historical Museum. May 2013. https://slah.us/james-weaver-and-hops/.

Reilly, Michael R. "Weaver Family: Ten Years in America—Life Highlights." Sussex-Lisbon Area Historical Museum. February 5, 2014. https://slah.us/weaver-family-highlights/.

Rentmeester, Jeanne, and Les Rentmeester. *De Vlamingen in Wisconsin / The Flemish in Wisconsin*. Published by the authors, 1985.

Riney-Kehrberg, Pamela. "Women in Agriculture." *Oxford Handbook of Agricultural History*. Oxford University Press, 2024.

Robichaud, Andrew. "Frozen Over: Making Ice and Knowing Nature in Nineteenth-Century America." *Environmental History* 27, no. 3 (2022). https://doi.org/10.1086/720343.

Rockman, Seth. *Plantation Goods: A Material History of American Slavery*. University of Chicago Press, 2024.

Rogerson, Christian M. "African Traditional Beer: Changing Organization and Spaces of South Africa's Sorghum Beer Industry." *African Geographical Review* 38, no. 3 (2019): 253–67.

Rolvenden History Group. *Hopping in Rolvenden*. Rolvenden History Group, 2018. Exhibition catalog. https://therolvendenhistorygroup.files.wordpress.com/2018/08/hop-exhibition-april-2018.pdf.

Ron, Ariel. *Grassroots Leviathan: Agricultural Reform and the Rural North in the Slaveholding Republic*. Johns Hopkins University Press, 2023.

Ron, Ariel. "When Hay Was King: Energy History and Economic Nationalism in the Nineteenth-Century United States." *American Historical Review* 128, no. 1 (2023): 177–213.

Ronnenberg, Herman Wiley. *Material Culture of Breweries*. Left Coast Press, 2011.
Rosholt, Malcolm. *Our County, Our Story: Portage County Wisconsin*. Portage County Board of Supervisors, 1959.
Rothman, Ellen K. "Sex and Self-Control: Middle-Class Courtship in America, 1770–1870." *Journal of Social History* 15, no. 3 (1982): 409–25.
Rück, Daniel. "The Continuity of Settler Colonial Narratives: The Diary of a Nineteenth-Century Dominion Land Surveyor and the Enduring Language of Harm." *Settler Colonial Studies* 14, no 3 (2024): 264–90.
Rudd, D. B., and E. O. Rudd. *The Cultivation of Hops, and Their Preparation for Market, As Practiced in Sauk County, Wisconsin*. Published by the authors, 1868.
Rumney, Thomas A. "Hops Cultivation in Wisconsin: A Nineteenth Century Interlude." *Wisconsin Geographer* 13–14 (1997): 49–55.
Sachs, Carolyn. *Gendered Fields: Rural Women, Agriculture, and Environment*. Westview Press, 1996.
Sasso, Robert F., and Dan Joyce. "Ethnohistory and Archaeology: The Removal Era Potawatomi Lifeway in Southeastern Wisconsin." *Midcontinental Journal of Archaeology* 31, no. 1 (2013): 165–202.
Sauk County Historical Society. "Yellow Thunder—Wakąjazi." Accessed August 6, 2025. https://saukcountyhistory.org/yellow-thunder.
Saunt, Claudio. *Unworthy Republic: The Dispossession of Native Americans and the Road to Indian Territory*. W. W. Norton, 2020.
Schlitz Audubon Nature Center. "Climate and the Tension Zone in Wisconsin." Accessed August 5, 2025. https://www.schlitzaudubon.org/2020/10/20/climate-and-the-tension-zone-in-wisconsin/.
Schuette, William C. *Loganville, Our Heritage: A History of Loganville, Wisconsin*. Village Press, 1980.
Schulte, Lisa A., and David J. Mladenoff. "The Original US Public Land Survey Records: Their Use and Limitations in Reconstructing Presettlement Vegetation." *Journal of Forestry* 99, no. 10 (2001): 5–10.
Scot, Reynolde. *A Perfite Platforme of a Hoppe Garden*. London, 1574.
Secchi, Silvia. "Compounded Extraction: An Examination of Early Agro-Extractivism in the US Heartland." *Environment and Planning E: Nature and Space* 8, no. 2 (2025): 791–814.
"Seymour Letters." *Wisconsin Magazine of History* 32, no. 2 (December 1948): 188–99.
Shipwrecks of Upstate NY. "Lake Ontario Ship Wrecks: S.S. Adiramled That Sunk in Lake Ontario on June 6, 1912." Accessed November 13, 2025. https://sonarguy.com/lake-ontario/#.
Simmonds, Peter Lund. *Hops: Their Cultivation, Commerce, and Uses in Various Countries*. Spon, 1877.
Simms, Muriel. *Settlin': Stories of Madison's Early African American Families*. Wisconsin Historical Society, 2018.

Sleeper-Smith, Susan. *Indigenous Prosperity and the American Conquest: Indian Women of the Ohio River Valley, 1690–1792*. Omohundro Institute of Early American History and Culture, 2018.

Slez, Adam. *The Making of the Populist Movement: State, Market, and Party on the Western Frontier*. Oxford University Press, 2020.

Smith, D. C. "Varietal Improvement in Hops." In *Yearbook of Agriculture*. US Department of Agriculture, 1937.

Smith, Henry Perry. *History of the City of Buffalo and Erie County*. D. Mason, 1884.

Smithsonian National Museum of Natural History Behring Center. "On the Water: Stories from Maritime America." Accessed August 6, 2025. https://americanhistory.si.edu/onthewater/exhibition/4_2.html.

"The Society and the State." *Wisconsin Magazine of History* 30, no. 4 (1947): 497–512.

Staller, Karen M. *New York's Newsboys: Charles Loring Brace and the Founding of the Children's Aid Society*. Oxford University Press, 2020.

Steeves, Paulette F. C. *The Indigenous Paleolithic of the Western Hemisphere*. University of Nebraska Press, 2021.

Steiner, S. S. *Steiner's Guide to American Hops*. Hopsteiner, 1973.

Stevens, Michael E. *The Making of Pioneer Wisconsin: Voices of Early Settlers*. Wisconsin Historical Society Press, 2018.

Street, Richard Steven. *Beasts of the Field: A Narrative History of California Farmworkers, 1769–1913*. Stanford University Press, 2004.

Street, Richard Steven. "'We Are Not Slaves': The Photographic Record of the Wheatland Hop Riot; The First Images of Protesting Farm Workers in America." *Southern California Quarterly* 64, no. 3 (1982): 205–226.

Suits, Robert. "Hoboes, Wheat, and Climate Precarity, 1870–1922." *Agricultural History* 97, no. 1 (2023): 1–47.

Summerhill, Thomas. "Farming on Shares: Landlords, Tenants, and the Rise of the Hop and Dairy Economies in Central New York." *New York History* 76, no. 2 (1995): 125–52.

Summerhill, Thomas. *Harvest of Dissent: Agrarianism in Nineteenth-Century New York*. University of Illinois Press, 2005.

Sunne, Daniel. "Abortion in Iowa in the Nineteenth Century." Master's thesis, Iowa State University, 2022.

Sussex-Lisbon Area Historical Museum. "David Topping." Accessed August 6, 2025. https://slah.us/david-topping/.

Sussex-Lisbon Area Historical Museum. "James Weaver Letter to Cousin John Hardeman (Son of Richard), May 2, 1873." Accessed August 6, 2025. https://slah.us/william-weaver-letter-to-cousin-john-hardeman-son-of-richard-may-2-1873/.

Sussex-Lisbon Area Historical Museum. "James Weaver Letter to Cousin Richard Hardeman, December 13, 1839." Accessed August 6, 2025. https://slah.us/james-weaver-letter-to-cousin-richard-hardeman-december-13-1839/.

Sutherland, Emma, and Robin A. E. Walton. *Hop Pickers' Hovels, Huts & Houses: Construction & History; Kent & Sussex*. Christine Swift, 1995.

Szucs, Loretto Dennis, and Matthew Wright. "Census Records." In *The Source: A Guidebook to American Genealogy*, 3rd ed., edited by Loretto Dennis Szucs and Sandra Hargreaves Luebking. Ancestry, 2006.

Tanzilo, Bobby. "Urban Spelunking: Schlitz Tied Houses, Like Dehne's Upper 90 Sports Pub." OnMilwaukee. March 2, 2017. https://onmilwaukee.com/articles/urban-spelunking-schlitz-tiedhouses.

Tetzloff, Jason M. "The Diminishing Winnebago Estate in Wisconsin: From White Contact to Removal." Master's thesis, University of Wisconsin–Eau Claire, 1991.

Tetzloff, Jason M. "'To Do Some Good Among the Indians': Henry Roe Cloud and Twentieth Century Native American Advocacy." PhD diss., Purdue University, 1996.

Thompson, John Giffin. *The Rise and Decline of the Wheat Growing Industry in Wisconsin*. University of Wisconsin, 1909.

Thurnell-Read, Thomas. "Craft, Tangibility, and Affect at Work in the Microbrewery." *Emotion, Space, and Society* 13 (November 2014): 46–54.

Thurnell-Read, Thomas, ed. *Drinking Dilemmas: Space, Culture and Identity*. Taylor & Francis, 2015.

Thwaites, Reuben Gold. *Bradbury's Travels in the Interior of America, 1809–1811*. Vol. 5 of *Early Western Travels 1748–1846*. Arthur H. Clark, 1904.

Tolan, Tom. "A Historical Perspective on Milwaukee's Brewing Renaissance." *Milwaukee Magazine*, April 12, 2017. https://www.milwaukeemag.com/historical-perspective-milwaukees-brewing-renaissance/.

Tomlan, Michael A. *Tinged with Gold: Hop Culture in the United States*. 1992. Reprint, University of Georgia Press, 2013.

Transactions of the Oneida Historical Society at Utica. The Society, 1889.

Transactions of the Wisconsin State Agricultural Society. Vol. 3. Wisconsin State Agricultural Society, 1853.

Transactions of the Wisconsin State Agricultural Society. Vol 7. Wisconsin State Agricultural Society, 1868.

Transactions of the Wisconsin State Agricultural Society. Vol. 12. Wisconsin State Agricultural Society, 1873–74.

Transactions of the Wisconsin State Agricultural Society: W. W. Field Secretary's Annual Report. Wisconsin State Agricultural Society, 1873–74.

Trimpey, Alice Kent. *Becky: My First Love; The Story of Becky and Other Dolls*. Remington House, 1946.

Tsing, Anna. *The Mushroom at the End of the World*. Princeton University Press, 2021.

Ulrich, Laurel Thatcher. *A Midwife's Tale: The Life of Martha Ballard, Based on Her Diary, 1785–1812*. Vintage, 1991.

Unger, Richard W. *Beer in the Middle Ages and the Renaissance*. University of Pennsylvania Press, 2004.

United States Census Bureau. "1870 Census Instructions to Assistant Marshals." Revised June 4, 2024. https://www.census.gov/programs-surveys/decennial-census/technical-documentation/questionnaires/1870/1870-instructions.html.

US Department of Agriculture. "Table I.—Summary for the Tenth Census, 1880." In *Statistics of Agriculture: Tabular Statements*. Accessed November 8, 2025. https://www.nass.usda.gov/AgCensus/archive/files/1880a_v3-02.pdf.

Usher, Ellis Baker. *Wisconsin: Its Story and Biography, 1848–1913*. Vol. 5. Lewis, 1914.

Varhola, Michael. *Shipwrecks and Lost Treasures: Great Lakes; Legends and More, Pirates and More!* Globe Pequot, 2007.

Vaught, David. *Cultivating California: Growers, Specialty Crops, and Labor, 1875–1920*. Johns Hopkins University Press, 2002.

Wade, Christina. *Filthy Queens: A History of Beer in Ireland*. Nine Bean Rows, 2025.

Waggoner, Linda, ed. *"Neither White Men Nor Indians": Affidavits from the Winnebago Mixed-Blood Claim Commissions, Prairie Du Chien, Wisconsin, 1838–1839*. Park Genealogical Books, 2002.

Waisanen, Pamela J., and Norman B. Bliss. "Changes in Population and Agricultural Land in Conterminous United States Counties, 1790 to 1997." *Global Biogeochemical Cycles* 16, no. 4 (2002): 1–19.

Walker, Francis A. *The Statistics of the Wealth and Industry of the United States, Embracing the Tables of* [. . .] *Agriculture;* [. . .] *Compiled, from the Original Returns of the Ninth Census (June 1, 1870)*. US Government Printing Office, 1872. https://www.nass.usda.gov/AgCensus/archive/files/1870c-04.pdf.

Walzer, Joseph B. "Beer Gardens and Beer Halls." *Encyclopedia of Milwaukee*. Accessed August 6, 2025. https://emke.uwm.edu/entry/beer-gardens-and-beer-halls/.

Watson, Ben. *Cider, Hard and Sweet: History, Traditions, and Making Your Own*. Countryman Press, 2013.

Weaver, Melinda Ann. *Memories of Early Days*. Published by the author, 1876.

Webb, James. *Tropical Pioneers: Human Agency and Ecological Change in the Highlands of Sri Lanka, 1800–1900*. Ohio University Press, 2002.

Western Historical Company. *The History of Jefferson County, Wisconsin: Containing a History of Jefferson County, Its Early Settlement, Growth, Development, Resources, Etc.* [. . .] Western Historical Company, 1879.

Western Historical Company. *History of Milwaukee, Wisconsin: From Pre-historic Times to the Present Date, Embracing a Summary Sketch of the Native Tribes, and an Exhaustive Record of Men and Events for the Past Century; Describing, the City, Its Commercial, Religious, Educational and Benevolent Institutions, Its Government, Courts, Press, and Public Affairs; and Including Nearly Four Thousand Biographical Sketches of Pioneers and Citizens*. Western Historical Company, 1881.

Western Historical Company. *History of Northern Wisconsin: Containing an Account of Its Settlement, Growth, Development, and Resources; an Extensive*

Sketch of Its Counties, Cities, Towns and Villages, Their Improvements, Industries, Manufactories; Biographical Sketches, Portraits of Prominent Men and Early Settlers; Views of County Seats, Etc. Western Historical Company, 1881.

Western Historical Company. *The History of Sauk County, Wisconsin: Containing an Account of Its Settlement, Growth, Development and Resources; an Extensive and Minute Sketch of Its Cities, Towns and Villages, Their Improvements, Industries, Manufactories, Churches, Schools and Societies; Its War Record, Biographical Sketches, Portraits of Prominent Men and Early Settlers; the Whole Preceded by a History of Wisconsin, Statistics of the State, and an Abstract of Its Laws and Constitution and of the Constitution of the United States.* Northern Micrographics, 1880.

Western Historical Company. *The History of Waukesha County, Wisconsin, Containing an Account of Its Settlement, Growth, Development, and Resources.* Waukesha County Historical Society, 1880.

Wherry, Frederick F. *The Culture of Markets.* Polity Press, 2012.

Wilkinson, Crystal. *Praisesong for the Kitchen Ghosts: Stories and Recipes from Five Generations of Black Country Cooks.* Clarkson Potter, 2024.

Wisconsin Historical Society. "Beer in Wisconsin." Accessed November 28, 2025. https://www.wisconsinhistory.org/Records/Article/CS1704.

Wisconsin Historical Society. "Brewing and Prohibition." Accessed August 6, 2025. https://www.wisconsinhistory.org/turningpoints/tp-051/.

Wisconsin Historical Society. "Dairy Farming in Wisconsin: How Wisconsin Became the Dairy State." Accessed August 6, 2025. https://www.wisconsinhistory.org/Records/Article/CS1744.

Wisconsin Historical Society. "Letters by Relatives of Laura Ingalls Wilder." Accessed August 6, 2025. https://www.wisconsinhistory.org/turningpoints/search.asp?id=1728.

Wisconsin Historical Society. "Property Record N5424 State Highway 26: Architecture and History Inventory; Joseph Spaulding Hop House." Accessed December 9, 2025. https://www.wisconsinhistory.org/Records/Property/HI93420.

Wisconsin Hop Exchange. "Quality First, Local Always." Accessed December 18, 2025. https://www.wisconsinhopexchange.com.

Wisconsin Oral History Project. "The Lands We Share: Farming, History, and Place in Five Wisconsin Communities." Accessed December 17, 2025. https://landsweshare.org.

Wisconsin Original Land Patents Database. "Wisconsin's Original Land Patent Data Provided by the General Land Office (GLO) and Bureau of Commissioners of Public Lands (BCPL), Mapped to the PLSS Quarter-Quarter Section." Updated March 29, 2024. https://wi-dnr.maps.arcgis.com/home/item.html?id=4da3c08881cb4bd880bf9f695840b29b.

Wood, J. David. *Making Ontario: Agricultural Colonization and Landscape Re-Creation Before the Railway.* McGill-Queen's University Press, 2000.

Xan, Erna Oleson. *Wisconsin, My Home: The Story of Thurine Oleson as Told to Her Daughter*. University of Wisconsin Press, 1975.

Zabinski, Catherine. *Amber Waves: The Extraordinary Biography of Wheat, from Wild Grass to World Megacrop*. University of Chicago Press, 2020.

Zappia, Natale A. "Frontiers of Grain: Indigenous Maize, Afroeurasian Wheat, and the Origins of Industrial Food." *Early American Studies* 17, no. 2 (2019): 215–55.

NEWSPAPERS AND OTHER HISTORICAL PERIODICALS

Note: Specific content from these periodicals is cited in the notes.

Baraboo News
Baraboo News Republic
Baraboo Republic
Daily Free Democrat (Milwaukee)
Daily Sentinel and Gazette (Milwaukee)
Das Tägliche Banner
Der Wanderer (St. Paul, MN)
Der Westbote
Evening Wisconsin
Evergreen City Times
The Farmer's Magazine
The Janesville Gazette
Madison Capitol Times
Madison Democrat
Milwaukee Daily Sentinel
Milwaukee Journal-Sentinel
Milwaukee Sentinel
The Practical Farmer and Rural Advertiser of the Middle States
Prairie Farmer
Racine Advocate
Reedsburg Free Press
Semi-Weekly Wisconsin
South Port American
Southport Telegraph
Sparta Eagle
Vernon County Censor
Watertown Democrat
Watertown News
Waukesha County Democrat
Waukesha Freeman
Waukesha Plain-Dealer
Weekly Wisconsin
Wisconsin and Iowa Farmer, and Northwestern Cultivator
Wisconsin Democrat (Green Bay)
Wisconsin Mirror
Wisconsin State Journal
Wisconsin State Register

INDEX

Page numbers in italics refer to figures.